ROBERTO MANCINI

ROBERTO MANCINI

A FOOTBALLING LIFE: THE FULL STORY

LUCA CAIOLI

CORINTHIAN BOOKS

Published in the UK in 2012 by
Corinthian Books, an imprint of
Icon Books Ltd, Omnibus Business Centre,
39–41 North Road, London N7 9DP
email: info@iconbooks.co.uk
www.corinthianbooks.net

Sold in the UK, Europe, South Africa and Asia
by Faber & Faber Ltd, Bloomsbury House,
74–77 Great Russell Street, London WC1B 3DA or their agents

Distributed in the UK, Europe, South Africa and Asia
by TBS Ltd, TBS Distribution Centre, Colchester Road
Frating Green, Colchester CO7 7DW

Published in Australia in 2012
by Allen & Unwin Pty Ltd,
PO Box 8500, 83 Alexander Street,
Crows Nest, NSW 2065

Distributed in Canada
by Penguin Books Canada,
90 Eglinton Avenue East, Suite 700,
Toronto, Ontario M4P 2Y3

Distributed to the trade in the USA
by Consortium Book Sales and Distribution,
The Keg House, 34 Thirteenth Avenue NE, Suite 101,
Minneapolis, MN 55413-1007

ISBN: 978-190685-044-9 (hardcover)
ISBN: 978-190685-051-7 (paperback)

Text copyright © 2012 Luca Caioli
Translated by Alia Nardini

Typeset in New Baskerville by Marie Doherty

Printed and bound in the UK by
CPI Group (UK) Ltd, Croydon, CR0 4YY

Contents

'In the Blue, Painted Blue'

Lesson five: Introduce yourself to your classmates.

'Hi. My name's Roberto. I'm 17. I live in Bologna, but I was born in Jesi. I've got one younger sister. I like football. I play for Bologna FC first team. I hope to play very well and score many goals. Besides football, I like watching basketball games. I love listening to music. My favourite singer is Renato Zero. I enjoy going to the movies with my teammates. My favourite actor is Sean Connery. I have seen all the James Bond films. My favourite dish is lasagne, cooked by my mother. My favourite drink is Coca-Cola. Thank you. Glad to meet you.'

Who knows, maybe this is how it all began – that is, Roberto Mancini's long flirtation with England: with an English course. *Il Bimbo* – 'The Boy' – as he is known in Casteldebole, Bologna's training headquarters, has given up school and is studying English at his club's request. If he passes his final exam, Bologna will pay for the course. This involves books, audio cassettes and taught classes. In his bedroom, Mancini listens and repeats sentences, idioms and phrasal verbs, a real pain for a 17-year-old boy whose only interest is football.

However, this will be his life one day. Two big names will describe to him what such a life might be like: Graeme Souness and Trevor Francis, both of whom will be teammates of Mancini in his early years at Sampdoria. The former won three European Cups with Liverpool; the latter two, with Nottingham Forest. Two legends of the 'beautiful game'.

1

With Trevor, Roberto will make feathers fly, and it will end in classic Old West style; still, his experience with such a high-profile player will prove invaluable.

Then later will come David Platt, who will be a close friend of Mancini and eventually his trusted first-team coach at Manchester City. Roberto having managed to persuade the Sampdoria president to sign Platt, the England midfielder will try to reciprocate the favour at a later date, arranging his transfer to Arsenal, where the pair will be reunited.

It is the beginning of November, 1995. Mancini, after a bad spell with referees and a harsh disqualification, is having dark thoughts. He believes that Sampdoria, his club for the past 13 years, have lost their ability to challenge for the Italian championship. The Gunners seem ready to do anything to bring him to Highbury. It is very tempting for Roberto, who had already entertained thoughts of a move earlier in the year. This time, Mancio is ready to go. Living in London is a very appealing thought. He reckons he can find new challenges and gain new experience: of a different football culture, with less stress; of the faster-paced British game. He believes his family could be more serene, his sons could learn English properly, and so could he. However, in the end he can't pluck up the courage to cut the strings attaching him to Sampdoria. His fascination for England lasts, though, and comes back in waves.

December 1996: Sven-Göran Eriksson, his manager at Samp, signs a preliminary contract with Blackburn Rovers and wants to take his playmaker with him. Again, nothing comes of it. Mancini hears good things about the UK from Gianluca Vialli, too, his former strike partner who moved to Chelsea in 1998. Mancini and Vialli have always shared their experiences in life, and they still do over the phone. But it will take some time yet for Mancini to follow his 'goal twin' (as the Samp fans would have it) to British shores.

In 2001, thanks to Eriksson's contacts (the Swede is now manager of the England national team), Mancini ends up at Leicester City. He is 36 when he makes his debut in the Premier League, against Arsenal, on 20 January. He starts with a bang, but then fizzles out: he hasn't played a proper match for eight months, since his final game for Lazio the previous May.

He enjoys his spell with the Foxes, but it doesn't last. Coaching, which Mancini is very keen to try, lures him to Florence. His style is already very British. In fact, Serse Cosmi, the Perugia manager – the first opponent Roberto faces – claims that 'some people wanted to picture this as a challenge between the butcher's son – i.e. me – and some newcomer from Buckingham Palace.' The fact is, Mancini has already defined his style. He is choosing the right clothes, custom-made by his Neapolitan tailor, or from the Giorgio Armani collection. His favourite colour is blue. On his wrist, classy watches. Tied around his neck, in a loose knot, those cashmere scarves that will become his trademark. His shoes are strictly made in England. He likes Ferraris and Bentleys – fast as James Bond.

Years go by, and Mancini masterfully perfects his image, while confirming his talent for winning. He looks over to England again. Rumours grow: there are mentions of Tottenham while he is still coaching Lazio, and later, after he departs Inter Milan, they speak of Portsmouth, Notts County, Chelsea, Liverpool, Sunderland.

The option is always there, at the door, because the footballing culture of England – the tradition, the stadiums, the supporters – is intriguing indeed for a manager. Then comes the right chance: Manchester City. 'I'd rather work to help bring success to those who haven't won anything for a while,' Mancio will say in an interview. That, after all, is what happened with Sampdoria, Lazio, Fiorentina and Inter

Milan. And history repeats itself with City. On 14 May 2012, in Manchester's Albert Square, fans are singing out loud, to the tune of '*Nel Blu Dipinto di Blu*' ('In the Blue, Painted Blue'), the famous song (also known as '*Volare*' – 'Flying') by Domenico Modugno:

Mancini oh oh
Mancini oh oh oh oh
He comes from Italy
To manage Man City
Mancini oh oh oh
Mancini came to win over here.

Mancini confesses, 'I love it when they sing that.' The story that has brought him to City has been an eventful one, taking in league-winning euphoria in Italy, cup final heartbreak in Europe, frustration on the international stage, and any number of twists, turns, bust-ups and lasting friendships.

It is a story that begins way back in a little town in the Marche region of Italy.

You can praise God with a football, too

It is five o'clock in the Piazza Federico II. The sun casts its light upon the golden stones of what used to be the old Roman Forum. This is where Frederick II of Hohenstaufen was born, on Boxing Day 1194. His mother, Constance of Hauteville, was travelling to meet her husband Henry VI, Holy Roman Emperor, and gave birth in a tent. The child would later be crowned King of Sicily, King of Germany and Holy Roman Emperor. He was the warrior, philosopher, legislator and architect who restored the Empire and attempted to solve all problems in southern Italy. His royal court in Palermo was a melting pot of three different cultures: Greek, Jewish and Arab. Today, he is remembered with a plaque and a circular inscription.

Two young boys are playing football behind the ornate, lion-adorned fountain, while the tall obelisk towers over them. It is not a market day, and there are only a few people walking about in the historic city centre, which is closed to cars. Suddenly, the ball crashes straight into the main door of the former Church of San Florián, where the Theatre Studio is now located. Paolo is seven years old; Marco is eight, and seems better at controlling the ball. When asked if he knows who Roberto Mancini is, he answers right away, without hesitating: 'Sure. The one who is in England.' But does he know where he is from? 'He's from here, from Jesi,' the boy answers proudly.

Jesi has been identified by Unesco as a World Heritage Site 'for its ability to preserve its artistic, architectural and cultural history.' According to tourist guides, it was founded by Esio, the King of Pelasgians, who brought the rampant lion as a gift to the city coat of arms. He was a mythological king, often thought to be the progenitor of Etruscans, Sabines and Picenes.

This small city in the Marche region, Ancona province, is home to about 42,000 people. The population has dramatically increased in recent years, due to immigration, particularly from Arab countries. It is going well for them because of Fileni, a company ranked third in Italy for poultry farming; Pieralisi, which produces cheese machines and oil presses; the oil refinery in Falconara Marittima, and a thriving range of small businesses. There are jobs here. The unemployment rate is lower than in other Italian provinces and that is record to be proud of, these days.

Inside and outside the Roman and Medieval walls of Jesi, the standard of living is good. You can get a real grasp of the city's wealth – not only in an economic sense, but also in terms of its culture – by walking leisurely along Corso Matteotti (the 'struscio') during the weekends, when everyone knows one another, everyone is out and about and says hello. Going out to one of the bars looking over Piazza della Repubblica for an aperitif gives a similar sense.

The Giovanni Battista Pergolesi theatre, a gem set deep in red velvet and gilded stuccos, opened in 1798 and has never missed a season in over 200 years of history – not even during the wars or when undergoing renovations. It is always fully booked, just like the Valeria Moriconi theatre studio.

The city art gallery and the Panettiana library are just two of the must-sees for sightseeing tours. Large canvases by Lorenzo Lotto, one of the most famous painters of the

Italian Renaissance, are among the range of antique and contemporary works of art that can be found here.

As the department of tourism proclaims on its webpage, Jesi 'believes in sport as its core value.' The city boasts one of the highest percentages of subscriptions to sports clubs, just as if everyone participated – while, in reality, many are non-playing members. This is a necessary consequence of the fact that the Aurora basketball team plays in A2, the volleyball team in B1, the Jesina football team in Serie D. And let us not forget fencing: there is a long tradition of fencing excellence in Jesi and an academy which has been training champions for the past thirty years.

This heritage is in evidence walking along the main street. In the conference centre, an exhibition is taking place: 'The Fencing Chromosome', photographs taken by Massimo Verdino at the World Championship in Paris's Gran Palais. Beautiful black and white images on spotless white walls hang opposite paintings of medieval duels and of Roman gladiator fights. Stefano Cerioni, who coaches Italy's national fencing team, and foil fencers Elisa di Francisca and Valentina Vezzali are noticeable among the crowd. They have just arrived from Budapest, where they made it to the top of the podium in the team competition during the World Fencing Championship.

Vezzali, 38, was born in Jesi. She won six consecutive Olympic gold medals in Sydney, Athens, Beijing, and London. 'Talking about fencing in Jesi is like taking about Verdicchio dei Castelli [the typical white wine of this region],' she says. 'Its roots go deep. It all started in 1947, when Ezio Triccoli, returning from the Zonderwater prisoner of war camp, South Africa, settled in a basement in the city centre and began teaching the art of fencing, which he had come to master during his internment. The Jesi Fencing Club was born out of his passion, and today it boasts great athletes, starting with Anna Rita Sparaciari, the winner of the first gold medal in the 1982/83 World Championship.'

We move on to a different football, and another star from Jesi: Roberto Mancini. 'I know him well,' adds Vezzali, 'and we were particularly close when he was coaching Inter Milan, because that's my team. Thanks to his skills, he managed to take the team where we supporters had for years been hoping to get to. My husband Domenico, a footballer who used to play in Serie C, reckons that midfielders, especially playmakers like Roberto, have a vision for football which only a few people possess. Mancini certainly knows his stuff. The fact that he excels at whatever he ends up doing proves it. Winning is in his DNA.'

It seems that in Jesi everyone knows and values Roberto Mancini, because 'everything he has achieved so far has been by virtue of his merits. No one ever gave him anything for free. He got where he is because of his class, and because he made many sacrifices, too.' These are the words of Elvio Cittadini, Roberto's hairdresser. 'He's a really decent person, he's funny, ironic … he always takes the mickey out of me. He's been coming here for a haircut since he was five or six. He comes in, sits down, reads some magazines … we'd have a coffee, talk about football and the latest news. Customers come in and say, "Hello Roberto, how are you?" They'll have a few words, then leave. He's at ease here because he is in his own environment; it's where he's from, where his parents and his sister live. As soon as he can, he's back.'

He is back where he belongs, the city where he was born on 27 November 1964, under Sagittarius, with Aquarius rising. His father Aldo was a carpenter and his mother Marianna had just turned 18. They met in Roccadaspide, a little village in the Salerno province, in the Campania region. Aldo had befriended some people from Salerno while working in Germany (it was hard to get by in Jesi after the Second World

War), and was visiting them when he met and fell in love with a local girl. So in love was he, in fact, that he decided to move back to Italy, and asked that beautiful southern girl to come with him to Jesi and marry him.

The wedding took place in 1963 and Roberto – their first son – was born a year later, but not without a great scare. He was delivered by caesarian section, and weighed 5 kilos and 100 grams (11lbs 4oz) – but he was not breathing, and was black all over. The doctor, tactless and overbearing, swiftly announced to the proud father that the baby was born but alas, he was dead. Luckily, he was not the only doctor on duty that day: a wiser doctor took the newborn child, immersed him in ice-cold water, slapped him two, three, four times and finally the champion-to-be started screaming.

It was Don Roberto Vico who baptised Roberto in the church of Saint Sebastian, in the Prato district, outside of the Medieval city walls. Today the 87-year-old clergyman resides in the Collegio Pergolesi, a nursing home where two football fields can be seen from the entrance – a little neglected, it must be said. Many years have passed, but the old priest still remembers the ceremony very well. The father and god-father came and asked when the little one could be baptised, and the whole family gathered around the rosy baby, who, at eight months of age, already weighed 13kg (28lbs).

Don Roberto also remembers with happiness Mancini's first holy communion: 'After the ceremony was over, once the service was finished and the office had been recited, off came the frock with two red stripes, in memory of the old Roman senators' laticlavius. While everyone was eating, drinking and partying, and parents and godparents alike were busy celebrating the occasion, I noticed that the boy was getting restless. He came up to me with a friend of his. The friend, who played football with him, did not hesitate to speak up: "Don Roberto, we're 2–0 down, you couldn't by any chance let Roberto come and play?" So I asked the boy if he was up to something. He said he would check with his daddy and come back. Well, apparently he couldn't get hold of his father, so I gave him permission to go and join his teammates, knowing how much he cared for the team. He already had everything he needed, hidden away in his locker: shirt, shorts and football boots, so that he would be ready to take the field at the right time.

'So after a while, parents and relatives young and old were standing in the square, chatting away and having their picture taken with the communion robes. His father came up to me, looking extremely worried. "I think I lost Roberto," he said, "he's nowhere to be found." "Don't worry," I answered, "he's not lost. Just think of where he could be." He said he didn't really know where he could have ended up. So I told him to look over to the football pitch … Roberto was wearing the number 9 shirt that day and his team won 6–2, thanks to him – I believe he scored two goals on that occasion. It really caused a stir that a boy would be allowed to kick a ball around on his holy communion. It just was not done; before receiving the sacrament there were catechism lessons to be attended, preparing for the sacrament of Eucharist, the spiritual retreat to be taken into account. But in the end,' the priest allows, 'that [playing football] was a way to praise the Lord, too.'

Roberto was nine at the time and he celebrated the day with his sister Stefania, a year and a half younger, all dressed up in white, her hair covered by a monastic bonnet.

At this time, Roberto was attending the Mazzini local elementary school, just a few steps away from his house. He was in class B: a nice, mixed-sex class with 27 pupils. Since the first day of class, his teacher is Annamaria Bevilacqua. She remembers him well:

'Roberto was quite lively, possibly among the liveliest boys in the school – and a bit of a rebel, too. At the beginning, I had some problems with him … Sometimes I was even forced to call his mother in. After a while though, I worked out that he simply didn't like being unjustly told off: because he was so naughty, he would sometimes get the blame, even if he had nothing to do with what had been going on. So I tried to give him responsibilities, and it turned out that that was just what he needed. From then on, I got real gratification from him. During the five years we spent together, I really felt his love for me.'

It was a mutual feeling for the little pupil wearing a light blue smock and a blue ribbon. Ms Bevilacqua was a fairy godmother to Roberto, sometimes even making him a cup of chamomile tea in the morning, just to keep him still – because the Mancini boy simply wouldn't sit quietly at his desk. He used to crack one joke after another.

He was not particularly keen on studying, but he managed to get by in just about every subject. He was just waiting for the bell to ring so that he could be out playing football. Ms Bevilacqua continues:

'I remember once, it must have been the beginning of the second year of class, in elementary school, I had assigned some reading and I called Roberto up to my desk to see what he had learned. It came out that he hadn't read anything. So I told him off, and one of his classmates, a girl called Emma, said, "Roberto couldn't do his homework because he was playing football all day on the Saint Sebastian pitch." I really went mad then, and I vividly recall saying to him, "What are you going to do with your life, if you don't study? Are you going to be kicking a ball around all day long?"'

Passing the ball

A Conversation with Aldo Mancini

'Roberto was just like any other kid. He was bright, lively, smart. But he wasn't hard work. He'd always have his football nearby. He was always playing: he used to come home from school at noon, he had his lunch and he was gone. At two o'clock he was already in front of Saint Sebastian church, kicking the ball around until dark. I would finish work, then go and get him for dinner. There were no dangers, back then: neither cars nor other hazards. All the boys in the neighbourhood would meet up there.'

Silver mane, rugged face made craggy by time, strong Marche accent, Aldo Mancini is wearing a blue tracksuit emblazoned with the Manchester City crest. He is Roberto's number one supporter, and he talks lovingly about him. At the Foro Boario football ground, outside Jesi city walls, the City manager's father is carefully watching the classes of 1999, 2000 and 2001 train. He spends his entire days there. Still, that's the norm, as he is honorary president of US Junior Jesina Roberto Mancini Football School, based here in Boario.

It is dusk, and the boys are swarming from the changing rooms onto the artificial turf football pitch, and back again. Mothers, fathers and older siblings are coming to pick them up or drop them off for their training session. Aldo is standing by the fence enclosure, shaking hands, smiling and chatting to those who are passing by.

Displayed on the fence is a picture of Roberto in his

playing days, wearing a light blue shirt and the captain's arm-band. His father talks to the coaching staff, listens to various opinions, offers advice. 'I am no coach,' he says, 'but after all these years I certainly know something about it.' He is so into football that, for the last administrative elections for the city of Jesi, he stood with the centre-left as a candidate for the Department of Sports.

'This is the city where world champions were raised,' he declared heartily in his address to the electorate, 'and I am not saying that because my son is from here. We excel in many sports, not only fencing. But in order to keep our name high and let Jesi shine, we need newer facilities, and most of all we must modernise school gyms. Sports survive thanks to volunteers, and sacrifices are made by those who passionately practise them; but we cannot do without public fundings. There is still very much to be done.'

His list lost the second ballot, but Aldo did not give up. He still likes to keep himself busy, although he is now over 77 years old. When he was young he used to run middle-distance races: the 7,000 metres cross-country, the 10,000 metres and the 5,000 metres on track and road. Many would remember him as the tall guy running the streets of Jesi. And, of course, he used to play football: he was a holding mid-fielder, a good player. And he swears he had a better left foot than Roberto. But then, with his carpentry work and his two children, there was not enough time for training anymore. But he has never forsaken the football stadiums and the city fields. In fact, talking to him, it soon becomes apparent that he is a real aficionado of the 'beautiful game'. He has seen the greatest champions play: from Alfredo Di Stefano and Ferenc Puskas to Lucidio Sentimenti, Omar Sivori, Pelé and Diego Maradona. To him there are only two players to watch out for right now: Lionel Messi and Cristiano Ronaldo: 'But Messi is above them all: he's humble and he never complains.'

Aldo had a role with the Aurora sports club as a tour manager, even before Roberto's birth. The club, started by Don Roberto as a parish recreational centre in 1955, catered for football, athletics and table tennis. Aldo stayed with them for 25 years until, after a few misunderstandings, he decided to leave to found Junior Jesina.

Everyone who has ever played football in Jesi hung out at the Aurora club. It is where the young Roberto Mancini took his first steps into the football universe. 'He started playing in the "Aurora Pulcini" when he was only five and a half …' begins Aldo.

So is it true what people say, that you lied about his age, because they wouldn't take children under six?
'It is true actually, but it didn't really matter. When he was at nursery, he would already be kicking any object he found lying around, and he spent hours in the church playground. Signing him up for Aurora was just a way for him to let off steam and have fun.'

Where did his passion for football come from?
'Who knows … maybe it happened because I used to play as well, or maybe it is because I have always found this sport fascinating, or perhaps even because there wasn't that much for those kids to do. There was football, period. I often took Roberto along to Serie A games; I supported Juventus and so did he. His idol was Roberto Bettega, so my wife had to go and buy him a black-and-white goalscorer's shirt, at all costs. When the Old Lady came to our Communal Stadium, we went to all the games. We wouldn't have missed them for the world. One time, in 1970, Bologna were playing Juventus in the quarter-finals of the Italy Cup. It was the day when Marino Perani scored the winning goal for Bologna, and I lost Roberto. I let him go forwards, but I got stuck behind

the crowd control barriers. I was caught in the crowd and I couldn't see him anywhere. The stadium was packed and in the end, when I finally managed to get out, he was standing with a woman who was holding his hand. He was crying, poor thing. He was only little, he wasn't even six at that time.'

What were his skills with the ball, at such a young age?
'He could kick the ball well, both with his left and with his right foot, and even as a child he had a good vision of the game. That is the reason why he was put in a team with older kids almost straight away.'

When did you realise that he really had a talent for football?
'When he was about ten, because he would do things that others couldn't do.'

What sort of things?
'Passing the ball. That, in my opinion, is the most vital thing when playing football. I don't like those great players who carry on regardless, ball glued to their feet, wearing blinkers like horses do, and they cannot see their free or unmarked teammates. Roberto used to play as a deep-lying centre forward. He could initiate an attacking sequence and he could always open up scoring chances for his teammates. I believe he used to play like Nandor Hidegkuti. I watched Hidegkuti play for Hungary in Rome in 1953, then I followed his career when he was coaching Fiorentina. Yes, Roberto was just like him: he was difficult to mark, as he would take up wide positions, and just like Hidegkuti, he scored goals by the bucketload.'

Your son was doing really well, so when he was 13 you gave him permission to move to Casteldebole, to the Bologna FC training camp.
'His mum, my wife, didn't want him to go because, you know, being away from home at a very young age … he needed

to carry on studying and obtain a high school diploma. Otherwise, what was he going to do in life? Also she feared drugs, it was a big threat in those days. I insisted, because I knew how much of an opportunity it could be for him; you just couldn't let it go. Roberto dreamt of being a footballer. So in the end we decided to give it a go. I remember that we were in Bologna when Roberto was 14, and I met Amedeo Biavati [the right-winger in the Azzurri's 1938 World Cup-winning side and winner of two Scudetti with Bologna in the 1930s and 40s]. After watching a game in San Lazzero di Savena, he asked who was the father of "that guy who moved so well on the field". I introduced myself, and he said to me, "Your son really has an edge over his teammates. He is good, very good." That's when I started believing, as one of the best footballers in Italy had said it.'

Apart from what Biavati said, would you have imagined Roberto's career then as it turned out to be?
'Not at the beginning, not really … but I did hope; that's what I was after all the time. I hoped he could become somebody, and I believed it could happen because of Roberto's personality. He never gave up. I see kids nowadays, I come across them at Jesina: they play football, but they don't really care. Roberto was different: it was really important to him. He always wanted to win. We lost a final in Ancona and he burst into tears, out of disappointment and anger. That's what always carried him forwards, making him stronger and stronger.'

Bologna, then Genoa, Rome, Florence, Milan …
'I was ever so happy when from Bologna he moved to Mantovani's Sampdoria, because in the football universe, I have never met any president like him. Mantovani turned the club into a family, and they won because they were so

close. Vujadin Boskov, the manager, was like a father to all those boys, and they all joined in to win the league.'

How strong was your influence, and that of your wife, on Roberto's choices? After all, he was only 17.
'He always made his own decisions. I advised him, and of course I had to sign his first contracts because he was under age, but he decided by himself, because he was the one who would be playing for one team or another, not me. The only thing I did was to make sure I never stood in the way of his career.'

And how do you see him today at Manchester City?
'He is happy, he has always liked English football. He enjoys it; it is not so stressful as it was in Milan, when he coached Inter. He was in a shambles then; things are quieter in Manchester. Once the match is over, it is "goodnight and good luck". Everyone shuts up, no one goes on and on about it, the press stays out of it all. Their football debates are not like ours. I've been to Manchester a few times; I've seen the team train in Carrington and I talked to Roberto many times. He's happy to be with City, and I really do hope he wins the Premier League. I believe it can happen, because where Roberto goes, success follows.'

Less than two months later, Aldo, excited and happy – 'over the moon' as he says – is on the Etihad Stadium pitch with Roberto, Marianna and the Premier League trophy, their thumbs up, celebrating victory. His heart, which has played tricks on him before, this time took the strain of one last, insane game. And it also managed the biggest strain of all: seeing his son win out in England.

Wrong address

It takes just ten minutes to walk from the Foro Boario football ground to Largo Granmercato. Here you can see the parish church of Saint Sebastian, consecrated in 1957, its stern-looking front, the crucifix overlooking the entrance. And, just to the side, the Aurora club badge, standing out against a rusty gate. This is the main entrance to the full-size football pitch where official matches are played on Saturdays and Sundays, and where the little ones train, moving the goalposts so that they can play across the pitch. There are neatly traced white lines, a lot of earth, and not much grass. Doriano Giuliani is filling the holes in the ground, and explains that this is where Mancini grew up.

'He lived just over there,' he says, pointing towards a big yellow building with long balconies, beyond the fence, in Via del Prato. The Mancinis have since built themselves a villa, but when Roberto was young they lived only a few yards from this pitch and he was here every afternoon. Even as a child, recalls Doriano, you could tell that he had class, and that he was born with a gift. 'My brother Valentino,' he says, 'who is a year older than Roberto, played as a defender in the same team, because Mancini played above his age.'

At the time, Roberto Pazienza was responsible for the youth team at Aurora. 'When I met Roberto, he was nine years old,' Pazienza says, 'and every afternoon, after training, he would then go and play on our other pitch, the concrete one.' The pitch he refers to is a tiny space, lined with ancient mulberry trees, with a basket at each end. Aurora basketball was born here. Pazienza continues, 'Roberto wouldn't go out without his football, and when our pitch was closed he used to go and play in front of the main doors of the church. He was different from everyone else – also personality-wise. He had that little extra something: he could dribble, he could run, he had the coordination. He played as an inside forward behind the strikers; he always found the space to move freely. As to what you teach a boy of that age – well, more than the technical skills, we tried to educate them to be team players and to respect their teammates. And, most of all, we wanted them to have fun.'

And Roberto surely had the time of his life. As a boy, he was a bundle of mischief: when he was nine, he smashed a tennis racket on his cousin's head, because they had had an argument. He broke his wrist while playing football; he rode his bike into a brick wall; he scratched his leg under a scooter. And he secretly smoked his first cigarette: it made him sick, so Roberto never grew up to be a smoker. Everyone called him a live wire. Indeed, so lively was he that his parents – who were by then both working to support the family (Marianna was a nurse in the local hospital) – decided to send him to a religious boarding school. But Roberto wouldn't have it and ran away, so in the end he moved back to his beloved old school in the neighbourhood, scuola media Federico Secondo. And of course, even at school, football was everywhere: the class team, with Mauro Bettarelli between the posts and Roberto playing as an inside forward, was going strong.

In June, once school broke up, the whole family headed off on holiday, to Senigallia on the Adriatic coast, 30km from Jesi. Aldo used to park his caravan in the pine forest. Roberto liked the seaside – he loved hanging out on the rocks, fishing for mussels and whatever else he happened to come across. But then September would come around again, school would restart, and so too would the football matches on the Saint Sebastian pitch.

Aldo Moretti, one of the directors of the Aurora club, remembers the competitions, the matches, the away games for which Aldo Mancini would set off at 6am. He even recalls Roberto's temper: an occasion in Colle Marino for example. After a number of fouls committed by a defender who was twice his size, Mancini couldn't take it anymore: he hit the roof and they ended up fighting. And it was the strapping defender who came off worst. Then came the prizes: the cups and the 'best player' trophies won by the young Mancini while wearing the yellow Aurora shirt. 'He was in love with football. It ran in his blood,' says Moretti.

Pulcini, esordienti, giovanissimi: Mancini, playing on the Saint Sebastian pitch, climbed the ranks of the amateur game one by one, up to the spring of 1978. Then came his first tantalising glimpse of a future in the professional game.

Silvio Cardinali, who used to work for Aurora, recalls: 'It was May, and Gabriele Cardinaletti, a disabled guy, one of the directors of Real Jesi, who gave his life to football and passed away when he was 38, set up a trial for all the best players in the city youth team. Luciano Tessari was there. He was assistant to Niels Liedholm, the Swedish manager of AC Milan.'

At the end of the game, Tessari went to say hello to Don Roberto. The clergyman asked his opinion on the match. The Milan scout whispered, 'Here's a secret for you, I spotted two: one is old, one is young.' 'The young one,' remembers Don Roberto, was Mancini.' The day he made an impression on Tessari, Roberto played as a left-winger. 'In fact,' adds Don Roberto, 'after the first half of the game, Tessari called him to one side and told him, "Little one, you must kick the ball through the posts more, and not pass it on to your mates so often."'

Together with Mancini, Tessari picked out three other

players: Roberto's classmate Bertarelli, Santoni and Ganzetti. The invitation to attend a final trial at Milanello football training camp was meant to arrive in a few days' time. But the letter, sent by registered post and with a return receipt, never came. It was sent to the wrong address: to Real Jesi, the club which had set up the trial. No one bothered forwarding it to Aurora, nor to the players' parents. An oversight perhaps; or, just maybe, a case of the green-eyed monster.

Aldo found out a few months later, when he met the AC Milan directors at the Adriano Spinelli trophy in Terni. 'We did send that letter, you know,' they said. 'But I never received it,' replied Mancini Senior. Unfortunately, by that time, the Red-and-Black academy was closed to applications, and Roberto had missed the boat, to everyone's disappointment – including the Aurora managers. Silvio Cardinali still wonders about that: 'By all means, they would have taken him [if he had attended the final trial]. I wonder what his career would have been like, had he started at a great club such as AC Milan.'

Aldo Mancini, convinced of his boy's talent, did not give up. And in September that same year, when Roberto started high school with a view to becoming an industrial technician, he phoned Alberto Barchiesi, a friend of his from Castenaso, only a few miles from Bologna, and asked him whether he knew anything about trials for the Red-and-Blues' Academy team. Barchiesi went to find out, and the answer came straight back: there was one scheduled for the following week.

Another player from Aurora was supposed to join in the big adventure: Valentino Giuliani, a defender. However, at the last minute, he was taken into hospital with appendicitis.

So, while Marianna went to a dentist's appointment, Aldo and Roberto headed towards Emilia, to Bologna's Casteldebole training ground, where they would report to Marino Perani.

Football intelligence

A conversation with Marino Perani

Sitting in front of a generous portion of steaming-hot tortellini, the former right-winger of the Red-and-Blues remembers a day back in September 1978. On the white tablecloth are a bottle of Lambrusco and starter leftovers: mortadella and Parmesan cheese. In this traditional trattoria where factory workers and clerks go on their lunch break, near Porta Saragozza in Bologna, everyone knows Marino Perani.

He comes from the Bergamo area, Ponte Nossa to be precise, where he was born in 1939. He went through the youth ranks with Atalanta and arrived at Bologna in 1958. It's mostly the elderly who remember him, as Perani was one of the leading players in the Bologna team that won the last of the club's seven championships to date.

It was 7 June 1964. At the Olympic Stadium in Rome, the winners of a play-off between Bologna and Inter Milan would be the Italian football champions. The two teams had finished the last round of Serie A fixtures on equal points (54), so everything was to be decided by this play-off. What's more, it was the epic Inter team of 'The Magician' Helenio Herrera; even today, many Black-and-Blue supporters can still recite its line-up by heart: Sarti, Burgnich, Facchetti, Tagnin, Guarneri, Picchi, Jair, Mazzola, Milani, Suárez. It was the same astonishing team that, only a few days earlier on 27 May, had defeated Real Madrid 3–1 in the European Cup final at the Prater Stadium in Vienna, with Alfredo Di Stefano,

Ferenc Puskas and Francisco Gento on the Real side. So the odds favoured the Black-and-Blues, while the Red-and-Blues were still grieving for the loss of Renato Dall'Ara, who had managed the team for more than 30 years.

Thirty minutes into the second half, the score was still 0–0. Then Giacomo Bulgarelli took a free-kick to Romano Fogli, who hit a powerful right-foot shot, which took a deflection off Facchetti – Sarti could do nothing about it. Bologna were 1–0 up. Still, Inter Milan hung in there and almost earned a draw. But Perani provided the pass for the Dane Harald Nielsen to score the clincher, and it ended 2–0.

It was a day worth remembering for Marino Perani. And it still is: to this day, a signed photo and a newspaper clipping from the occasion take pride of place on the wall of the trattoria.

'In those days, Bologna were a great team,' says the former winger, 'we never surrendered. Even when the match took a turn for the worse and we were under the cosh, all we had to do was look into each other's eyes and begin recovering.'

Wearing the Bologna shirt, Perani also won two Italian Cups and one Anglo-Italian League Cup – against Manchester City, strangely enough, in 1970. He ended his football career in Canada, in 1975, playing with Toronto Metros-Croatia, and then started his new life as a coach. This decision would take him all around Italy, from Udine to Salerno, from Brescia to Reggio Emilia, from Ravenna to Padua.

He learned this profession in his adopted Bologna, coaching the lower divisions first, then managing the youth team. This is how he met Roberto Mancini. A glass of red wine to rinse his mouth, and then comes the story: 'The clubs in the area knew me. They often phoned me to recommend their best boys. We made them come to the Casteldebole training ground for a trial. Pietro Battara, the goalkeeping coach, Romano Fogli and I would examine them and then draw our conclusions. If we saw that the guy had potential, we signed a deal straight away, both with the club and the parents. It would have been a pity to let a young talent slip away.'

Was that the case with Mancini, too?
'To tell you the truth, someone had mentioned the guy to me before. If I remember correctly, it was one of Roberto's father's friends. He said that he had this boy who looked promising, so I asked him to bring him in to Casteldebole. Roberto came with his father Aldo. I welcomed him and said: 'Come on boy, hurry up, go and get changed because you're playing next.' I have always thought the best way to assess young players is to get them involved in a friendly match, especially if they are competing against older boys. Better than making them run, or dribble the ball, or impose some kind of exercise on them. After fifteen minutes or so on the field, I call Mancini over and I say to him: "Off you go son, go and get changed. I've seen all I needed to see."'

How did he take it?
'He froze on the spot, literally. And his father, too.'

What happened next?
'Nothing. I told them to pop into my office before they left, as I had something to say to them. When Aldo sat down in front of Martelli, the secretary, and me, he was almost in tears. "What did he do? What did he do wrong? Why did you make him leave so early, while everyone else carried on playing?" he asked me, with real concern. "I'll tell you right away. I have already seen what I wanted to see: this guy would suit us, so if the terms we are setting are OK with you, he can stay."'

And what were those terms?
'700,000 lira on the spot, which would go to the Aurora club

for his player registration, and a five million lira deal, in the event that he made his debut in Serie A before turning 18.'

What did Aldo Mancini say to that?
'"Good, great," he immediately answered. But you could tell he was nervous, too. "How are we going to manage? We are in Jesi, and Roberto goes to school there." So we told him he needn't worry: if Roberto were to accept the deal, he would move to the halls of residence in Casteldebole, he would go to school there and he would be looked after in every way. "We'll just see how it goes, how he grows up, how he develops." Such words were immediately soothing for his father. So we agreed that we would call them on the following day, to tell them what kind of papers were needed, and when he needed to show up in Casteldebole. And so we did.'

The tortellini are getting cold and the landlord looks worried. He comes over to the table and asks Signor Perani, with a pleading look on his face, whether they are not to his liking. So as not to hurt his feelings, the tortellini are swiftly dispatched.

Perani has an unquestioned ability to tell the future from the evidence of the present. Other than Mancini, he scouted players like Macina, Bergossi, Zinetti, Pazzagli and Boschin, just to quote a few names. Still, when you are assessing a 13-year-old boy, you can get it wrong.

'You can indeed, but in my opinion there really are hard and fast rules about football. At that age, it's easy to spot talents that other people might not notice.'

So what did you see in 'Mancio'?
'He was able to use both feet well, especially his right foot, and he had a real vision of the game. As soon as he saw a free teammate, he would pass the ball on to him, with the inside

of his foot, with the outside, always with great precision. He played as a wing half and had a good sense of manoeuvring, remarkable individual skills and a sharp shot. What impressed me most about him was his football intelligence, not to mention his good fundamentals and his natural talent, which were all shining bright. In short, he was already a proper footballer, and I believe that you are born a footballer. Then, with the right advice and tips from your coach, you can become a better player.'

What was Mancini like, when he got to your place?
'His head was really screwed on. Mancini had a strong personality, he was quite sensible and he understood that we took things very seriously in Casteldebole. We kept telling the boys that being a footballer didn't mean kicking the ball around, earning a lot of money and living it up. We said many times that sacrifices were needed – a great deal of them, too, if you want to be a professional player. Some got it, others didn't. Roberto was among those who had this concept clear in his head. He was enthusiastic and determined. He wanted to seize the opportunity. We never had any issues with him. We didn't need to tell him off, ever, because he was the first to know his duties.

'He was a man of few words, and he was good friends with my son Paolo, who used to play with him. He was a fine man and showed what he could do day after day, proving to us the skills we had noticed in his trial. He believed in himself, he trusted his talent. That's why coaches like Franco Bonini and Andrea Soncini, who worked with him when I went on to coach the first team, put their trust in him.'

What did you teach him in Casteldebole?
'It's easy enough to teach someone who has good fundamentals. With such guys we usually teach them how to kick

the ball in certain ways, how to give the opponents a hard time, how to implement a pattern of play, how to play as a team, how to get your teammates to help you, and how to help them back. And mostly, we correct mistakes. After a match, if a player has done something wrong and he really screwed up, you take him to one side and you tell him how and where to make things better. Still, I'm not one of those coaches who want to impose their view at all costs and end up ruining players. A footballer, especially one like Roberto Mancini, must have complete freedom of expression.'

Dessert, coffee and spirits – a well-deserved break before the final part of the conversation.

Would you have ever imagined Mancini at the level he ultimately reached?
'He had the skills and he had the character, and what's more he wasn't afraid.'

Afraid?
'That's right, he wasn't scared to take on responsibilities, or ride one tackle too many. Some guys just don't jump in; they go all shy and find it hard to show what they can do on the field. And the first time they face an opponent, they become frightened and move their leg away. Still, I believe that Mancini must have been gifted with both will-power and brains, even as a child: they are essential, in order to achieve all that he has achieved so far.'

The Boy

He is 13 years and nine months old, bobbed brown hair, like the Beatles, and the hint of a moustache. The youngest in Casteldebole; that is how he gets his nickname, *Il Bimbo* – 'The Boy'. The memories of his trial, 'an unforgettable moment, a permanent feeling that will stay with me forever,' and Perani's assent, are behind him now. The Boy now needs to face up to the reality of the training camp. Sure, Bologna Academy is one of the best in Italy: there are four luscious green football fields, changing rooms and facilities which Aurora could only dream of; there are trainers and technical teams, champions that you might have only seen from a distance in a football stadium, or close up in the Panini stickers collection; the halls of residence are spacious, with only 15 guests; everything is beautiful, a dream come true for anyone who wants to be a footballer – but it is not enough. The first days for little Roberto are not easy at all. He is really missing home, and homesickness is a scourge, showing up at dusk, creeping up behind you all of a sudden when you least expect it, and it won't let go. The only solution is calling home; so he pushes his coins into the payphone up on the wall, again and again.

Mother Marianna and father Aldo, who made a hard decision when they let him go, spoke for a long time with those in charge ('I would never allow my children to leave home at thirteen and a half,' Roberto would say many years later, after becoming a father). His parents tried to reassure themselves about the school being good, they enquired about the food, the teammates, the way their son would be treated; and at the same time, they told Roberto that, if he felt he couldn't do it, it only needed one phone call and they'd be on their way to bring him back home. Sometimes Roberto, when the jokes and the bullying are too much to take (being the youngest makes him a target, although on the football pitch he knows his stuff), is tempted to send out an SOS to Jesi; but he does not give up. He speaks to Aldo and Marianna, but he tries not to let sadness show in his voice, he pretends to be happy, so that they do not worry. He knows his parents won't let him stay, otherwise.

He acts the same with his coaches and those who surround him. 'I never saw him cry, never heard a complaint,' says Franco Bonini, now 77 having spent a lifetime in Bologna as a player and youth team manager. 'On a daily basis, Roberto was good, very good and responsible. A credit to his parents, who educated him well; to himself, who was already as conscientious as a grown-up; but also to us. We tried to make sure, in every way possible, that the boys didn't feel out of their depths, detached from their own reality. And right from the start, we tried to put across to Roberto that, if he followed the rules, if he behaved like he was expected to, he would go far in the football world.'

So Roberto is 'good, very good' – apart from the times when he skips school. This happens on his very first day. The bus picks up all the boys at 6.30am sharp and drops them off a few kilometres away, in Casalecchio di Reno. They have breakfast in the bar, then everyone takes public transport to get to their own schools in Bologna. Mancini is the newcomer, and Walter Bicocchi, the administrator, nicknamed 'The Magician', acts as a kind of tutor for the young ones, so he is taking care of Roberto that day. Standing in front of the industrial technicians high school, a thousand doubts strike Mancini. New school, new classmates, new teachers, his strong Marche accent, which sounds completely out of place in Bologna – he really does not feel like going in. So he asks 'The Magician' not to walk him to his class, because he is embarrassed: he is not a kid on his first day in elementary school. And as soon as Bicocchi turns the corner, Mancini is gone. He retraces his steps, heads back towards Casalecchio. He buys a sports paper, sits on a bench and reads to kill time, thinking that he can wait there until the bus comes to take him back to Casteldebole. He convinces himself that no one will notice he has skipped school. But it is not his day, for who should chance upon him there but Bicocchi, who gives him a good telling off and takes him straight back to school.

School and books are not really his thing, as the Boy does not like studying. He reads the sports pages in *Resto del Carlino*, he reads *Stadio* and *Guerin Sportivo*, so he knows every-thing about football; he devours comics, such as *Intrepido*, *Il Monello*, *Tex Willer*, *Diabolik*, *Mickey Mouse* – anything, except school books. And during his second year in Casteldebole, he decides that he has had enough. He does not want to go to school anymore.

Pietro Battara phones Roberto's family to discuss the matter with them. 'Yes, we talked about it,' says Aldo, 'he says he wants to devote himself completely to football.' At first Battara thinks, if the boy's father is okay with it, there is not much he can do; but he can't stomach the fact that while everybody else is getting up, having breakfast and going to school, Roberto is lazing about in bed. He must act, so he goes and speaks to Mancini. 'Right,' he says, 'at 7am tomorrow you must report to the warehouse. You'll go down there every day and I'm sure they'll find you something to do.' And so the Boy ends up brushing the first-team play-ers' boots, folding up shirts, sweeping floors and generally tidying up everyone else's mess, a morning routine which will last until the following year, when Mancini decides to go back to school and study in a technical school for surveyors. He passes his first-year exams, but by his second year he is already part of the first-team squad, so he packs it all in for good to start the famous English course.

His school education may have had its highs and lows, but his football career is going great guns. He starts in Giovanissimi, then moves to Allievi. His coach there is Antonio Soncini, a true Parma man, who used to play in Serie B (Alessandria, Salernitana, Modena, Parma) as a midfielder – and a very reliable one – before becoming a youth coach for Parma, Varese, Bologna and Sampdoria. Today, Soncini, now 74 years old, recounts his impressions of the young Mancini. 'He already had distinct technical and tactical ability,' he says. 'He stood out because of his vision of the game, his movements without the ball, his remarkable ability to shake off markers. And, most of all, for his character: he was a born leader.' Bonini adds, 'On the field, he acted like a manager: very demanding, but also capable of giving a lot to others. If someone made a mistake, he never stopped grudging. And he would do that with me, too. For example, when a free-kick could not be taken from his side (he is right-footed, so taking a free-kick on the left side wasn't the best for him), I told him to let someone else have a go. And he would wander off in a temper.'

On that Allievi team, there were a lot of stars of the future. Soncini recalls:

'There were Claudio Treggia and Omar Martelli, who made it to Serie C; Francesco Gazzaneo, who would later play in Serie A and B; Riccardo Bellotto, who went on to play for Pistoiese; Giancarlo Marocchi, a midfielder who got lucky with Juventus; Antonio Paganin, who ended up with Inter Milan after playing for Sampdoria and Udinese; Paolo Perani – Marino's son – a good defender; and there at the front, we had Mancini and Macina.'

This impressive pair of strikers – 'Bologna's Brazilians' – left in amazement all those who attended Allievi's home games on Saturday afternoons on the main football pitch in Casteldebole. Mancini was the team captain; Macina, skinny and sublime, dominated on the wing. 'He [Macina] was great, but he didn't have the willpower. He drove me mad,' admits Bonini.

The two forwards shared a room in Casteldebole, and later moved into the same flat in Bologna, in via Valeriani. The city was welcoming, the people were warm, open and honest, and here Mancini found good friends who helped him overcome his homesickness and settle into the new environment: people such as Macina, Bonini, Soncini, even Walter Bicocchi, who, after that scolding on Roberto's first day at school, took him under his wing. The boys could go out in Bologna in the evenings, provided they asked their coach for permission. They typically went to the movies or to basketball games (watching Fortitudo, the team supported by some of their new friends). They did not go out for dinner very often, as money was scarce. The club paid Mancini 40,000 lira per month as travel allowance, later increased to 90,000. His generous and caring parents, whenever they could, gave him a little something. But there was no money to fritter away.

During the day, they trained with Soncini and Bonini, who made them work really hard, practising both technical and athletic skills. They ran a lot and they performed the same drills over and over again: passing, dribbling, controlling the ball, shooting ... to the players, the coach seemed stern and strict, hard like an iron sergeant in an American movie. But the man who would become 'Grumpy' in Sampdoria's 'Snow White and the Seven Dwarves' club had a heart of gold. He taught Mancini the basics, affectionately calling him Robertino. He moulded him into an attacking midfielder, someone who could play in the 'hole' behind the two strikers. Unfortunately, circumstances would prevent Mancini from playing in this role at either Bologna or Sampdoria, as he was needed up front.

Once a fortnight, on the Saturday night after the match, the Boy used to catch a train back to Jesi. Over three hours on a clanging wagon, just to be with mum, dad and Stefania. Oh, and to stuff his face with 'vincisgrassi', a pasta dish typical of the Marche region and Marianna's speciality. Here he would recount all his latest news, of his victories and his adventures in Emilia. He would meet up with his friends, who were proud of what he was achieving. Then, on the Monday, off he would go again, his case full of clean clothes – and plenty of food. In fact, the Boy was growing up quickly, and he was always ravenous, prompting Aldo to intercede: he turned up at the restaurant in Casalecchio with which the club had a partnership, and left a tip to the waiters, entreating them to ensure Roberto did not starve (there was also a threatening phone call from Marianna!).

And if he was hungry for food, the Boy was equally ravenous for success on the pitch. The Allievi team won everything, hands down, and Mancini scored 37 goals. The next step was Primavera, but Roberto played only one game with them – he had already been called up for the first team. 'Do I go, or don't I?' he asked Soncini. 'I'll kick your butt if you don't,' his coach replied.

The best years

A conversation with Marco Macina

He was 'the better one', better than Roberto Mancini. 'Pure talent. Never seen anyone with such class,' the Manchester City manager used to say. Marco Macina was an ambidextrous winger, quicker with the ball than without, a rebel genius. He loved nimble dribbling and beautiful goals, girls and nights out clubbing, cards and horses. 'And in such cases,' Mancini said, 'football – which [for most of us] is great, because it allows you to do a well-paid job that is also fun – becomes a bad thing. Football is not forgiving. Even talent may not be enough for you to find the way back home. It has you lost in the sands.'

Marco and Roberto are opposite characters, each balancing the other out. The Boy's roommate came from San Marino. After his apprenticeship in Bologna and his first-team debut (24 appearances, three goals), he was sent to Serie B: one season with Arezzo, one with Parma. Then, in 1985, came his chance: the call from Nils Liedholm's AC Milan.

It was not the best of times, as the club had run into financial difficulties and Giussy Farina would soon hand over to Silvio Berlusconi, the new president. Macina made five appearances without scoring. The boy was not doing well, so there came another change of direction, downwards this time, on loan to Reggiana. For a player who has walked the San Siro fields, Serie C1 is a hard place to be. The following year he was in Ancona, C1 again.

One Sunday, in Ospitaletto, his right knee started tingling: the doctor told him it must be his meniscus, and that he might need surgery. Macina carried on training, and the pain became worse. More detailed examinations showed that he had torn a ligament. The operation was difficult and the convalescence long; he came back just in time for the last matches of the league. His contract with AC Milan came to an end, Ancona did not make him an offer and, at 25, he who was considered to be the best Italian talent of his generation gave up playing football.

Today, Marco Macina works for the tourist office in the San Marino Republic. It is not easy to get hold of him. In the football world, not many people know what happened to him. He speaks happily about Mancini, and while he is wary of telling his own story, he agrees to share his memories of his early career:

'I wasn't even fourteen. I started kicking the ball around in Tre Penne, a sports club in San Marino. I was meant to go for a trial with Inter Milan, but I had some problems with my throat, so I couldn't take part. So I ended up in Bologna. There I met Mancini, he was two months younger than me, and they took us both. At exactly the same time. It was Perani who wanted us.'

What was your initial reaction, when you arrived at Casteldebole?
'The same that any 14 year old would have. Bologna was in Serie A. The people and the facilities were up to standard, but at that age one is still a child. It was probably easier for me, because I was from there. For Mancini it was harder; he lived further away.'

What was Mancini like, at that age?
'We were always together, same room, same team. We shared everything, both in Bologna and in the national team. We

went through the youth teams, Allievi, then the selections for the national team at Under-15, Under-16 level. Many scouts came along – one of them was Nils Liedholm, who liked us a lot. We were very good, so we soon reached a higher level; so by the time we were 16 we were already knocking on the first-team door. Basically, Roberto and I lived together until he moved to Sampdoria.'

So what were things like with the Boy?
'He was just like everybody else, he was a good guy, like everyone else there.'

Did he miss home really badly?
'I suppose that's normal, at the beginning ... at our age, we weren't used to being away from our parents, from our friends. As far as the environment is concerned: one can go and play wherever he likes, but if he comes home to his family in the evenings, everything's different. But if you're living away from home, in halls of residence, everything is harder. Also, we were the youngest ones: in Casteldebole, the Beretti team was still up and running; there were guys who were 21–22 and wouldn't let you get away with anything at all.'

What was your daily routine like?
'At the time, Bologna was a nice place to be. And the Magician, Martelli, Soncini, the whole club were looking after us. We led a very quiet life.'

Still, when you turned 16, you both let loose ... or at least that's what Mancini said in an interview, comparing his youth to Mario Balotelli's
'Look, things are very simple. When, in spite of your wishes, you become someone, and fame hits you at 16 years of age; when you're all over the newspapers; when you're worth

four or five billion; when you're centre stage at an age where you are prone to mistakes … well, you can screw up. But I still think that ours were small, venial sins. We never did anything outrageous, we stayed within the boundaries and we were checked upon.'

Let's go back to football. It is true what everyone says, that you were stronger than Mancini?
'We played two different roles. Even if eventually he did really well as a striker, when we played together, Roberto was an attacking midfielder; he played right behind the strikers. And he was very good at the offensive and the tactical side of things – he was the perfect attacking midfielder. I was a forward, a pure winger. I could play on the left or the right side alike. Perhaps I was better at dribbling and neutralising opponents. I played differently, probably in a more flamboyant way. He had a stronger character, he was more mature and put more effort into things.'

Did you fight for long for a place on the first team?
'No, we didn't compete at all, because Roberto made it before me. He played right from the start; he totalled up more appearances than me in the league, he scored nine goals that year and was confirmed on the first team straight away. And he did work his way up to the top, didn't he?'

So why did you lose your way?
'Mainly, I lost my way because I was unlucky at the most important moments of my football career. And I suffered with injuries. Possibly, it might have been bad luck to arrive at AC Milan when I was still so young; maybe I needed some father-figure president like Paolo Mantovani was to Mancini. And, obviously, at AC Milan there were Paolo Rossi, Pietro Paolo Virdis and Mark Hateley, who were ahead of me, so I

didn't have much of a chance. In that respect, if I had gone to a slightly weaker team, I might have had more opportunities. Then I went to Ancona and suffered a knee injury, and of course that happened in the last year of my contract. That was hard. You need somebody to trust in you and push you forward, and no one stepped in. I thought I'd stop for a year, to sever all the ties and become the master of my own destiny, free to decide my future. However, after that, although I only heard nice words, no club wanted me. It might sound predictable but I was unlucky at the most important times of my life, and I paid for that. By God, there were surely faults on my side, too. Of course I made mistakes, but could you name any young footballer who is not out there clubbing and on the pull on a Sunday night? On some matters, the press really blew it out of proportion … I paid for my early fame. I couldn't understand what was going on. In any case, that's how it went.'

Let's go back to Mancini. How do you judge his career?
'As a footballer, he was one of the strongest Italian players ever. And he won staying where he was – it is much easier to win the league or a cup with AC Milan, Juve, Inter, than with Sampdoria or Lazio. As a manager, the facts speak for themselves: three Scudetti with Inter Milan, the Premier League with City … Roberto has always been able to get back into the game, at Manchester City, for instance. A lot of money was being spent, but money is not enough to lead a team to victory – Mancini did that. He is doing really well. And he was lucky to work with good teams, too, where there are a lot of players to choose from – that goes to his advantage.'

Macina pauses, then ends the conversation with one last sentence: 'In Bologna, Roberto and I spent our best years. These memories will never fade away.'

1981

Prince Charles and Lady Diana Spencer marry on 29 July in St Paul's Cathedral. Three-and-a-half thousand people are invited, 60,000 more fill the streets of London, and 750 million follow the event on TV. Bobby Sands dies on a hunger strike he started on 1 May in HM Prison Maze. John McEnroe avenges his previous defeat, beating Bjorn Borg both at Wimbledon and in the US Open, and also wins his third Davis Cup. As he leaves a hotel in Washington DC, Ronald Reagan, the new President of the United States, is shot and wounded by the insane John Hinckley Jr. In Spain, there is a failed coup d'état when Lieutenant-Colonel Antonio Tejero interrupts the Congress of Deputies who are finalising the appointment of the new President Leopoldo Calvo Sotelo. Henry Fonda wins the Academy Award for Best Actor for his performance in *On Golden Pond*. Best Picture goes to *Chariots of Fire*, directed by Hugh Hudson, but the movie bagging four awards in Hollywood is *Raiders of the Lost Ark* by the duo of Steven Spielberg and George Lucas, starring Harrison Ford as Indiana Jones. Françoise Mitterrand is elected President of France. Peter Sutcliffe, the Yorkshire Ripper, is arrested by the police. IBM releases its first personal computer: the IBM 515. As he enters St Peter's Square, Pope John Paul II is shot and critically wounded by Mehmet Ali Ağca, a Turkish terrorist who is a member of the militant fascist group Grey Wolves. King Crimson release 'Discipline', while Nikka Costa, eight years old, climbs the world charts with '(Out Here) On My Own'. Liverpool win their third European Cup at Parc des

Princes in Paris, beating Real Madrid 1–0. On 11 May, Bob Marley dies in Miami.

It is 1981, and in Italy the P2 scandal is brought to light: a Masonic Lodge is running a shadow cabinet with the participation of the country's main politicians and economists. Gilles Villeneuve wins the first Grand Prix of the turbo era, in Monaco, on behalf of the Maranello team, driving Ferrari fans crazy. The Red Brigades abduct the American General James Lee Dozier. Umberto Eco's first novel *The Name of the Rose* is a number one bestseller, and not only in Italy. Giovanni Trapattoni's Juventus, with Zoff, Bettega, Gentile, Cabrini, Scirea, Causio and Liam Brady, wins the league ahead of Roma. The country is glued to the television as the tragedy in Vermicino unfolds: little Alfredo Rampi, having fallen in an artesian well, dies after three days, more than 60m below the surface, while rescuers try desperately to save him.

On 13 September 1981, the eightieth Italian championship begins. The usual suspects are deemed to be the main contenders: Juventus, pursuing their second star (which they will add to their badge upon achieving their 20th Scudetto); Rome, wanting to make up for wrongs suffered during the previous season; Beccalossi and Altobelli's Inter Milan, Franco Baresi and Joe 'The Shark' Jordan's AC Milan, and Giancarlo Antonioni's Fiorentina.

At the Communal Stadium, Bologna are playing Cagliari. Tarcisio Burgnich, manager of the Red-and-Blues, tells Mancini to warm up. There are 17 minutes remaining, and the score is 1–1. The Boy, 16 years, nine months and 16 days old, warms up and enters the field of play, replacing Giuliano Fiorini. Roberto's entrance is a positive move by Burgnich, an attempt to find a winning goal, but the scoreline does not change. Mancini does not see much of the ball but his father Aldo, in the stands, is over the moon. He almost missed his son's debut. Roberto hadn't told him – not even a phone call home, so Aldo was placidly setting off to watch the Allievi match against Rimini. Luckily, Soncini phoned him and said, 'Go to the Communal Stadium. Robertino is on the bench and maybe it will be his day.' From now on, he will be playing all the games.

Mancini had already been getting close to some of Bologna's big names. In Casteldebole, the boys would sometimes train with the first team. For a 15-year-old kid, standing side by side with the likes of Savoldi, Chiarugi, Pileggi, Dossena and Colomba was a real honour. Still, those times were rough due to the emergence of the betting scandal, one of the sorriest chapters in Italian football history. The story came to light in the 1979/80 season. In the aftermath, footballers and managers alike received jail sentences, AC Milan were relegated to Serie B, Paolo Rossi – the hero of the Spanish Mundial – along with 26 other players received a two-year ban, and Bologna had to start the 1980/81 season with a five-point penalty. Mancini later recalled that, at the time, players and management talked about it incessantly.

Despite the penalty points, Bologna's new coach Gigi Radice – who had won the league with Paolo Pulici and Ciccio Graziani's Torino – took the team to seventh place in Serie A. When the team travelled away to Ascoli, Mancini was brought along as a substitute. The intention had been to take Marco Macina instead, but when they went to pick him up from school, he wasn't there – he had gone to bet on the horses. In the event, Mancini did not get the opportunity to play in Ascoli. His chance would come with the New Year's Day Football Tournament in 1981.

With the Azzurri in Uruguay to play the Mundialito, the Italian football authorities decide to stage an additional competition between the 16 Serie A teams. It's a filler tournament, but it gives Mancini the opportunity to play. On 4 January at the Dall'Ara Stadium, he features for a whole half against Torino. Amilcare Ferretti, Gigi Radice's assistant, needs to compensate for the players he has missing, and he puts his trust in Roberto. The match ends in a 2–1 defeat, but the Red-and-Blue supporters will remember the magic touch and the confidence that the would-be star shows during the game.

The New Year's Day Football Tournament is only a pleasant interlude, as there are no other chances for Roberto to shine until 13 September that year, a day that marks the beginning of a fabulous season, at least on an individual level. Burgnich gives him the number 7 shirt, then the number 13, and later the number 9 as the Boy becomes a central player for Bologna. The coach pairs him with Chiodi, Chiorri or Fiorini. He plays him carefully, that's for sure: 12 minutes in Turin against the Granatas on the second match day of the season; 28 minutes the following Sunday against Catanzaro. Then, on 4 October, San Petronio's (the patron saint of Bologna's) Day, the Red-and-Blues are playing Como in an away game. After three league matches, the situation is critical: two points in total. Against Como, Bologna are playing for safety. It begins badly when Nicoletti scores straight away for Como. The score is still 1–0 to the home side when Mancini replaces Chiorri after 57 minutes. Como then double their lead with a penalty and it looks like the match is over. But Pileggi reduces the deficit in the 74th minute and, four minutes later, Mancini scores the equaliser after a defensive mistake. 'I happened to be on a ball passed to me by Neumann. The keeper was out, and I lobbed him,' Mancini would say at the end of the season, in front of the cameras, as he reflected on his first goal in the highest division.

By the time he turns 17 on 27 November, he is already in the line-up on a regular basis and has scored his first two goals. The second was against Roma, in their eighth league game of the season. Bologna got a good hiding, 3–1 after a goal by Bruno Conti and a double by Pruzzo, but the Boy got one back for his team. Around the dressing-room, Liedholm the Baron pays him compliments, and Burgnich starts naming him in the starting XI rather than on the bench. By Christmas, the kid from Jesi has already scored three goals in his first season in Serie A, the most recent coming in the Friuli Stadium against Udinese on 20 December: Colomba delivered a cross from the left; Mancini got to the ball before everyone else and put it away.

Photographs of the Bologna Christmas party show him toasting with Chiodi, Benedetti and Burgnich. Under the tree for the Boy is a present from the club: one and a half million liras, for the outstanding job he has done. It is a generous Christmas gift, and an amount of money he has never seen before in his entire life.

I'll play him

A conversation with Tarcisio Burgnich

His opponents used to call him 'The Rock'. The nickname was given him by Armando Picchi, the great Inter Milan captain, when the team was coached by Helenio Herrera. During a match against Spal, an opponent, Carlo Novelli, collided with Burgnich and was knocked out on the ground. When Novelli pulled himself up, he saw his ex-teammate Picchi smiling at him: 'Don't say anything, I know how you're feeling: you just hit a rock.' From that time onwards, Tarcisio Burgnich became 'The Rock'.

Giacinto Facchetti and Burgnich were the most admired pair of full-backs in the 1960s and 70s, the pillars of Herrera's Inter and Ferruccio Valcareggi's Italian national team. In twelve years wearing the black and blue stripes, Burgnich had really seen it all: four league championships, two European Cups and two Intercontinental Cups. This defender was the man who managed to score the momentous equaliser for the Italian national team in the 'game of the century', the 1970 Mexican World Cup semi-final with West Germany (it ended 4–3 to Italy). To this man, in the final at the Azteca Stadium on 20 June 1970, fell the hardest task: marking Pelé at the top of his form. Burgnich was the full-back who allowed 'O Rei' ('The King') to fly high and score the goal that put Brazil 1–0 up, leaving him in mid-air like El Greco's Christ on the Cross. That mistake would be thrown back in his face for a long time, but his nickname stayed on. He was

'The Rock' to his opponents, and a good egg to his mates. After his decision to end his incredibly long professional career in Naples in 1977, he went on to coach many players with that same philosophy.

His first experiences were in Livorno and Catanzaro, then he landed a coaching role at Bologna for the 1981/82 season, taking the place of Gigi Radice, who was on his way to AC Milan. Tarcisio Burgnich, who is now 73, retired to Altopascio, Tuscany, after his last season as Pescara's manager – eleven years ago. He distanced himself from the game of football, although he has not given up watching it on TV. His voice is steady and resolute, just as he was in tackles on the football pitch. You can tell he comes from Friuli (he's from Ruda) from his slight accent when he speaks. He gladly talks about Roberto Mancini, who still calls him occasionally to say hi.

How come you decided to field a boy of just 16 years and 9 months in the first team?
'We had two players from the Academy team, Mancini and Macina, who were both phenomenal. The president, Fabretti, was very keen on Marco. He was a fast and cunning right-winger, he would easily overcome opponents, and when I played him, he would turn the game around for us. It's such a pity that he lost his way afterwards, but that's the way he was: he was a hothead. Roberto was a conscientious midfielder, very mature for his age. If he had always played in the midfield, he would have become the new Michel Platini. Antonio Soncini, my second manager who also trained the academy team, had already told me about him several times, saying he was first-rate.

'The president wanted to loan him to Forlì, in the third division, so that he could cut his teeth. Vulcano Bianchi, one of the directors there, really tried hard: he wanted him at all costs. Nevertheless, I went to Fabretti and told him: "Look, I'd rather have Mancini here, and I'll play him." We took him to our first-team training camp for the championship, and also to Rome for the Coppa Italia, although he watched the game from the stands.'

What was Mancini like at that time, technically speaking?
'He used to play as a wing half in the academy team. He was a midfielder like Valentino Mazzola, one of the best number 10s in Italian football history [the captain of the great Torino team that perished in the Superga air disaster back in 1949, and father of Sandro, who later played for Inter Milan]. Mancini was a sort of jack-of-all-trades, truly capable of setting the pace of the game, but also great at scoring goals. When he came to me, I had to change his position, because I needed someone up front. Fiorini, our centre forward, was injured; Chiodi, the other striker, had some problems too, so I needed the guy there, in a forward position, as second striker. I must admit, though, if I had played Mancini back to goal, he would have been in trouble. That was what happened with Sampdoria, especially in the early days under Ulivieri. Afterwards, when Boskov came and decided to play him further back, he had more passing options and could happily distribute the ball to the strikers without giving up scoring goals himself.'

Let's go back to 13 September 1981, when he made his debut against Cagliari at the Communal Stadium in Bologna, with 17 minutes of the game remaining.
'I remember it well. Mancini was meant to go to Rimini to play with the academy team that day. However, on the Saturday – the day before the match – I told Soncini to make

him available for the first team. On the following day, I had him come off the bench to replace Fiorini.'

You put your trust in him, and Mancini paid you back with a wonderful season.
'Yes, he did. He scored nine goals and became top scorer for the team. His first one was against Como, with only a few minutes left in the game. And that was in a 2–2 draw, a key result for us. The best goal? The one he kicked in Rome, picking up a really long pass by Baldini. The ball came from way behind the midfield: Roberto, stuck between two defenders, lifted a side-foot shot with a volley, over Tancredi and into the net. An extraordinary goal, for his coordination and precision.'

How did the youngster get along with his older teammates in the dressing-room?
'That year, Bologna, together with Massimo Giacomini's Torino, had the youngest team in the division; so Mancini found himself at ease, surrounded by other young players. Also, he was a quality player, so older teammates got along well with him. Let's not forget that, at the time, the first-team squad did not have 30 or so names on the list like it has now. Relationships between teammates were a lot easier.'

How was he with you?
'He was a good guy, quiet and peaceful. I wouldn't call him shy, but surely reserved. You could tell that he came from a good family who raised him strictly. I tried to encourage him, to give him advice that could be helpful to his career, and he appreciated that. Off the pitch, out of interest, I could tell you that Mancini and Macina, the reckless one in the bunch, used to go to the same school as my daughter. They were always surrounded by girls.'

Unfortunately for you and for Bologna, that season ended badly. You were relieved of your duties as manager, and Bologna, for the first time in history, were relegated to Serie B.

'We were missing two key players: Danilo Pileggi and Herbert Neumann. The German, who was supposed to be the brains of the team, injured himself during summer training, he struggled with a heel problem that whole year – basically he was never available. Neumann and Pileggi were our coordinators, pulling the strings in midfield, so the team suffered greatly without them. And we had no money for new acquisitions. Actually, before the season began, the president had sold a striker to Sampdoria, Salvatore Garritano, while Giuseppe Dossena had gone back to Torino. We need to pay wages, we were told. I was dispensed with, and the person who came after me, Franco Liguori, still didn't save Bologna from relegation.'

So, Mancini went to the highest bidder …
'I had already spoken of Mancini to Sandro Mazzola and to Giancarlo Beltrami, director of football at Inter Milan. I went to Milan and said to them: "You must take this guy, come on, you have Klaus Bachlechner, a defender that Bologna really want. You can consider a loan or a swap." They didn't pay any heed. They answered that they already had young players in their youth team, so no dice there. I also went to Turin, as I had known Giampiero Boniperti, the Juventus president, for a long time. We used to play together, you know. I suggested trading Pier Paolo Virdis for Mancini, but no dice there, either. And at the end of the season, when money was a bit tight for president Fabretti, he sold Mancini to Sampdoria.'

You were one of the pillars of the Italian national team that won the European Championship in 1968 and that were runners-up in the 1970 World Cup in 1970. How do you explain Mancini's lack of success wearing national colours?

'It was because he had to come to terms with Roberto Baggio. Managers didn't trust Mancini and Baggio in the same team: it could have resulted in the kind of rivalry that we saw during the 1970 World Cup, between Gianni Rivera and Sandro Mazzola [two players who, according to their manager Valcareggi, simply could not be on the field at the same time – hence, there was a 'relay' whereby one would start the game and the other would come on later to replace him].

What do you think of him now, as a team manager?

'I remember him as a child. I could never have imagined that he would show such a strong temperament and character, and establish himself as a leader off the pitch, in such a demanding job. He must have learnt the basics of coaching in his long years with Sampdoria, where he was always the one in charge. He also had the chance to learn a lot from Boskov, and above all from Eriksson. Today, in Roberto's case, results speak for themselves.'

Enfant prodige

A conversation with Franco Colomba

'Watch out for him, that "cinno",' the Magician Walter Bicocchi said to him. 'He's a bouncy one.' And as a good captain, as a veteran midfielder, as the team's standard-bearer and as the 'wise metronome, who made Bologna fly high' (as the papers described him), Franco Colomba did watch out for Mancini.

The 26-year-old (nine years older than Roberto) did so willingly, because he liked 'playing with the young ones' – and because Bologna was his life. He spent over 17 years there as a player, starting with the youth teams and progressing to the first team, and went back as a manager for the 2009/10 season, saving the team from relegation to Serie B.

Born in Grosseto, 57-year-old Franco Colomba's most recent managerial role was with Parma. He was relieved of his duties there on 9 January 2012 after four draws and a bad defeat (5–0) against Inter Milan at San Siro. Having spent 22 years in management, on various benches around Italy (from Salernitana and Verona to Cagliari, Napoli, Novara and Vicenza), he knows how things turn out in the world of football. He knows that the manager will be the first to pay. There is plenty of time for him to find another club; for now, speaking in Bologna, where he has lived since 1961, he can take the time to remember the young boy he bonded so well with on and off the pitch.

'Out of training, I would sometimes give him a lift in my car, and some advice,' reflects Colomba. 'We were in tune on the pitch, especially when I played further back. I managed to play a few decent balls towards him, so that he could score.' He is right: in a game in Udine, Mancini slotted home after he was first to a Colomba cross from the left. Likewise against Avellino: another cross, and the Boy scored with a header.

What was the Boy like?
'He was our *enfant prodige*. You could tell straight away that he was very good, a world-beater. We saw it in the New Year's Day Football Tournament, but Radice didn't play him during that season. Burgnich, though, was brave and put him in. He needed him, as many players had left during the summer, and some of the newcomers had physical problems to resolve.'

How did Mancini react to the first team?
'He was 17; he was just a boy, and we treated him as such. But he was very mature on the field. It was a pleasure to watch him move, lose his marker and ask for the ball. He used to do well as a striker, too – he immediately became the main attacking threat in the team. He was a born leader, who would make his presence felt during the game. He was also a generous player, very good at passing the ball. To sum up, he was a born champion, he had a clear head and he knew exactly what he wanted. He was very focused: he trained properly and listened to the manager's advice.

Mancini was so good that you put his name forward to Enzo Bearzot, the Italy manager, who led the Azzurri to victory in the 1982 World Cup in Spain.
'That's right. Even considering his young age, Mancini could have been one of the 22 players who made up the squad. It

is a pity that he didn't get real satisfaction from the national team as everyone expected him to. Perhaps Roberto Baggio stood in his way. Still, it is unquestionable that Mancini really moved into the spotlight during that season in Bologna. He exploded on to the scene. He played in all of the 30 matches, and was the team's top goalscorer.'

That season ended badly, though ...
'We looked safe with six games to go. Then everything went pear-shaped and we ended up in Serie B.'

And Mancini moved to Sampdoria.
'Just as they did with Eraldo Pecci and Gianluca Pagliuca, Bologna sold their gem, the one who could have secured the team's future. From then on, it all spiralled downwards and Bologna ended up in Serie C1.'

You also played against him, when he was wearing the Sampdoria shirt and you played for Avellino.
'We always gave a hard time both to him and to Vialli, when they played against us – to my entire satisfaction.'

Could you have pictured him as a manager?
'Yes, I could indeed. He loved football and he liked the logic behind matches; he liked looking at patterns and roles on the pitch ... he was very promising, and in the end he made a smashing career. Sure, luck was on his side at the beginning, and that is not the case for everyone. It is hard to begin at a Serie A club. But he made the most of his luck.'

Let's speak about Manchester City.
'They hadn't won anything for years, and Mancini brought them back into the limelight. It took him two years, but that's the norm. It takes time to lay out patterns, to perfect

the tactics. You must decide who to play and who to leave out, which players to bring in. And you need to instil the right frame of mind, too. I believe that Mancini worked hard in this respect, in order to motivate his players and relieve them of the pressure surrounding the Premier League title.'

In Europe though, City didn't succeed against either Napoli or Sporting.
'It is not easy to be a top team in Europe. It takes time and, in this case, money, too. But in the coming season, I believe that City will be there, among the top teams.'

Can you still see that boy who made his debut in 1981?
'We sometimes meet at the seaside, in Sardinia. We play a couple of games, like retired footballers do. And Roberto still plays wonderfully.'

Mister Five Billion

End of January, 1982. It is snowing in Casteldebole, but the football training carries on regardless. Halfway through the season, everyone is on a tight schedule, because it is already clear that Bologna must fight to avoid relegation. The team is on a bad run, but there is one player who has been playing well and drawing everyone's attention. He has played 16 games in the league so far, many of them coming off the bench. He has scored six goals. The latest one, on 17 January in the Sant'Elia Stadium in Cagliari, earned Bologna a draw. Gigi Riva, nicknamed 'Roll of Thunder', the undisputed striker of the Italian national team, whose goals fired Cagliari to the league championship in 1970, complimented Mancini on that goal. And Riva is not the only one to marvel at the boy. All the supporters in the Communal Stadium are madly in love with him. They consider him the new Angelo Schiavio (the Bologna centre forward of the 1920s and 30s, who never wore another club shirt, and who won the World Cup in 1934 with the national team, coached by Vittorio Pozzo) or Giacomo Bulgarelli (the Bologna captain of the 1960s and 70s). Newspapers and magazines devote entire pages to him. They describe him as 'the boy of the whirling goal, waiting to seize the fleeting moment'; and they prophesise about his future: 'he will do great things, marvellous, unique things.' They write, 'Everyone wants to tap with their blessed sword the head of this holy terror from Marche, this leaping fawn.' They wonder – in baffling jargon – about his position on the field: 'passing player on the wing, centre-forward manoeuvre, or else?'

They take a wild guess at numbers: 5 billion liras, this is his market value – or so they say. It is really something, as Diego Armando Maradona is worth 10–12 billion. Bologna managers say that it is the press who is setting the price, because 'the boy is not on the market.' Famous last words.

Rai TV dedicates a ten-minute special to him, titled *Goals, Love and a Little Bit of Fantasy.* They go and see him in Casteldebole, they ask him how it feels, what it is like to see all those figures and get so much attention from the media. 'It is a great thing, a wonderful thing, but I'm feeling just the same as ever. It won't go to my head,' Mancini answers. And he really does not look worried in the slightest. However, Burgnich does worry, and very much so. He fears the boomerang effect of such massive media coverage; he is afraid that the press will lift him to riches, only to plunge him back into rags at his first mistake.

It won't happen. Bologna, though, will be plunged into rags, as on 16 May 1982, for the first time in its 73 years of football history, the club is sucked into the quagmire of the lower divisions.

Let us take a closer look at those four tragic months. On 28 February, Serie A match day 20, a head-to-head match to secure safety is held at San Siro. AC Milan are second from bottom of the table, with 13 points; Bologna are third from bottom, with 16 points. It is a great opportunity to open up a significant gap, but Bologna fluff their lines. They lose 2–1, thereby losing ground, and momentum, in the race to avoid relegation. Following this, Bologna get a sound beating from Cesena as well: 4–1. This defeat costs Tarcisio Burgnich his job. On 15 March, with eight match days remaining before the end of the season, his assistant, Franco Liguori, takes over. A former Bologna holding midfielder, Liguori's career ended at a very young age because of a serious injury.

The first match under the new manager is deceiving: 2–0 at the Olympic Stadium against Roma, Mancini scoring the second goal to secure the result. 'We really picked ourselves up with today's win. We left behind teams such as AC Milan and Cagliari, who could have caused us some trouble. Let's hope we carry on like this,' announces 'the holy terror from Marche' on television. On the following Sunday, Bologna draw 0–0 against the champions Juventus. Things are starting to look up, or so it seems. Quite the contrary: the Red-and-Blues come crashing to the ground and chalk up one loss after another, four in total, against Napoli, Fiorentina, Udinese and Genoa respectively. On 9 May, a home match against Inter Milan – sitting fourth in the league – is played on the next-to-last match day of the season. Azeglio Vicini is sitting in the stands, checking on Mancini's progress with an eye on his Under-21 team. Eight minutes into the game, the ghost of relegation hovers over the old Communal Stadium after Centi scores the opening goal for the Black-and-Blues. Only three minutes later, Bordon, the Inter Milan keeper, saves a shot by Mancini. In the nineteenth minute though, Fiorini equalises, before firing Bologna into a 2–1 lead six minutes later. At the same time, however, Cagliari and Genoa – who are both one point ahead of Bologna in the league table – are winning, so the pecking order remains the same. Inter Milan give up the ghost, and Mancini scores on a long lone run from midfield: 3–1, and Mancini's ninth goal of the season. When the championship began, he was only hoping to play in some of the matches; in the end, he has played in all of them.

So we come to 16 May, the 30th and final match day. Bologna have accumulated 23 points, AC Milan 22, Cagliari and Genoa 24. Four teams within two points of each other, two relegation places to be assigned, and 90 minutes for the final verdict. All the matches will start at three o'clock sharp. The Red-and-Blues think they can manage, because they are playing a relatively peaceful Ascoli with no particular ranking aspirations. Nine minutes into the game, Mozzini scores the goal of hope for Bologna. Still, at the end of the game, the result is a 2–1 defeat and Bologna are relegated to Serie B, together with AC Milan and Como.

It is a tragedy for the team and for the city as a whole. It is a terrible disappointment for Mancini too, although, unlike his teammates, he gets a chance to make up for it straight away.

He wins the national league championship with the Allievi team, beating Bari in the final. Mancini is the captain and top goalscorer in a team of promising young players: Turchi, Salice, Nobile, Martelli, Treggia, De Bianco, Macina, Bellotto, Marocchi, Mancini and Gazzaneo. And together with Treggia and Macina, he is capped for Vicini's national youth football team.

At the end of the season, he is asked whether, all in all, this has been a positive experience. Mancini smiles wryly and asserts, 'Well, in a way it has, because the Allievi trophy came right after our relegation, when I needed it most. But it would have been better to avoid relegation and win the title, too.'

He says that he gave his all in the championship: he ran a lot, he played a lot. What really struck him about his first Serie A season was 'the Italian defenders' grit; I believe it is unparalleled in Europe. It is really difficult to score over here.'

He says that he is tired and he is going on holiday: at first to Jesi, then, as usual, to the seaside in Senigallia. When he leaves Casteldebole, the Boy is convinced he will be back 20 days later, for the beginning of his next season in Serie B. However, only a few hours later, an auction between Fiorentina, Udinese, Sampdoria and Juventus is under way for the Bologna baby-centre-forward (as the newspapers are now calling him).

In Assago – transfer market paradise for Italian football – hefty sums are thrown around: Sampdoria offer 4–5 billion, an amount deemed excessive only a few months earlier. People will find out about the deal for the new Red-and-Blue superstar only on 6 July, when Gigi Radice, the manager hastily recalled to sweeten the bitter pill of relegation to supporters, hands in his resignation, together with all his coaching staff, after finding out that the president's promises to strengthen the team are nothing more than empty words, and that Mancini is going to be sold. The news is spreading fast in town and supporters begin their protests, with demonstrations along the streets and hails of stones, which break the windows of Tommaso Fabretti's insurance offices. Some hothead even tries to set fire to the president's house. Some time later, in a newspaper interview, president Fabretti will respond by accusing Radice, who 'in person and at length had been negotiating Mancini's transfer to Juventus. He only got so worked up because I was the one who finalised the deal – and in any case, I got a bigger sum than what Juventus had been willing to spend. Every single person in the world of football has agreed with me since.'

On 14 July 1982, three days after Enzo Bearzot's Italy win the Mundial in Madrid, the transfer market closes in Assago. Giacomo Bulgarelli officially announces that the baby-striker Mancini is being sold to Sampdoria. The actual transfer fee is unknown. It is understood that only four players (Galdiolo, Logozzo, Rosselli and Brondi in co-ownership) will come to Bologna. Fifty supporters hang a banner off the trees in Bologna. It says, 'Operation clean city. Fabretti must go. With a travel warrant.'

Nevertheless, the player who could have brightened the Red-and-Blues' future is now heading for Genoa and the club of the oil tycoon Paolo Mantovani.

'You will be Sampdoria's standard-bearer'

A conversation with Paolo Bórea

The outside tables at the Cafetteria Drogheria Giusti are an ideal vantage point for admiring the front façade of Modena's Palazzo Ducale. Baroque, solemn and elegant, the 16th-century building, once the official residence of the Estense Court, has hosted the Military Academy since the unification of Italy. Against this backdrop, with a cup of coffee and a glass of water in front of him, the former Bologna and Sampdoria director of football begins his tale.

'I came to Bologna in 1980, halfway through the season, and there I found Mancini. I remember that I was watching some trials with the first-team manager, Gigi Radice. At one point, he said to me, "Look, that one over there, he really is a good one." It was obvious that he didn't follow the youth teams a lot. "That one" was Roberto Mancini, who played for the Red-and-Blue academy team. He stood out among them all. For a boy of that age, he had an astonishing change of pace and an amazing shot. He was the complete striker. That was my first contact with "Mancio".'

Paolo Boréa comes from Ferrara. When he was younger, he used to support Spal. With his silver mane, sunglasses and checked jumper, he definitely does not look his age. He has an excellent memory, and with him questions are unnecessary.

'Shortly afterwards, Tommaso Fabretti, the team owner, asked me to go and check out the academy team. Fabretti didn't know anything about football, but he did know how to make money. If he had good players, he could sell them, or build the first team around them without spending a penny. So I went to Treviso and watched Roberto play in an official match. I came back and told the president, "Mister, that team is phenomenal." Antonio Paganin was there, and Giancarlo Marocchi; between the posts was Marco Ballotta, who later played for Parma and Lazio, and up front, Mancini and Marco Macina, genius and rowdiness. Roberto could be a wild horse: my first clash with him happened in Bologna, of all places. The European Under-21 Championship was taking place in Jesi, and Italy were playing Spain on the Saturday. It was their most decisive match. Meanwhile, Bologna were due to play Inter Milan on the Sunday, and Burgnich wanted him on the first team. "Mancio" wanted to play both games. "How will you manage that?" I asked him. And he replied in earnest, "I will, Dr Borea, I will play both." He locked himself up in his room in Casteldebole and didn't want to let me in. It is surely difficult to get such things across to a 16-year-old boy. At his age, as they say here in Ferrara, you jump over ditches lengthways.'

Still, how was the first year in Serie A for 'Mancio'?
'It was a cursed championship for Bologna, with their relegation to Serie B, the lower division, for the first time in their history. Nevertheless, they had a good team: Chiorri, Chiodi, Fiorini, Baldini. Bad luck had a hand in it, that year, and so did injuries. And then came the biggest mistake, the dismissal of Burgnich at a time when Bologna were still in the safety zone. Bologna's best chance to stay in Serie A would have been with a pragmatic man like Tarcisio. And Roberto? He was of few words – he is still like that – but he fitted in

straight away, by virtue of his unquestionable technical excellence and his assertive personality. The records will state that he was only a boy, but it surely didn't show on the pitch. He wasn't the kind of guy everyone had to take care of. He pulled the chestnuts out of the fire for us several times.'

And at the end of that season, Mancini moved to Sampdoria.
'The deal had already been sealed by Claudio Nassi, Sampdoria's director of football, who had brought the team up from the lower division to Serie A, and who mentioned me to Paolo Mantovani upon leaving his job. The first time I met the president, he asked me to persuade Mancini to come to Genoa. The clubs already had the deal in the bag, and only the player's consent was needed.'

Still, during that summer, many papers mentioned the fact that other teams were interested in Mancini: Juventus, Udinese, Inter Milan, Roma …
'Everyone wanted Mancini. Udinese were surely further ahead of us in the negotiations. The president Franco Dal Cin was really pressing forward, even though it was hard to compete against Mantovani, the oil tycoon, who had brought Sampdoria up to Serie A. Maybe Juventus would have succeeded, if they had tried hard enough. I went to see Mancini at the beginning of June, in Senigallia, where he used to spend his holidays. I met with him and his father Aldo in a restaurant called "da Peppino", where they served great seafood. I only said to him that, if he went to Juventus, he would end up as one of the many wallflowers to past champions. If he chose Samp instead, he would become what Gianni Rivera had been to AC Milan, Giancarlo Antognoni to Fiorentina, Sandro Mazzola to Inter Milan: "You will be the club standard-bearer, the Blucerchiati's totem," I told him. And I was right – it really turned out that way. I won him

over, and we signed a four-year contract that very night: a deal worth 40 million liras for the first year, 60 for the second year, 80 for the third and 100 for the fourth. His monthly salary was guaranteed, and he had a match bonus on Tuesdays.'

His move caused an uproar, because rumour had it that Samp paid four and a half billion liras for him, while Diego Armando Maradona was worth 10–12 billion at the time.
'To tell you the truth, we paid one-and-a-half billion "Black & Decker", and four players on top of that.'

What does "Black & Decker" mean?
'Under the counter. I remember driving the money to Piacenza station, under escort, in an armoured car, so that Fabretti would take it from my own hands.'

Mancini's transfer caused uproar among Red-and-Blue supporters and also enraged the new team manager, Gigi Radice.
'Yes, there was a lot of controversy because it looked like Mancini was traded for four players. The one-and-a-half billion liras didn't appear in the equation, maybe because some of Fabretti's companies were broke – I am only making assumptions here. Still, it was the supporters' opinion that Mancini was sold out.'

And so we come to Sampdoria, where at the beginning it was not all roses for Mancini. In fact, there were rumours about a possible further transfer to Torino, Roma or Juventus; even back to Bologna …
'There were a few issues there. First of all, his physical condition. Roberto was in an explosive phase [that is, he was rapidly growing bigger and stronger] – he was still growing up, of course. He had skinny ankles, which meant more sprains; and muscly thighs, which meant more strains. But

he had a good turn of pace, and great style, too. You could tell he would make it, one day. I remember his first derby match against Genoa. I was sitting under the south terrace in the old stadium, right behind the goal Samp were attacking. Roberto came over at full speed, sprinting away from the others and scoring with the tip of his foot – he pulled his muscle doing it. He did have some physical problems, you see, and you must also take into account that he was a 17-year-old boy, catapulted into a big city. You could try as much you wanted to keep a close eye on him but, at that age, things happen. Monica was his sweetheart back in Bologna but he fell for this beautiful girl in Genoa, who really hurt him … his mind was set on her, you see.'

Romantic issues aside, there were misunderstandings with his coach, too …
'Renzo Ulivieri wasn't really fond of him, possibly because of the amount of money that had been spent on the guy. It was always the same old thing: "Here comes the golden boy", "Who do you think you are?" '

Instead, with Vujadin Boskov, Mancini started working wonders.
'Boskov was first and foremost a psychologist, before being a team manager. He had a way with players; he could get the most out of them. In all my years of football, I have never met anyone like him. He was like Nils Liedholm, but more straightforward. If Roberto told him to go to hell, "Uncle Vujadin" wouldn't mind: he knew that the player would go and give him a hug later. He also knew how to get on someone's good side. Just to give you an example: one morning Boskov might call me to his office and say, "What's wrong with Vierchowod today?" And I would answer, "Nothing, Mister, nothing at all." "No," he would insist, "he's not his usual self; go and find out what's wrong. I bet there's something up with his family." And

it would be true: one of the player's kids would be ill or something. Vujadin was always right.'

Roberto Mancini arrived, and Samp won the league.

'We had amazing players on that team, such as Toninho Cerezo and Giuseppe Dossena. They were the real coaches. Cerezo, playing midfield, used to set the pace, organise the marking and dictate the play. Dossena had originally been an attacking midfielder, but Boskov reinvented him as a left-back, and in that position, with his amazing feet, he could do whatever he wished. He could be a real menace, right when the opponents least expected it. Still, Mancini was the heart and soul of the team, for his goals and also because he could inspire his teammates. Indeed, he was Mantovani's unchallenged protégé. Mantovani loved the guy, he really cherished him. When I told him that Roberto was fed up with the team and wanted to move to Roma, the president answered, "Tell him to come over to mine tonight, and I'll make pizza." And everything would be all right. Mantovani was like a second father to him. For instance, I remember when Sampdoria travelled away to Juventus. The president was asked whether he would attend the game. He said he wouldn't, because Mancini wasn't playing. He shouldn't have said that: it was all over the papers, and Vialli went mad. Still, Gianluca and Roberto got on well. They had opposite personalities: Vialli was thoughtful and he would choose every word carefully, while Mancini was all heart and soul. Both were very much loved by the Blucerchiati fans; but Mancini, because of his passion, was a supporter's dream come true.'

Was the defeat to Barcelona in the 1992 Champions League final the biggest disappointment for Mancini in the Boskov era?

'I suppose it was. You couldn't say that Barcelona stole the game, but if we had won, no one could have complained.

Vialli missed two chances – because he already knew he was going to Juventus, he wasn't himself. In fact, for the first time in his career with the Blucerchiati, he got cramp. When Gianluca, with only Zubizarreta to beat, delivered a lob, Boskov came to hug us all. We all saw the ball nestling against the net, but it was on the wrong side: it had brushed the crossbar and gone over. It just wasn't meant to be. If you remember, only seven minutes before the end of extra time, the referee called a free-kick the wrong way (it should have been given to Samp), and Koeman scored from it. Samp would have won on penalties, we were sure about that, because Pagliuca had studied the Barcelona players one by one and he was a great penalty stopper.'

Tell me about Sven-Göran Eriksson and Mancini.
'Roberto always gave Eriksson enormous credit for his coaching skills. He learned a great deal from him – in fact, Mancio's teams play exactly like Eriksson's Samp used to play. All the midfielders close to one another, short passing, ball possession and sudden breaks forward. That year [1993/94], under Eriksson, we played fantastic football: our wing halves on the team were David Platt and Vladimir Jugovicic, with Ruud Gullit, Mancini and Lombardo as our strikers. They scored 51 goals between the five of them. We finished third in Serie A and won the Coppa Italia. Maybe, if our president hadn't died, we would have won the league, too.'

And in 1997, after 15 years wearing the Sampdoria shirt,
Mancini moved to Lazio.
'I met Sergio Cragnotti, the president, in a hotel in Milan. Eriksson was there, too. We talked about Verón, Mihajlovic and Mancini. A deal was signed for Mihajlovic, who would move to Lazio for 15 billion liras, and I drew up Mancini's new contract myself: 5 billion for the first two seasons, 4 bil-

lion for the third. Then we went on to discuss a deal for me to go to Rome as well: the agreement seemed in the bag, I shook hands with Cragnotti, but he didn't keep his word. So I didn't follow Mancini in his new adventure.'

Three years at the highest level, then a short spell in the UK before
he started his coaching career. What did you think about that?
'To tell you the truth, I didn't believe it at first. I wasn't sure about the coaching, mainly because of Roberto's passionate, impulsive disposition. How can you manage a team if you get carried away at every opportunity? On the contrary: he knows the game so well that he is now one of the best coaches, too. Just like he was when he used to play. He can make teams play good football. As Boskov used to say, Mancio seems to have eyes in the back of his head. And Eriksson swore that Roberto could see what other people could not. He has intuition and genius, and he has managed to transfer those qualities on to the training field.'

Genoa for us

With that face just so
the expression just so
that we have before we go to Genoa
and every time we wonder
if that place where we are going
will not swallow us so that we never go back home
And yet, we are in some ways relatives
of those people that live down there
that, deep inside, are a bit wild, like us
and how afraid we are of that dark sea
that moves even at night and never stands still
Genoa for us
we who live in the bottom of the countryside
we who rarely have sunshine in the city square
and the rest is rain that soaks us.
Genoa, I said, is an idea like any other one.

This song, 'Genova Per Noi', is by Paolo Conte. Bruno Lauzi used to sing it, an artist who was born in Italian Eritrea, but grew up in Genoa. The record was released in 1975, and made a real fortune. On the sleeve, under the title, there is an image of the symbol of the city: 'La Lanterna', the lighthouse overlooking the harbour. Delicate and nostalgic piano sounds, a hoarse voice: the boy from Jesi knows this tune well, as do many others of his age. It also somehow describes his feelings on the summer day, when, accompanied by his parents, the Boy travels towards his new city and his new team.

Mancini had been to Genoa the previous year, while play-ing for Bologna. From the coach, he only saw flyovers, over-passes and gloomy outskirts. Altogether, he got the wrong impression of the city, and he thought, 'I would never live here.' It must be added that, despite Paolo Borea's promises and substantial contract offer, Roberto's dream was to play for Juventus, the club he had supported since he was a child; the club of his hero Roberto Bettega. He came close, too: a scout for the Old Lady came to the campsite in Senigallia where Roberto was staying, just after Aldo had signed a contract with Sampdoria. He came to say that Giampiero Boniperti wanted Mancini at all costs; he pleaded with him not to accept any other offers or make any commitments, because the deal was on. He had just come to accompany him to Turin. Mancini could do nothing but decline, saying, 'Sorry, I already signed for Samp.'

So, on a sultry afternoon in late July, the young forward arrives in Genoa. Driving past Nervi, they bump into the new Blucerchiati acquisition: Irishman Liam Brady, who has just arrived from Juventus. Mario Rebuffa, the club secretary-general, welcomes Marianna, Aldo and Roberto. He goes with them to the city centre, to Via XX Settembre. At the club's headquarters at number 33, a crowd of supporters has gathered to take a look at the new arrivals, who are supposed to be securing a bright future for Sampdoria, now that the team is back in Serie A after five years in the lower division.

They are met with great anticipation, especially Brady and Alviero Chiorri, who is returning to the Blucerchiati after a season-long loan to Bologna. There is also someone who, seeing the *enfant prodige*, shouts 'Bobby Goal, Bobby Goal' – a chant that will be heard often during the following 15 years.

Inside, the club directors meet the newcomers. Francesca and Filippo Mantovani are there in place of their father

Paolo: the president is confined to Switzerland, in exile, after his name was linked to a big oil industry scandal. With Mancini are Brady, Chiorri, Dario Bonetti, Alessandro Renica, Francesco Casagrade and Domenico Maggiora, the backup troops called in by the president. Only the 28-year-old England forward Trevor Francis is missing. Paolo Mantovani watched him play in the World Cup in Spain, and fell in love with him. He sent his private aircraft to Malaga, where the footballer and his wife were spending their holidays, and less than an hour later the plane was landing at Nice Côte d'Azur airport. A limousine drove Francis to Monte Carlo, where the Sampdoria president was staying. It took Mantovani just under three hours to persuade him to leave Manchester City, where Francis had had an undoubtedly good season (26 appearances, 12 goals), and move to Genoa. The rumours talk about a £580,000 fee, on top of a salary of 300 billion liras per year. The Englishman will join his teammates at their training camp in Arcidosso, Tuscany.

In Via XX Settembre, after greetings and ceremonies, it is time for photos and interviews. It is Marianna who helps Roberto into his Blucerchiati shirt, with the Phonola logo on the front (the team sponsor, one of the Philips brands). If she is totally honest, at first she was angry about her son's move. The deal was closed by Aldo, Paolo Bórea and Roberto, without anyone asking for her opinion. However, in the club headquarters, in her new flowery dress, she is just as happy and excited as, or even more than, her son.

Photographers' flashes go off and the recent acquisition is now under the TV spotlights. Mancini, bobbed wavy hair and a gold medallion around his neck (it is not a cross, nor an image of the Holy Mary, but an indicator of his blood group, as his mum dreads accidents), talks about his first impressions. His fee, the famous 4 billion paid for him, does not weigh on him: 'These are considerations which are up to the clubs … I am only here to play, better and better. I accepted [the offer] to come to Sampdoria straight away, because they are among the most reliable clubs.' Asked for his opinion on the new acquisitions, he replies, 'On paper, it is a good team which shouldn't have any problems with rankings. With such a line-up, we could even aim at a place in the Uefa Cup.' And then the question regarding his role in the team: is he a striker, or an inside forward? 'Neither,' he answers decisively, 'I am a midfielder, joining the attack from deep.' He will say this more than once, but the fateful question will linger over his career, starting with his new coach, Renzo Ulivieri. The Tuscan manager, from San Miniato, arrived at Mantovani's court in 1981 and, in his first year, accomplished the miracle of bringing Samp back up to Serie A.

In Arcidosso, Ulivieri takes the boy from Jesi to one side and asks him, 'What position do you play, Boy?' Roberto answers that he likes playing behind the strikers, joining up with the attack from a deep position. The coach laughs, and walks away without a word. The nine Serie A goals Roberto already has to his name, from his debut season, weigh heavily on him. They will end up becoming his worst nightmare; or rather, they will serve as smoke and mirrors, deceiving managers and experts alike.

Ulivieri will be among them: after all, the numbers speak for themselves, don't they? The Tuscan coach is persuaded that Mancini is a central forward, a Roberto Bonisegna-type player (the famous Bonimba, Inter Milan and Juventus number 9 who, together with Gigi Riva, got Italy to the final of the 1970 World Cup). So Ulivieri gives him the number 11 shirt and, at first, the player seems to prove him right. In his second match, on 9 September 1982 at the Meazza Stadium, he partners Francis up front and, from a corner on the right, he strikes a flying volley to beat the Inter Milan keeper Ivano Bordon.

Sampdoria are the surprise package of the season: after three matches, they are top of the league, having drawn against Juventus, beaten Inter Milan at San Siro and won 1–0 against Roma, the goal coming from Mancini – his 11th in Serie A. After the match, he says to the press, 'I am over the moon; we thought we would gain two points in the last two matches against such difficult opponents, and we secured six instead. Let's hope we can carry on like this.' 'Everyone says you're the best,' suggests the reporter to Mancini, who has just come out of the shower wearing the club dressing gown. The Boy replies modestly, 'That can't be right. It's the team that's great.'

Roberto scores his 12th Serie A goal against Pisa, but it is not enough to avoid a defeat. The following Sunday, 10 October, in a match against Catanzaro, he plays beautifully, but suffers an injury: a muscle strain in his left thigh. He misses the match against Torino, but the problem reappears in Ascoli, and then flares up once more on 28 November, straight after he scores the equaliser against Genoa in the Lanterna derby.

Physical problems will trouble him to the end of the season. But it is not only the injuries – which are due in part to his growing up – that trouble him. The Boy also has an uneasy relationship with Ulivieri. The blue-eyed manager with the thin moustache would like to set the gem into a cast; he wants to mould him, to constrain him. This is easier said than done. Ulivieri goes ballistic when the Boy overdoes it and loses the ball. He wants him to play more for the team. He expects him to put aside stylistic mannerisms and get on with business. He tries the carrot as well as the stick: he invites him over to his house for lunch, worries about his nights out – he even suggests that the Boy can stay over for a few nights. But Mancini can show quite a fiery temper, as even big-name overseas signings like Brady and Francis are bound to find out. Roberto has an argument on the field with Trevor, about a pass he didn't receive, and in the dressing-room the two come to blows.

Then there is Genoa. The impact is traumatic because it is a strange city; its people are more reserved than those of Bologna, and Mancini has very little time to get to know them well. He goes to live in Nervi, bonding at first with those he already knows from his former team: Chiorri and Salvatore Vullo. They then reach out to other newcomers, such as Bonetti and Renica.

As soon as Roberto gets his driving licence, he buys his first car, a white second-hand A112, which he will soon trade in for a more sporty Golf GTD. In his car, he often drives to Bologna, the city of the Two Towers, to eat some tortellini, as he is not keen on pesto, and to meet up with his friends. He has already broken up with Monica, his sweetheart in Bologna – they broke up shortly after his arrival in Genoa.

At the end of the season, the Boy has played 22 matches in the league and scored four goals. He is not the out-and-out striker Ulivieri wanted him to be; he is not the goalscorer the fans were expecting – and now many start advancing doubts. Sampdoria end up seventh in the league, in a season in which Roma win their second Scudetto. All in all, it is not a bad result for a newly promoted team. In fact, Mantovani asserts, 'We have been specialising in suffering for many years. Now we can try to specialise in joy.'

In order to achieve this aim, the Sampdoria president adds other building blocks to his work-in-progress team during the summer of 1983. Pietro Vierchowod returns home after winning the Italian championship in a Roma shirt; Bordon and Marocchino join him, arriving from Inter Milan; Roberto Galia joins from Como and Fausto Pari from Parma. Still, the final outcome doesn't change much compared to the previous year: Samp rank seventh in the league again, with 32 points – the same as Verona and AC Milan and 21 points behind Juventus, who achieve their 21st Scudetto. The league's top goalscorer, with 20 goals, is Michel Platini for the Old Lady. Mancini leads the goalscoring charts for his club with eight, having played in all 30 matches. A goal to remember? The one scored in the 2–0 derby win against Genoa. This will prove to be the first of many Christmas presents to the Blucerchiati supporters.

The seventh-place finish is deemed an underachievement on the part of Ulivieri, so Eugenio Bersellini takes his place as Sampdoria manager. He joins from Torino but he has already coached the Blucerchiati team from 1975 to 1977, so the club knows him well. He's an iron sergeant from the old school, an old-fashioned man with his own beliefs and methods. He does not trust young players very much. Mancini does not get along with him at all.

The manager from Emilia tries to tame the Boy, to restrain him tactically. He wants Mancini to fall back and defend when he does not have the ball. He hates Roberto's leaps of imagination, he hates his backheels, even when they succeed. He wants to impose his own rules, on and off the pitch. For instance, he weighs the players every morning, because he wants to see whether they have been out for a big meal the night before. Mancini can't take it: he holds out, he opposes every decision, and clashes are frequent. Years later, he would comment, 'Instead of reacting like a man and putting some effort into it all, instead of fighting, I used to go and train with a smug look on my face, like some kind of Mister Know-it-All.'

To cut a long story short, he becomes a rebel as far as his coach and the papers are concerned. Used sparingly from the bench, he scores only three league goals all season.

The problem is not only the manager though, it is the line-up. With 'Bersa', others have arrived: Moreno Mannini,

Fausto Salsano, Graeme Souness, Evaristo Beccalossi and, from Cremonese, Gianluca Vialli – the man who in a few years' time will make up, together with 'Bobby Goal', one of the most famous strike partnerships in Italy. Beccalossi, a former Inter Milan player, is a number 10 by trade, an attacking midfielder, a playmaker – just the role the boy from Jesi would like to play. But Roberto is only 20, and the manager reckons he is still too young for such a decisive role. Just like his predecessor, Bersellini sees 'Mancio' as a striker or a right-winger. But Francis is ahead of him in the pecking order, not to mention the newcomer Vialli. There is not much room for the Boy. However, Francis suffers an injury in the first half of the season, and then again during the last game of the championship.

In the meantime, Sampdoria play nice football, neat and assertive, creating plenty of chances. They finish in fourth place, equalling the club's highest-ever league finish, recorded in 1960/61. And in Genoa, on 3 July 1985, the club wins the first trophy in its history. In front of 'the man with the pipe' Sandro Pertini, President of the Italian Republic, Sampdoria win the Coppa Italia, beating the AC Milan of Ray Wilkins, Mark Hateley and 'the Baron' Liedholm in both legs. In the first leg, a goal by Graeme Souness just before the end of the first half secures the 1–0 win for Sampdoria. In the return game, Mancini, wearing the number 9 shirt because of Francis's injury, partners Vialli and converts the penalty that puts his team ahead after 42 minutes. Vialli then doubles the lead for Samp but AC Milan halve the deficit through Virdis. The last minutes of play are really tough, but the Sampdoria defence holds firm, and the southern stands in the Marassi erupt as the final whistle sounds. The supporters' chants of 'Doria, Doria' turn into a massive roar when Alessandro Scanziani, the captain, lifts the golden cup. Not only is it Sampdoria's first trophy in its 40-year history, it is also the first trophy for many of the players, Roberto Mancini among them.

'The cup belongs to Samp, and rightly so,' the papers will say the following day. 'Great team, a new dimension in Italian football. Their last one was a big game, and with that, the title is theirs by right.' President Mantovani takes the pitch and applauds the supporters and players alike. Very composed, he says that everything is wonderful and that he is happy to attend the Cup Winners' Cup draw the following day. That's right, because Sampdoria's first trophy is also a ticket to European football. Sampdoria Football Union, the club founded on 1 August 1946 after the merge of Sampierdarenese (1891) and Andrea Doria (1895), has never competed in an official competition outside of Italy. Sure, there have been a few informal competitions, some summer matches, a couple of invitations to play here and there, but never as part of a high-profile event. President, players and supporters alike can't wait to show the world what they can do, what they are worth, out there beyond the Alps.

Their first adventure finishes early though, on 6 November 1985 to be precise. Having reached the last 16 of the Cup Winners' Cup, Sampdoria win the home leg of their tie against Benfica 1–0, but the away leg at the Da Luz Stadium in Lisbon (a 2–0 victory for the Portuguese club) has already decided the outcome. Mancini has already made a request to the president in September, after a defeat against Fiorentina in Sampdoria's first league game; now he repeats it: 'Please let me go on loan, to Bologna.'

Back in June, there had been rumours about his possible departure. Roma, Torino and Fiorentina were all interested in him. Nothing happened back then with the advent of the new season, the rumours became more frequent. 'I would like to stay here, but I want to play as well,' says Mancini to the press, 'so if there's a chance to move, I would rather take it.' The rebel does not want to be a bench player anymore, coming on for Francis, Vialli or Pino Lorenzo, who arrived during the summer transfer season from Catanzaro. 'We already had three strikers, now we have four, and I can't figure out why,' says Mancini. 'Bersellini can't really say that he tried me out, or that he knows me well. I played 24 matches for him last year, but only 14 from start to finish. He clearly doesn't believe in me.'

The papers write that he has fallen out with the manager and the team. Everyone swears that it is only a matter of days, of hours, before a new transfer is made. So when Bologna step in, ready to pay 6 billion, Mancini – on an all-time low because of the cup knockout – is willing to go back to his former love, even though they are in Serie B. He is insistent with Mantovani, who does not mince words but simply tells him to go to hell. The president explains that, when the boat is sinking, everyone is needed. In other words, he shows the grumpy, shy and unruly young man that he really thinks highly of him, that he values him and cares about him very much. Almost as if Roberto was his son. And it is here, in this refusal to let him go, that the special bond between Mancini and Mantovani is forged. The bond which will partly lay the foundations for Sampdoria's future achievements.

The 1985/86 season ends badly. In the league, the team avoid relegation with only five games to go. And in the Coppa Italia, where they again reach the final, they are defeated by Sven-Göran Eriksson's Roma. It is Toninho Cerezo who scores the decisive goal in the Olympic Stadium, the very same player who will later become a key man for the Blucerchiati.

And what about the iron sergeant Bersellini? He has long since lost Mantovani's trust, possibly as long ago as that cup defeat to Benfica. So he packs his bags and leaves.

When I was 19 I was just the same

A conversation with Graeme Souness

In the Olympic Stadium in Rome on 30 May 1984, the Liverpool captain lifts the Reds' fourth European Cup. It is the most recent success of an impressive season: the league championship, the League Cup, and now a European trophy. All this in Joe Fagan's first season as manager, after succeeding the legendary Bob Paisley the previous summer.

Roma were the favourites, in all respects. They could call on players like Bruno Conti, Paulo Roberto Falcao, Ciccio Graziani, Roberto Pruzzo and a young Carlo Ancelotti; the game was at their home ground, so the crowd would be on their side; and they had already shown, in their title-winning season the previous year, that they could play effectively and win with flying colours. Their coach Liedholm had them playing a well-implemented zonal defence system.

Still, in spite of the predictions, the score was 1–1 at the end of the 90 minutes (Phil Neal scored for Liverpool, Pruzzo equalised for Roma), and extra time came and went without any further scoring. Finally, the Red-and-Yellows lost on penalties (4–2), bowing to the perseverance of the team from England. Graeme Souness, wearing number 11, put his penalty away, Liverpool's third, sending it into the top corner of the net, to the left of Roma keeper Franco Tancredi. Bruce Grobbelaar, the South African, ingeniously came up with his legendary 'spaghetti legs' and made poor Graziani lose his nerve, firing his penalty over the bar and into the terraces. The European Cup is Liverpool's.

Souness, the captain of the Merseyside team, has played his last match in a red shirt. Eleven days later, the moustached Scotsman, the midfielder with class and determination to spare, lands at Genova airport, where 2,000 Blucerchiati supporters are expecting him. In Via XX Settembre, he first meets Trevor Francis, then president Mantovani, and the deal is in the bag. For £650,000, the Scotsman joins Sampdoria. He will take Liam Brady's place in the team, the Irishman having moved to Inter Milan. Souness will stay in Genova for two seasons, 1984/85 and 1985/86, before returning to Rangers as player-manager, taking with him a strong knowledge of Italian football.

Twenty-six years on, Souness is 59 and a commentator for Sky Sports. He has a game of golf to attend shortly, but he finds the time to talk about the former teammate he now watches in the Manchester City dugout, from his vantage point in the press box.

Why did you come to Sampdoria?
'They bought me because I was an experienced player. At that time, I was 31. Sampdoria was a team of young boys … if you look at Vialli, Mancini, Mannini, they were basically young players and the president needed someone who could bring experience to the team.'

How do you remember Roberto Mancini from that time?
'Extremely talented. He didn't want to listen to much advice, and that could be a little frustrating at times. He thought he knew all the answers, which is quite normal at that age. I was the same – in fact, all 19-year-olds are like that. Obviously he was exceptionally talented and he knew that he was going to be a star in Italian football.'

*In what way did you contribute to making this team, and
Mancini, grow?*

'Well, you would have to ask that question to somebody
else ... I think there would be no doubt that they needed
some experience in that team. There was me, there was
Bordon, there was Trevor Francis, and Scanziani the captain,
we were the oldest in the team ... I was the most experienced, coming into a very young team, and obviously you
have something different to offer. I saw that as part of my
role and I did help looking after the younger ones. I believe
that my style of play helped to do that anyway, I was reason-
ably aggressive at football.'

*You scored against AC Milan in the first leg of the Coppa Italia
final, and you helped the team to win their first title in years and
years. How was it?*

'A good goal in San Siro, and an incredible fiesta in Marassi.
For me, the whole experience – my two years in Italy, working with the people there, especially with a top coach like
Bersellini, and all the young guys – was a real pleasure. The
city I lived in was fantastic, the supporters were great. It was
a fantastic experience for me and my family.'

*You describe Bersellini as a top coach, but between him and
Mancini the relationship was not so good*

'Yeah ... all sorts of 19-year-olds, myself included, don't like
being told off, or being told to do things that we don't agree
with. I'm surprised that Roberto Mancini has developed into
such a mature, intelligent, footballing man. I look at him
now on English television and he handles the press really,
really well. He's always calm, always collected. He's got a
real charming influence, when you see him interviewed on
television. Obviously, over the years, with all the different
people he's worked with, and the success he had as a player,

he's learnt and he's done a lot. Still, I'm quite surprised he's turned out the way he has, because he's a very impressive football person now.'

Let's talk about Mancini today and his successful story with City.
'Well, that's a big surprise for me because managing Manchester City is a very, very difficult job.'

Why?
'I think coaching today is hard, because of the players, the money they earn and the independence it has given them. Not all, but a large percentage of them don't have a very good attitude to being told something – because they think that they have all the answers and people should listen to them rather than them listening to people. I think that if you look at the situation at Manchester City, they had to deal with Craig Bellamy, they had to deal with Tevez, they had to deal with Balotelli … if you had one of those in your club, it would make your job as a coach very difficult indeed. Mancini has had four very, very tricky individuals. Adebayor may come back [following loan spells at Real Madrid and Tottenham Hotspur], because he's still a Manchester City player, so Roberto may have to work with him again … Bellamy is gone and I'm not sure if Tevez will be there next year, but I think Mancini handled the situation with him very well. That was a nightmare scenario, and I felt that he handled it brilliantly. He was super.'

In what way do you think Mancini has adapted to the mentality, the media and the reality of English football?
'The Manchester City dressing-room is not full of English people, they have people from all over Europe like all the big clubs today, so that's not such a big problem. I think if you are a football person you quickly understand what's needed,

and what you have to do to be successful, and Mancini understood the challenge ahead of him very quickly. He's had some good advice ... and so it's not been that difficult for him.'

What about his style of play?
'I think a coach's job is to get the best out of his group of players, and his style of play for me is a winning style, I think last year they scored the most goals in the league and conceded the fewest. For me there were no problems. I know that there was some criticism that maybe he was coming with an Italian mindset, being a little too defensive. I couldn't agree with that; I think he was working with the group of players he had and he was getting the most from those players, and he turned out to be very successful. So there's no criticism, he's done very well.'

But all along, throughout the year, the press has been speculating about all the managers who could take his place.
'This is normal. You lose a game and if you're a big manager they want to replace you. It's the usual bullshit. I think he has the confidence [to deal with that kind of speculation]; if he didn't before, he certainly has now.'

What do you think about the war of words with Manchester United and with Sir Alex Ferguson in particular?
'I think they make more of it than it is – it sells newspapers. They are two professionals, two top professional coaches. It's like a little game and I don't attach much importance to that.'

And the Premier League win, in injury time, what was your take on that?
'I was in the stadium working for Sky. It was the most dramatic end to any season I have ever known. When you think

it was the final game, and in the last kick of the ball you win the league ... it's a script. It's just theatre.'

And now Mancini is a hero at Manchester City?
'If you're a Manchester City supporter, you're the happiest among any English supporters, and you love Roberto Mancini.'

How do you see the future for Man City?
'As long as the people in Abu Dhabi have a real desire to be successful, Man City will be one of the world's biggest football clubs. I see success for them. Big things are ahead for Man City. Because they have the finances to do it, and now having won the FA Cup and the Premier League gives the manager great strength in the dressing-room.'

Azzurro pallido

Thirty-six, and no more, are the international appearances totalled by a playmaker who played in Serie A for almost 20 years, challenging for – and winning – top honours and notching up 541 club appearances. The relationship between Mancini and the blue shirt of the Azzurri is indeed a curious one. Anything and everything has been written on the subject, an adventure which started under a lucky star, but ended in a bad way. Let us take a look.

At just 17, Mancini is named on the 40-strong list of players that Enzo Bearzot presents as a pre-selection for the 1982 World Cup. His name is crossed out when the list is whittled down to the 22 who will leave for the Spanish expedition. Bearzot chooses Cagliari striker Franco Selvaggi ahead of him. 'Fine,' is Mancini's comment. 'In Spain, I would only be watching, anyway.' In Italy, on the other hand, he has the opportunity to play and win the Allievi title. Such a response is quite telling of Roberto's personality.

Still, in October 1982, Sampdoria's new acquisition is capped for the Italy Under-21 side by Azeglio Vicini, appearing in a friendly match. It is the natural development of a path that Mancini has trodden since he first turned out for the Azzurri in 1978, at 15 years of age. In 1980–1982 (the competition was played over 18 months), he was part of the team that won the European Under-16 Championship; then came the Under-17s, followed by a third-place finish in the 1983 European Under-18 Championship, won by France. Eventually, he comes to the 'Azzurrini', the Under-21 team.

The first match is in Enns, against Austria. It ends 1–1. The manager is happy with the team and with his latest acquisition. He tells the press: 'I can rest easy up front. Mancini and [Juventus forward Giuseppe] Galderisi require no credentials. They are two great strikers.'

So it is only natural that Bearzot – the manager of the senior Italy side – should also cast a glance at Mancini. After the World Cup in Spain, he is trying to bring new blood into the team, with one eye on Mexico 1986. He tries out the young emerging players in Serie A. And at the end of the season, after a test game with the Olympic team, against Rumania in March 1984, Mancini is picked for the Azzurri's North American tour. Roberto is the youngest in a group including the more famous Tardelli, Gentile, Scirea, Collovati, Altobelli, and, representing the new generation, Baresi, Bagni, Battistini and Fanna.

The first match is against Canada in Toronto, on 26 May at Varsity Stadium. Mancini, having started the game on the bench, makes his debut in the blue shirt at the beginning of the second half, replacing Lazio's Bruno Giordano. He partners 'Spillo' ('Pin') Altobelli, the scorer of Italy's first goal, 30 minutes into the game. The match ends 2–0 to the Azzurri, Mancini doing all that is expected of him.

On Wednesday 30 May at Giants Stadium, New Jersey, home of the New York Giants, Italy's second friendly game, this time against the United States, takes place in front of 31,000 supporters, among them many Italian immigrants. History repeats itself: in the 46th minute, Mancini is brought on in place of Giordano. The final score is 0–0: no guts, no glory. Still, Bearzot can draw useful conclusions: for one thing, Roberto appeals to him. The next day, however, things between the manager and the Boy will change, permanently.

The Azzurri party returns to their hotel in the Central Park area. They have dinner, then Tardelli, Gentile, Dossena,

Giordano and Mancini meet in the lobby and go for a walk. They stop at a nearby bar, then an Italian resident who has joined them suggests they pop over to number 254 West 54th Street – Studio 54. It is New York's most famous club, and Mancini is wide-eyed at the big wide world he is experiencing. But the party doesn't stay for long: the older guys realise that it is getting late, and wisely decide to leave the music behind and head back to base. The boy from Jesi though, mesmerised by the Big Apple, chooses to roam the streets downtown.

'New York was beautiful, full of lights; it was heaven for a boy like me, not even 20,' he would say, years later. He arrives back at the hotel at six in the morning, gets changed and is off again, wandering about and waiting for the shops to open, so that he can buy a little something for his family. When he returns, at about eleven o'clock, he bumps into Marco Tardelli, who warns him, 'Be careful, the coach has gone ballistic.' It proves to be an understatement: when Mancini enters the hall, Bearzot confronts him. He knows of Roberto's little escapade, and he has been worried sick about the young man. Now he's angry, furious. He calls him every name under the sun. He assails him with a barrage of choice words, so that the Boy does not dare reply. Bearzot's last words to Mancini are 'You're done with me and with the national team. I won't call you again.' And so it goes.

In hindsight, perhaps it might have been prudent to apologise on the spot, or to call Bearzot later to clear the matter up. But Mancini is proud, and he does neither – because he is ashamed of his behaviour but, at the same time, he feels that he did nothing wrong. All he did was go out at night in the city of lights – an opportunity that nobody of his age would have forgone. Still, the die is cast and Mancini, still in the international wilderness two years later, misses the 1986 World Cup in Mexico.

In order to wear the blue jersey again, he must wait until 8 October 1986, when Vicini replaces Bearzot as Italy manager. It is a friendly match against Greece, in Bologna. Roberto starts the game on the bench, but comes on to replace Altobelli. In order to obtain a first XI shirt – the number 7 – he will have to wait for almost a year. It finally happens on 18 April 1987 in a match against West Germany.

Less than two months later, he draws cutting remarks from the critics after an incident in the Rasunda Stadium in Stockholm. Italy are playing Sweden in a qualifying game for the next European Championship. Fifteen minutes into the game, the referee Mr Pauly awards a penalty kick to the Azzurri. It is Italy's number 7 who steps up to the penalty spot. Mancini faces Thomas Ravelli. The Blucerchiati player shoots to the left of the keeper, a swerving shot, but it is not enough: Ravelli gets a hand to the ball, which hits the post and rolls out. It is a bad mistake, and it is compounded when Larsson scores to secure a 1–0 win for the Swedes. The press crucify the Sampdoria player. Everyone is better than him: Altobelli, Aldo Serena, Pietro Paolo Virdis or Roma's Rizzitelli. Not many critics want to see Mancini in a blue jersey again.

On 5 December 1987, on a dark and rainy afternoon at San Siro, the last qualifying match for the European Championship is being played. Italy, who are already through, are playing Portugal, who are already out and playing without their star, Paulo Futre. The Boy comes off the bench again, as usual to replace Spillo Altobelli. This time, however, in his 22 minutes on the field, playing alongside Gianluca Vialli, he shows that he can really shine wearing blue. Mancini's best spell with the national team begins here, leading him all the way to the 1988 European Championship in Germany.

Fast-forward to the night before the first match of the tournament, Italy against the host nation in Düsseldorf's

Rheinstadion. Mancini is given the star treatment: hundreds of autographs are signed; the foreign press want to know everything about the man who is supposed to be the best player in Serie A. And he is always asked about the same thing: that blessed goal that he has not scored yet, after 14 appearances for the Azzurri.

'Why do I always need to repeat myself? Am I no good at scoring goals? This is not a worry to me, I am not bothered,' says Roberto during the press conference. 'During a match, I am not interested in scoring only. I try to be a complete player. For example, I often worry about tracking the opposition wing-back who goes up in attack; this way I am doing something useful for my teammates. But this is not something you find interesting, is it?'

He also comments on criticism that he received in the papers after a friendly match against Wales in the build-up to the tournament: 'I am used to it by now. I've developed a thick skin. I am under a little pressure, I won't deny it. When we arrived at the airport and I saw all those people, I realised that something has changed, that things are not like they used to be. I can now feel the European Championship in my guts: Germany, the supporters, the matches.'

So he feels the pressure, but that is a good thing, because 52 minutes into the Germany game, Roberto Donadoni steals the ball on the left, runs to the byline and crosses; Mancio is in the box and beats the German keeper with a sharp diagonal shot. It is an important goal, both for the Azzurri and for Roberto, who – as the commentators will say – has finally loosened up. His first goal in the blue of Italy has come after a total of 675 minutes' play, and he runs towards the press gallery, where he shouts out all of his anger to the journalists who have been attacking him. A hand conveniently placed over his mouth ensures a scandal is averted.

Three minutes later, a free-kick is awarded to Germany. Andreas Brehme fools his Inter Milan teammate Walter Zenga and scores to secure a 1–1 draw. Nevertheless, Mancini has passed his test, and the following day he is swarmed by microphones and notebooks. 'I didn't celebrate, I was too tired,' he tells the press. Of his behaviour after scoring, he says, 'Just leave that episode aside; I didn't hold any grudges last night. It was only a liberating scream, something I had been holding back for quite some time. What about my goal? I cannot deny that scoring had somehow become an issue, but only to a certain extent.' He goes on to thank Gigi Riva, the Azzurri's tour manager, who has stood by him and advised him, telling him to keep calm and repeating that, sooner or later, a goal will come.

Still, his goal against Germany does not guarantee him a full 90 minutes. Azeglio Vicini has got into the habit of bringing him on for Altobelli for the final 20 minutes of every match. In terms of results, it delivers against Spain (1–0, Vialli scoring the goal) and Denmark (2–0 to the Azzurri), but it ends badly against the Soviet Union, when Italy are defeated 2–0, bringing their – and Mancini's – adventure to an end. Roberto Baggio's star is rising, but it is not only the 'Divin Codino' ('The Divine Ponytail') who will restrict Mancio: Serena, Borgonovo, Carnevale and Rizzitelli will all be preferred to him at one time or another.

'Vicini and I have known each other forever. And he knows me like only a few people do, so it is only right for him to try other players,' states Mancini, gloomily, while the papers talk about an indifferent, misunderstood footballer. They say that, by now, he has been cast aside by the national team. And they wonder when he will finally grow up, take responsibility, and reciprocate the trust the coach has put in him. Fourteen months and eleven international matches pass without Mancini getting on the pitch. However, the

Blucerchiati playmaker does feature on the list of 22 players picked for Italia 90. It is the first World Cup he might actually figure at, having been denied the chance in 1982 and 1986.

He is not sure to make the starting XI, as competition is fierce. In attack, Totó Schillaci, Roberto Baggio and Andrea Carnevale have all been picked ahead of Mancini at one time or another. Nevertheless, on the eve of the first match, against Austria, Vicini proclaims, 'Mancini will be the greatest surprise in this World Cup.' Still, nothing happens. Nothing at all. Out of the seven games played by Italy, Mancini plays none, not a minute, not even a fraction. Right to the end, he is hoping. He trains meticulously, and he does not complain. He even talks up Schillaci, saying, 'He is particularly suited to this World Cup. Italy is playing at home, he is very attack-minded and his skills are appropriate here. He has a very high scoring record, whenever the team creates an opportunity. It is only fair that he plays right now, he is a true striker and goals run in his blood.'

He believes that Vicini has nothing against him – 'He would have said it to my face,' Mancini explains. He waits, and hopes to at least make an appearance in the Italy–England match for third place, against David Platt and Gary Lineker. But that is not the case either. He does not utter a word, despite his bitter disappointment, but years later he will not be so inclined to hold his tongue. 'It's crazy,' he says, '70 days on a training camp, just to be watching. Vicini behaved really badly with me: he didn't even have the guts to explain.' Trying to find an explanation, Mancini speculates, 'Possibly my problem, like Vialli's or Vierchowod's, was that I played for Sampdoria and not for one of the more politically influential clubs.'

The 1990 World Cup, hosted by Italy, has gone. And the following year, Italy miss the train to Euro 92 as well. During the sixth qualifying match in Moscow, on 12 October, the Azzurri can do no better than draw 0–0 against the Soviet Union. Roberto, who since the World Cup is in and around the Italy team again, comes on in the 58th minute, replacing Giannini, Roma's deep-lying playmaker. Mancini does his best to support Rizzitelli, Lentini and Vialli in attack, but to no avail: the Soviets' net, it seems, is charmed.

The Vicini era ends here. He is succeeded by Arrigo Sacchi, the man from Fusignano, the prophet of zonal defence, the coach who took the Milan of Maldini, Baresi, Gullit and Van Basten to European and Intercontinental success. The new manager has a very clear picture of Mancini's role, and when he takes him to the United States for the 1992 US Cup, he tells him straight away, 'For me, you are Baggio's deputy. When he is out, you're in.' Roberto appreciates this, and he makes himself available to the new coach. 'Every person, in any job in the world, deserves trust. In the Italian national team, I have had few opportunities,' reflects the Sampdoria captain. 'I played well during the European Championship in 1988. Then, after Italia 90, when I didn't play even for a minute, I thought it was all over. I was tired and disappointed. Now my motivation is right again. The environment is better, things are clearer. I know I can give something to this team. Sacchi asked me if I am ready to lend a hand to his Italy team; if that had meant being used and then discarded, I wouldn't have accepted. Instead, he persuaded me with his straightforwardness, and I'm happy to be here.'

His mood seems to be lifting again, the former golden boy knows his place and what is expected of him. Sacchi, obsessed with tactics, is certain that the overall structure of the team is more important than the roles of individual players. He reckons that Baggio and Mancini cannot play together in a normal formation, but, if the rest of the team were set up perfectly, it might be worth a try. And he does just that, in a friendly game against Mexico, on 23 January 1993, his 12th match in charge. 'If the pairing works, I'll be the happiest coach in the world,' says the manager before the game. 'Otherwise, Mancini will go back to being Roberto Baggio's deputy.' Actually, it does not work: it takes a lot of effort to get them going. Baggio scores but Mancini performs only in fits and starts. So Mancio goes back to being, to use the coach's expression, the twelfth first-string player. Or, as the papers say, the Ponytail's deputy.

When Baggio is injured, Mancini plays. It happens on 24 March 1993 in the match against Malta, in Palermo. He scores two goals: a real turning point for the Sampdoria player. But then Baggio returns, and again there is no room for Mancini. Sacchi makes other attempts at having both of them on the field: in Berne, against Switzerland for example; but even before the match, he says, 'I am not sure whether Baggio and Mancini are the best pairing.'

And so we come to the end of the story: a friendly match against Germany in Stuttgart, on 23 March 1994. Baggio is not there, so Mancini plays from the start. But at the beginning of the second half, with the score locked at 1–1, Sacchi replaces him with Gianfranco Zola, the Parma pixie who will later become the darling of the Chelsea fans. Italy play horribly and lose the match 2–1, their second defeat in the run up to the World Cup, having also lost to France. 'Sacchi's national team is still not worth watching,' the papers write. They call Mancini's performance 'ugly' and they 'cry out for Baggio'. The Sampdoria player asserts, 'If I must play half a match, under these conditions, I can't do any better: they always had the ball. If Baggio plays first string, surely that must mean something, although I don't think that even he could have made a difference to this game. We experimented, in a difficult match. What about my future, you ask? Well, I shall try and learn something from this defeat, too.'

That 'something' is that he'll be quietly slipping away from the national team, turning down commitments, or maybe stepping aside before Arrigo Sacchi can leave him out of the World Cup squad – or worse, keep him on the sidelines watching others play. In any case, something has happened in Stuttgart, and Roberto's snagged and tangled blue thread breaks, after 36 appearances, 2,053 minutes of play and four goals.

It is the one great regret of his otherwise brilliant career. Why did the player described as one of the best Italian play-makers not succeed for the national team? Mancini's most fervent supporters talk about a conspiracy between football superpowers such as AC Milan, Inter, Juventus and Roma, fuelled by the sports press which pays lip service to them. They cite Sampdoria's scarce relevance to important issues. They get worked up over blind managers who failed to unlock his potential, preferring to him players who never made a difference.

Still, fate and bad luck maybe played their part, too. For example, fortune smiled on Totò Schillaci when he was capped for the national team: he brushed the ball, put it in the goal and became a hero in the popular imagination. Mancini, on the other hand, missed a penalty in Stockholm and history took a wrong turn. He was unlucky to be playing at the same time as Roberto Baggio, with whom all managers deemed him incompatible, even though the player always denied it. But maybe the reason is simpler: outside of his Sampdoria, Mancini did not feel loved, cherished and pampered. He did not command the leading role that was always his with the Blucerchiati, and to which he always aspired.

A tough nut

A conversation with Azeglio Vicini

There were only three teams in his career as a midfielder: Vicenza, where he made his debut; Brescia, where he ended his playing days; and Sampdoria, where he played from 1956 to 1963. Wearing the Blucerchiati shirt, Azeglio Vicini helped his team reach fourth place in the league in 1960/61, their highest placing until the Mantovani era. Vicini began his coaching career in Brescia but his sole season there ended badly, with the Swallows relegated to Serie B. Still, that same year, 1968, the national team opened their doors to the 35-year-old born and raised in Cesena. He joined the technical staff, before being made coach of the Under-21 and Under-23 sides, a role he fulfilled for ten years. After the 1986 World Cup in Mexico, he was named manager of the senior Italy team.

Vicini led them to Euro 88 and then Italia 90. The World Cup remembered by England supporters for Gazza's tears and Pavarotti's rendition of *Nessun dorma* is recalled by Italians as the tournament of Totó Schillaci's goals and the song 'Notti magiche' ('Magic Nights') by Gianna Nannini and Edoardo Bennato. For the Azzurri though, the dream of becoming world champions faded on a none-too-magical night in Naples, losing in the semi-finals to Diego Armando Maradona's Argentina on penalty kicks.

Italy earned the consolation of beating England 2–1 in the third-place play-off and Vicini remained in charge until the following year, when the side failed to win qualification to the 1992 Euros and he was replaced by Arrigo Sacchi. Today, in his home in Brescia, the former Italy coach, now 79, reflects on his relationship with 'Mancio', and their ups and downs – because he surely played an important role in the frustrating love story between Sampdoria's captain and the blue jersey, warts and all.

On 6 October 1982 you played Roberto Mancini for the first time in your Under-21 team. Had you been keeping an eye on him?
'Mancini had already stood out in the youth and Juniores [Under-18] teams. He was team captain for Italy Under-16 and Under-17. He was an imaginative player with a good shot; he was one of the main footballers of his generation, together with Zenga, Bergomi, Ferri, Vialli, Giannini, De Napoli and Donadoni.'

Your Under-21 side did well; and after Bearzot's veto, you again picked Mancini to wear the blue shirt.
'It is true that Bearzot didn't call him again after that first time [the 1984 North American tour], but he was also very young. Still, Mancini was one of the players I brought through from my Under-21 team. He was certainly one of the most promising players in Italian football – he deserved to be picked for his country. That Under-21 team, the team I knew so well, became the backbone of the senior team.'

Sure. But Mancini was never an indisputable first-string player; very often he was 'Spillo' Altobelli's replacement. Wasn't he any good in blue?
'He was very good. In fact, he played all the matches in the 1988 European Championship in Germany. He even scored his first international goal on his tournament debut, against West Germany. He played against Spain, Denmark and the first half of the semi-final against the Soviet Union. We lost

that match, and that shut the door to the final against the Netherlands for us.'

That's right. Still, after that, Mancini disappeared from the international scene. Why?
'Because others came, for example Roberto Baggio. There was a lot of competition, and for Mancini there was also the issue of his position, which had never been defined in relation to what he did for Sampdoria. He was an untypical player, and it was hard to line him up with Baggio. Nevertheless, Mancini made most of his appearances for the national team when I was coaching. He never had much of a role with the Azzurri before or after.'

So we come to the 1990 World Cup in Italy, when Mancini was among the squad of 22 but did not play, not even a minute – this was surely one of the most upsetting moments in Mancini's adventure with Italy. In later years, he harshly criticised you for that.
'It is strange indeed, because at the beginning of the World Cup I also thought he could be one of the leading players, coming off the bench. I had hoped he could play a little. Was that my mistake? No, it wasn't, as there were choices to make and every time I preferred other players who I thought would do better under those particular circumstances. Let us not forget either, that players like Schillaci blossomed during that World Cup, taking hold of the scene and thrilling all Italians. Nevertheless, someone like Roberto, who had been among the best players during the past season, and who felt very close to the national team (I remember he exempted himself, so that he could play with Italy Under-18s), he deserved more. I totally understand his bitterness: if I had been him, I would have felt awful. I must admit though, despite his disappointment, he behaved in exemplary fashion. He never spoke out of turn, he didn't complain or cause any trouble.'

At the time, there were rumours about the national team being influenced by the great powers in Italian football – AC Milan, Juventus, Inter – and the partisan press. They said that Sampdoria's political influence was limited, so the Blucerchiati players were not held in much consideration.

'It's only words, compounded hearsay, because there were four Sampdoria players in that Italy team: Vierchowod, Mancini, Vialli and Pagliuca. Four players – just as many as Juventus and AC Milan had.'

And after the World Cup, you played him again …

'Yes I did, I played him in other matches, many of them. He came back for a friendly game against the Netherlands in September 1990, and he was there for the match against Russia, too – the one that kept us out of the 1992 European Championship. That was the last match for me, as well.'

Sure. But perhaps the Samp leader – the captain of that team who won the league in 1991 – well, maybe he expected something more from a former fellow Sampdoria player, like you were.

'Maybe … but I can also say that I expected more from Mancini, too, while I was coaching – definitely more than one single goal in the 22 matches he played.'

Ten years later, in 2001, another issue came up between you and Mancini. You were president of the Football Coaches Association, and you resigned from your job as vice-president of the Football Federation technical team. You disagreed with Gianni Petrucci, the special commissioner who exempted Fiorentina from the ban on having Mancini as their manager.

'I resigned because I didn't share the decision made by the Federation. The issue concerned both Fiorentina and Lazio. I had nothing against Mancini, who was perfectly able to coach; still, he could not change team, with the championship already under way. He could not do it [that is, move from one club to another as coach] within Italy. Those were the rules, and they were changed for that one time. Nothing else.'

The rumours are now in the past and reconciliation has been made: in 2008, as president of the Football Federation technical team, you presented Mancini with the Golden Bench award, after his contemporaries voted him the best manager of the season.
'Look, I never had any problems with Roberto. Every time we meet, we smile and hug warmly.'

Coach to coach now, how do you rate Mancini's performance as a manager?
'He has managed great teams, and he's been highly successful. Even in England, where it is not easy to win a title, he did it. He's a tough nut, Mancini.'

Unfinished beauty

'I believe you must shoot, if you want to score.'

'In order to win a match, you must score the most goals.'

'The ball is in, if God so wills it.'

'A penalty kick is awarded only when the referee blows his whistle.'

'The match lasts 90 minutes, and it is over only when the referee blows his whistle.'

'The team making fewer mistakes wins; we made more and we lost.'

'If we win we're winners, if we lose we're losers.'

'It is better to lose a game 6–0 than to lose six matches 1–0.'

'A player must keep his eyes on the ball, and his other two on his opponent.'

'A great player sees a highway where others only see paths.'

'Managers are like skirts: one year miniskirts are in, the following year you stick them at the back of your wardrobe.'

These are just a few of the quotes, or pearls of wisdom if you like, that Vujadin Boskov bequeathed to the football world. The 'Grandpa' arrived in Genoa in the summer of 1986. His story is a long one, beginning in Begec, Serbia. He spent his youth among modest people: his father fixed cars in a garage on the outskirts of Novi Sad. And it was with the Novi Sad team, FK Vojvodina, that Vujadin started playing football, as a midfielder. He eventually totalled up 57 appearances for the Yugoslavia national team, and emigrated when his country's laws allowed it, upon turning 30. He then spent a season at Sampdoria, followed by two in Switzerland, with Young Boys.

He started coaching in Berne, the outset of a career that would take him all over Europe – he would go on to earn him the nickname of 'Gypsy Rover'. His first involvement was with Young Boys, then he returned to his hometown team, winning the league in 1966. More yet: in the Netherlands, he coached Den Haag and Feyenoord; then on to Real Zaragoza, Sporting Gijón and Real Madrid in Spain, with whom he won two cups and a league championship.

He taught coaching to people such as Vicente del Bosque, the manager who made Spain World and European Champions, and José Antonio Camacho, who went on to manage China. In 1984, Boskov finally arrived in Italy, at Ascoli, where his brief was to save the team from relegation. He did not succeed, but he led them straight back up the following year, before leaving the Lantern city.

The Serbian was not among the most valued coaches in the Italian championship. Despite him being 56, and notwithstanding his very respectable CV, they still considered him an 'emerging' manager. However, it fell to him to impose a vision and a mentality on Mantovani's team under construction at Sampdoria. Under construction, that is, until that moment. It would be Grandpa Boskov, with his good-natured manners, with his rural wisdom, with his odd assertions, who would turn potential into results, and a good-willed team into a contender in European football. It would take time though, and for a while yet, Mancini and Vialli's Samp would still be an unfinished beauty.

Mancini's first impression of the new coach is not exactly great when Boskov turns up at the 'Il Ciocco' training camp with an iron-sergeant stance. He gathers all the players in the middle of the pitch, as he will do every day before training for the following five years, and starts giving his lecture. He doesn't want to see sunglasses, long hair, badly shaved faced, shabby clothes. He wants them up bright and early, all lined up, ready for work. And on he goes with a set of rules and prohibitions that should be followed to the letter. Mancini, perplexed, catches Vialli's eye. Those who will become known as the 'Goal Twins' are thinking the same thing: here comes another Bersellini.

Nevertheless, as days go by, they come to see what the man is made of. He knows anything and everything about football. He is a cunning old fox, as far as the game is concerned. His Italian is comically bad, but he speaks every language and everyone understands him. He knows exactly how to get on the right side of people. Criticisms, insults, whatever comes at him from left, right and centre, none of it seems to affect him in the slightest.

Once he gets to know him properly, Mancini will explain, 'We were used to sergeant Bersellini's barracks. Training sessions had to be so quiet you could hear the grass growing. When Boskov arrived, it was like coming back to life: you were actually looking forward to training, because you were having fun, joking, and that smart-ass Vujadin would surprise us every day – he would make us sweat with a smile on our faces. He's the kind of guy who really puts his trusts in you; he helps you believe in yourself. Off the pitch he will lend you a hand: if you have a problem he tries to work it out with you, maybe in the bar, buying you a drink. You never talked to Bersellini. Boskov, though, was an important anchor for us, especially for the young ones like me – far from my family, and always on the go.'

Boskov trusts Roberto, and he is generally popular with the young ones. He promotes from the youth team players like Maurizio Ganz, Antonio Paganin and Gianluca Pagliuca, who came from the Bologna youth ranks and little by little will go on to replace the first-string keeper. Hans-Peter Briegel arrives from Verona, the Italian champions; Luca Fusi comes in from Como. Toninho Cerezo joins from Roma to replace Graeme Souness in the midfield. The Brazilian, contemporary of Falcao and Zico, is 31; the Red-and-Yellows have traded him, because they are sure he has nothing more to give. They are wrong: he is just what Samp needs, the missing piece of the jigsaw.

However, although the foundations for the season are good, the beginning is terrifying: Sampdoria are knocked out of the Coppa Italia, and in the league, after six games, they are still stuck on three points. But the team recovers, and although it proves to be Napoli's year (led by Diego Maradona, they will go on to win the league), the Blucerchiati finish fifth, on equal points with AC Milan. This necessitates a play-off to determine which side will qualify for the Uefa Cup. At a neutral venue in Turin, Sampdoria are beaten 1–0 by the Red-and-Blacks, the goal coming from Daniele Massaro on the counter-attack. Europe will have to wait. During the season, Samp have played well in spells but they still don't have that maturity, that ruthlessness, which would allow them to compete with more experienced opponents.

One of the season's low points came after the Atalanta–Sampdoria match on 18 January 1987. The referee, Mr Boschi from Parma, had wrongly awarded a penalty to the Bergamo club, which was converted by Magrin for the only goal of the game. Afterwards, Mancini, blood still boiling, announced to reporters, 'Boschi is useless. He targeted eleven players wearing white and gave them a hard time throughout the match. He doesn't even deserve refereeing the third division – maybe he could referee a married men v. bachelors match. We complain about football violence, but supporters really ought to think about beating up referees instead of clobbering each other. Then we could really start thinking about playing football, because today, thanks to Mr Boschi, we haven't actually seen much of that.' A rant, completely out of place and completely over the top.

The next day, in Bogliasco, Mancini apologised for the outburst: he had been angry and had lost his temper. Expecting a fine, he was instead referred to the Football Disciplinary Commission 'because of comments to the press, considered harmful to the referee's reputation' and given a three-match suspension. Azeglio Vicini, who had named Mancini in his squad for an international match, was forced to reconsider his decision amid a storm of criticism.

Mancini asked for understanding: 'It was madness, I would have never said anything like that in cold blood. But those of you who call me "a football terrorist" should try walking in my shoes. When I was 13, I was taken to Bologna, where I had to grow up on the spot because of football. I studied for a couple of years in school, I didn't read very much, because football doesn't leave much room for anything: one or two training sessions per day, you eat, you sleep, you go on a training camp … there is never time to live normally, like other boys of that age do. And all the time, the next match is inside your mind, that match you just cannot afford to lose … then you do lose it, in such a way that – for once in your life – you just blow up. I acted properly until last Sunday, then I couldn't take it anymore.'

Taking stock of his life, he swore he would never talk about referees again. But in the years that follow, he will find himself unable to keep his word: his temper won't let him.

The good news of the season has come in the shape of the guys who are being called the 'Goal Twins' – the pair that Vujadin immediately promoted to the first team, at Pino Lorenzo's expense (Lorenzo will, in fact, be sold to Cesena the following year). Gianluca Vialli, with 12 goals, is the league's second top scorer, behind AC Milan's Pietro Paolo Virdis (17 goals). Roberto Mancini now says he does not want to leave Genoa anymore. 'I'm doing well now,' he says, 'I live by the sea, people are not in my face the whole time, everything is alright with president Mantovani. I'm happy here … I used to feel bad because I felt useless; they showered me with money but I wasn't playing. Now everything has changed – and the best is yet to come!' He is at peace with himself, and on the football pitch it has been showing. Since the ties imposed by Ulivieri and Bersellini were broken, he has become a true number 10, an attacking midfielder, a man for all seasons. The Serbian coach understands what Mancini's best position is: he was a wing half who had been playing as a striker out of necessity, but finally, he has become the playmaker, capable of a stroke of genius, and of scoring improbable goals all over the place.

So at the beginning of the 1987/88 season, the general feeling is that 'the naughty kids' team, the on-and-off champions, have started playing for real.' Discreetly, people start to talk about a possible scudetto. 'A scudetto? Why not?' asks Boskov. 'I believe that this team, with Mancini and Vialli's growth, with the arrival of two well-known champions such as Briegel and Toninho Cerezo, playing alongside real strong athletes like Vierchowod and Pellegrini, could face up to any opponent. On a technical level, my team can measure up to any other; they are determined, I see them play courageously and with a lot of self-abnegation. These are the qualities that make a team great, and Sampdoria now have the right to be called such. They only need to learn to be more ruthless, tougher in the box.'

Roberto Mancini agrees entirely. 'I like this new Sampdoria more and more,' he says, 'and I think no aims are unachievable for us. I said earlier that Napoli were favourites, and AC Milan their best opponents. I haven't changed my mind. Still, considering that we have been marching in step with Napoli for over a season, in the championship and in the Coppa Italia, I can't see why we cannot dream, too. Once we used to panic when we were classed as favourites. Not anymore. We could really be this year's biggest surprise.'

The dream, though, remains just out of reach, as AC Milan take the championship – their first of the Berlusconi era. Sampdoria repeat their achievement of 1985, finishing fourth, eight points off the top, to earn themselves a ticket to Europe. And on 19 May 1988, at the Communal Stadium in Turin, Salsano's beautiful left-foot shot beats Torino's keeper Lorieri and flies in just under the crossbar in the seventh minute of the second period of extra time. With this goal, Sampdoria with their second Coppa Italia.

Fast forward to 10 May 1989. Berne. Barcelona v. Sampdoria in the final of the European Cup-Winners' Cup. The Samp boys got here by beating the Swedes of Norrköping, the Germans of Carl Zeiss Jena, Romania's Dinamo Bucaresti in the quarter-final and the Belgians of Mechelen in the semi-final. In the stands of the Wankdorf Stadium, there are over 20,000 Sampdoria supporters. It is their European dream come true, and no one wants to miss it.

They are facing the Blaugrana, coached by Johann Cruyff – a club with two Cup-Winners' Cups in their cupboard already (1975 and 1982), and a more experienced line-up than Samp. But it is not only a matter of experience: hit by injuries and disqualifications, the Blucerchiati are missing half of their defence. Vierchowod and Carboni are not playing, and Mannini is returning after a long period of absence – in fact, he will be replaced 27 minutes into the game. Vialli and Cerezo are also in bad shape.

Perhaps due to these ailments, or the charisma of their opponents, or nerves at reaching the unknown territory of a major European final, the Blucerchiati enter the arena like sacrificial lambs. Just three minutes into the game, Sampdoria go behind: a defensive mistake, and Julio Salinas, with a header, scores the opening goal. It stays like this for the rest of the first half: the team from Genoa remain timid, while the Catalans launch many dangerous counter-attacks.

In the second half, Sampdoria's efforts improve, and they almost grab an equaliser. But with 15 minutes remaining, Barcelona's Lopez Rekarte – on for Beguiristain – wraps up the 2–0 win with a perfect diagonal shot. On the stands, supporters are throwing stones and chanting 'Thanks, thanks anyway'.

Both on the field and in the locker room, tears are shed, together with recriminations and reflections. Mancini is the most critical: 'Two penalty kicks should have been awarded to me, but the referee didn't see any. Did we have a weak bench? I don't think so, we had too many injuries. In the future we will have to plan better for that.'

Vujadin Boskov is more relaxed about it. 'Barcelona deserved to win,' he says, 'we flunked the second half, when we exposed ourselves, giving them the opportunity to counter-attack. I would also like to add that, with our team lined up properly, Barcelona would have never won. Is this the end of an era? Don't you say that. We have the chance to do great things.' He will be proved correct, but the next day, the headlines still read, 'In Europe, too, Samp are an unfinished beauty.'

Luckily, the championship is far from over, and likewise the Uefa Super Cup and the Coppa Italia. Sampdoria's league position has not been looking too healthy, but with an angry recovery they manage to grab fifth place, which means they are off to Europe again. The Super Cup final doesn't go so well: AC Milan deny the unfinished beauty time and space on the ball, and they win the trophy. However, at the Giovanni Zini Stadium in Cremona (Marassi is undergoing renovation work ahead of the 1990 World Cup), Sampdoria beat Maradona's Napoli by an impressive four goals to nil, overturning a first-leg deficit to claim their third Coppa Italia. The last goal, the one that wraps up the match, is a penalty kick taken by Mancini, who is then sent from the pitch in the final minutes, together with the team masseur, following a brawl. But the cup is Sampdoria's, and 'The Czar' Vierchowod makes sure it is lifted up to the sky.

'First, you win the scudetto, then you can leave'

A conversation with Pietro Vierchowod

'AC Milan contacted me and offered me twice as much as I was making at Sampdoria. So I go to Mantovani and say, look, they are offering me twice as much. He replies, "Come on Pietro, if we are talking about money, you know I can't match those offers. Just think about it, though." We still had to play the second leg of the Coppa Italia final against Napoli in Cremona, and we went on a training camp in Salsomaggiore. Mancini and Vialli gave me a hard time all week. During the meals, on the football field, in the evenings – they'd come up to me and say "you can't go". They would knock on my door at any given time, saying I couldn't leave them: "First, you win the scudetto with Sampdoria," they would say, "then you can leave." They would call me a traitor, or beg me to stay with a pleading look on their faces. So, in the end, I changed my mind. The cup final came and we won 4–0. I scored the third goal and Mantovani came on to the pitch, made me lift the trophy up high and told me, "I'll renew your contract for three more years – Mancini and Vialli, your backers, gave me an enormous amount of hassle, so I agreed to that."

He laughs out loud, remembering that week. Pietro Vierchowod, also known as 'The Czar'. His nickname comes from his Ukrainian father Ivan, who was a factory worker in the engineering industry and was formerly a deportee soldier. He smiles at the memory of the 'Goal Twins' making his life impossible. And it didn't just happen once: Mancini managed to block his transfer on the following year, too: 'It was 1990, and Mantovani sold me to Juventus, together with Vialli. The president was a good friend of Juve president Giovanni Agnelli, and he couldn't take his word back. Under Mancini's insistent pressure, he made me and Gianluca pull out.'

This is the story of the failed transfer that allowed the Blucerchiati to win their much-wanted championship, of which more later. The former centre-back, one of the best in the Italian league during the 1980s and 90s, joined Sampdoria a year after the arrival of Roberto Mancini, following a title-winning season with Roma in 1983.

'He was very young, but he already had a strong personality,' says Vierchowod of Mancini. 'He was very talented, and afterwards he went on to become the champion we all know. He was perhaps the key to the success of our team, which grew little by little and won everything there was for us to win.' Vierchowod, 53, is now far from the football world. He stood for mayor in the latest administrative elections in Como, the city where he has been living for many years. He got 2.53 per cent of the vote. 'A decent result,' he suggests, 'if you consider that I am no expert, and it was the first time that I did anything of the sort. It was a good experience.' So will he carry on with politics? 'We shall see ... we still have time on our hands. We created an association, Il Faro ('The Lighthouse') for Como, and we shall continue our work.' So let us leave politics aside and go back to football.

Mancini was a talented player; however, in his first years, with Ulivieri and Bersellini, he was unable to get going ...
'He didn't have the same opportunities he got later on. That one was a team under construction, and it was better to let

the experienced footballers play, leaving the young ones to one side. The time with Bersellini was the year when Roberto played the least.'

There was also an issue about his position?
'Sometimes, when you are young, your ideas on your role on the football field might not be totally clear. Then you mature, and you find your place on the pitch. That is just what Roberto did, making the most of his talent.'

What did you see as his best position?
'I preferred him as an attacking midfielder, because he had the right skills and he would continuously try out new stuff. He didn't score much, but he liked to be on the ball. He would ask for it, even though he was surrounded by three opponents.'

You saw many champions play: Maradona, Van Basten, Falcao, Gullit, Platini, Ronaldo … who would you compare Mancini with, as a player?
'Every player has his own distinctive traits, and Mancini had those of several champions in him. When he carried the ball, he could keep it, but also pass it to his teammates the right way; and when he was attacking, he was excellent at creating trouble for any defence. From midfield onwards, he could do anything. In the defensive areas, he was better off not getting involved …'

Talking about defending, apparently your arguments were quite popular, and they would end with Mancini saying 'Pietro, you are the best defender in the world, but you don't know anything about football.' And you would answer the same back.
'We were all quite close, but we wouldn't mince our words. Mancini and I had a few arguments, it's true, but everyone

had quite a temper and we all wanted Sampdoria to win. And in the end, we did it. We were all willing to give 100 per cent, but occasionally someone did not manage to do so, or maybe was a bit selfish, so we inevitably ended up arguing. Mancini and I almost came to blows many a time; still, once the match ended, we went for dinner together that same night, regardless of anything that had happened a few hours before. That was our strength.'

Grandpa Vujadin was another of your strengths …
'That's right. Before him, we'd had other managers who didn't succeed in turning us into a real team. It's not that Boskov gave us new tactics, or some amazing new skills … we basically played man-to-man. It was individual skills that made our team. Still, he was very good at handling the dressing-room, he was fair and easygoing; we used to train in a serene mood, happily and with pleasure. Boskov was always quick-witted, and we gave our all for him.'

What about Sven-Göran Eriksson?
'Eriksson tried to introduce a different system: he wanted us to play zonal. But in my opinion, in order to hold our group together and get the concepts through to us, more of an iron grip was needed – that was what Sacchi, one of the best managers ever, did with AC Milan. Sampdoria has always been a happy, jaunty club, which could have won much more than it did. Although it didn't turn out that way, we still had a great time and we have all remained friends.'

Let's talk briefly about the national team and Italia 90 …
'I believe we threw that one away in Naples against Argentina. It was a really important semi-final; we had some footballers who were in good shape, but who weren't playing. The match ended badly also because, with half an hour remaining,

substitutions that seemed obvious to me simply didn't happen: Carlo Ancelotti, to strengthen the midfield, and me on Maradona. We were both kept out, and Mancini didn't find any space.'

Roberto had been calling for a substitute for a long time in that match, seeing you as the ideal solution against 'El Pibe de Oro' ('The Golden Boy')…

'We completely agreed on that. Azeglio Vicini had selected me for the national team after four years out. When he first encountered trouble, he said to me, 'Do you want to come and play in the World Cup? I'll be straight, though: I'll play you only when it comes down to marking players such as Van Basten, Careca, Maradona.' I said that was all right with me. So that was the ideal game for me. I was in good condition, I had played in three matches only, I'd had some rest and, in the championship, I had always done a good job marking Maradona. I had stopped him – he acknowledged that himself. But nothing happened. I ended up playing the match in Bari for third place, when there was no point anymore.'

So, after the disappointment in the World Cup, You went on holiday with Mancini, Vialli and your respective wives and girlfriends, to the Seychelles.

'We were glad to get away. We went to a wonderful resort. We really needed that holiday, to get rid of the tension and recharge – as a matter of fact, the following year we won the league.'

What was that like?

'It was a great ride. Even though we lost the derby against Genoa just before Christmas and the match against Lecce, we won the league convincingly. We didn't mess up a single game in the second half of the season; everything went smoothly. We went to Milan and won against Inter, we went to San Paolo put four past Napoli – Mancini's goal was brilliant. We played great football, with great simplicity. And the scudetto gave us the chance to play in the European Cup. It would have been amazing to be the first club to win both the league and the European Cup without a proper tradition on its back. Unfortunately, that match went as it did … we missed four chances and Barcelona scored against us 14 minutes into extra time – a 40-metre shot by Koeman. Maybe that's the way it had to go, but we were stronger than Barcelona. Maybe some of us, including Mancini, were a bit too nervous. That final was a bit too uncomfortable.'

It was also one of the saddest memories for many Sampdoria fans. Anyway, what is your happiest memory with Mancini?
'Winning the Cup-Winners' Cup, the first European trophy we ever gained. We had lost the final in Berne the previous year, but we did it the second time round. It was like a dream come true. When we returned to Genoa, I got off the plane first, walking down the steps holding the cup. Mancini gave it to me. He knew the president wanted to sell me to Juventus. But I didn't leave, because Roberto made Mantovani change his mind.'

The Snow White Club

Once upon a time, there lived Snow White and the Seven Dwarves.

Edilio Buscaglia, one of the great supporters of the Blucerchiati, who left us in 1999 at the age of 53, owned a restaurant that carried his name, right behind the Marassi Stadium. He was Snow White.

Roberto Mancini is Dopey, because he looks so boyish and innocent, in fact his nickname – 'The Boy' – totally reflects his personality. Gianluca Vialli is Sleepy, because he is a sleepyhead and his eyes are always half-closed, giving him the appearance of being permanently on the verge of sleep. Moreno Mannini is Sneezy, because he runs as fast as the wind; Paolo Bórea is Doc, because he is grown up and has a degree. Antonio Soncini, who coaches the youth team, is Grumpy, because of his disposition, although according to him he is 'stern, not grumpy'. Domenico Arnuzzo, in charge of the Academy team, is Bashful; and Guido Montali, who is responsible for liaising with the referees, is Happy.

This is Sampdoria's Snow White and the Seven Dwarves Club, a very odd gathering indeed.

The club was founded in 1987, before the Blucerchiati started competing in Europe, and its members meet once a week, no exceptions, rain or shine. At first the meetings were every Wednesday, but then they move to Thursdays because of the players' European commitments. The guys have dinner and watch European Cup matches, telling each other that that's what they are aiming for, too. And they play cards:

they play 'Ciapa no'. Sometimes there are other attendees: Fausto Pari, Beppe Dossena, Giorgio Parri – the cook who takes care of team meals on away trips. Doc – Bórea – invariably tells the president about these evenings, but 'Pope Paul VII', as his fans call him, is not interested in the football details, he wants to know who has a steady girlfriend, whether she is pretty, where his boys go for dinner and what they are having ... in other words, he is like a father, revelling in his sons' lives. Just as well, because when he is in his office, Mancini, Vialli, Mannini and Vierchowod – and later, also Pagliuca and Lombardo – have right of admission. Even if he were talking to Jesus Christ in there, his players would still have come through the door.

Mantovani wants to know all about their evenings; he is ever so curious. So one night he just shows up at Edilio's: 'Can I sit down?' he asks. 'Please, take a seat,' everyone answers, bashfully. He has dinner with his team, then asks nonchalantly whether they can all have a game of cards. No one denies the club president a seat at the card table. But Mantovani is a born player – he is in another league. Snow White and the Seven Dwarves don't know that; they'll realise only when the evening is over, and their president has fleeced them right to the bone, making it home with 180,000 liras. Sleepy – Vialli – rests his head on the table, saying, over and over again, 'He conned us! He pinched all our money!'

This is only an anecdote, but it gives a good impression of what the atmosphere at Sampdoria was like at the time. Each man has an embroidered bib with his nickname on it, and for Christmas, Vialli buys everyone a dressing gown with a picture of Snow White, while Roberto purchases seven garden gnomes in Sampdoria's team colours. Even when the club is deciding on the colours of the away kit, everyone gets a say in the matter.

'You may not believe it,' Mancini would say, years later,

'but that team was also a gathering of true friends.' A group of young boys, all single, meeting regularly away from the football club, to have a nice fish dinner together, for a trip to the seaside, or even to go and listen to Father Mario Galli preach – the Augustinian lay brother who will become a friend and father confessor to Mancini et al, and who will in fact conduct a service before all noteworthy European matches, in front of the whole team, in whatever hotel they are staying.

Real friends then, and a core group of players, a hard kernel that gathers around the idea of loyalty to the team colours. Roberto and Gianluca, the 'Goal Twins', exemplify this bond, and become the symbol of the club. They live in Quinto, only a few metres away from each other, in a quiet and unobtrusive town that Mancio has learnt to love. Here he has found his place in life and his reason for being. The Twins' life is happy and carefree. They race around on their jet skis in the bay that their home overlooks. They go for dinner at Piedigrotta or La Ruota, they hang out at the Covo club or the Carillon, between Santa Margherita and Portofino. Luca drives a Saab, Roberto a Thema Ferrari 328 GTS – both black. Supporters chase them everywhere, girls sigh.

Vialli could have gone to AC Milan, Mancini to Juventus; they could be winning championships and trophies by now, but it wouldn't be the same. 'I don't have fun without Roberto,' says Vialli, and Mancini thinks the same. The two of them are inseparable; they even spend their holidays together. The first time this happens is in 1988, in Barbados, after the European Championship in Germany. Fausto Pari, Fausto Salsano and Roberto Bocchino join the party, together with their respective partners. Roberto has invited Federica Morelli, his girlfriend who he met around Christmas the previous year. They met in Cortina, the skiing resort where she was on holiday with her friends. She is from Naples, where her father runs a leather manufacturing business; and she studies in Milan. Mancini, who had taken a few days off with Marco Branca and an old friend of his, saw her in the hall, then in the restaurant and in the club. He was completely charmed by her presence but was too shy to approach her. Beppe Dossena and Paolo Berutta, the two Samp players who were there with their wives, helped him out. Introducing himself as a footballer would have been far too easy, so Roberto told her he was a clothing salesperson. She invited him skiing, but Roberto refused, with an apology. He is not good at skiing like he is at football. When Federica found out that he was a footballer, and a famous one, too, she did not wince. Football is just not her thing.

Their holidays over, she went back to Milan and he returned to Genoa. He managed to get her number, so he simply kept calling her and as soon as he had a day off, he drove fast down the Genoa–Milan motorway to meet her.

True love blossomed, so after two years' engagement, on 30 April 1990, in the church of San Giovanni Battista at Castagna di Quarto, Roberto and Federica tie the knot. Father Galli conducts the wedding; the best men are Paolo Mantovani, Paolo Bórea and Mancini's 'twin' Luca Vialli. Roberto is wearing a dark suit, Federica is in white, wearing a bridal veil and a train. Vialli, with a goatee beard and wearing round glasses, and Federica Mantovani take turns reading in the church. Outside, cheering for Bobby Goal – or rather Bobby Pass – there are many supporters. Inside, besides his family, are his entire team.

The Serie A season only finished the day before, on Sunday 29 April. Sampdoria scored three goals in a win over Cremonese, taking their points total to 43 and securing fifth place in the league, eight points behind Maradona's Napoli, who claimed their second title. Samp's new signings for 1989/90 (Attilio Lombardo, Gabriele Invernizzi, Giulio Nuciari and Srecko Katanec, the Slovenian midfielder who joined from Stuttgart) had made the Blucerchiati stronger and more compact, and the team started off well, but in the end, once again, winning the title proved beyond them and a ticket to Europe would have to do.

The 1989/90 season also saw Grandpa Vujadin squabble with Samp's Genoa neighbours. One of his most famous remarks, which almost cost him his job, was 'Genoa paid one-and-a-half billion for [Uruguayan midfielder José] Perdomo but my dog is a better player, when I let it loose.' Luckily, Bórea patches things up and the Serbian can carry on with his work.

But let us go back to Federica and Roberto. The newly-weds have had to postpone their honeymoon; Roberto only has two days off before starting to prepare for the Anderlecht match – because Sampdoria, for the second year in a row, have qualified for the Cup-Winners' Cup final. The road has been long, and the Blucerchiati have had to defeat Norway's Brann, Borussia Dortmund of Germany, Switzerland's Grasshopper and, in the semi-final, Monaco, for whom one George Weah has been beginning to attract attention.

The final is on 9 May in Gothenburg. Sampdoria fans take up more than 12,000 of the 20,000 seats available in the Ullevi Stadium. Twenty-five charter flights and hundreds of coaches, cars and motorbikes have taken the Blucerchiati supporters from Liguria to Sweden, hoping that this might be their day. The players believe it, too, as they want to assert themselves in Europe once and for all, after winning three cups at home.

Pagliuca, Mannini, Carboni, Pellegrini Vierchowod, Katanec, Dossena, Pari, Vialli, Mancini, Invernizzi. This is Boskov's line-up. Toninho Cerezo is injured, so he misses the match. He is sitting on the bench, next to Nuciari, Lanna,

Victor and Salsano, and cannot stop giving advice to those on the pitch. Samp are playing in their traditional blue-ringed shirts, Anderlecht are in white.

After the first few minutes, everyone can tell that there is no comparison: all the opportunities are Sampdoria's. Mancini crosses the ball into the middle, and Carboni connects with a volley, but misses the goal. Vialli gets the ball upfield to Mancini, who shoots from inside the box, but his effort is similarly off-target. Again, Mancini curls a corner kick from the right side; Vierchowod, up from the back, meets it with a powerful header, but Filip de Wilde saves – 'miraculously', according to Rai TV commentator Bruno Pizzul.

The game carries on. Pagliuca takes a very long goal kick and Mancini, wearing the number 10 shirt, goes to meet it. The keeper comes out but Mancini gets there before him and shoots with his left foot. The ball is heading towards the net at full speed, but Guy Marchoul manages to keep it out.

Sampdoria keep trying, but the Belgians defend their goal meticulously. The score is locked at 0–0. After 90 minutes, the Swiss referee, Mr Galler, sends the teams to the changing rooms.

Sampdoria shine through extra time, too. Mancini, then Vialli, then Pari; Pari faces de Wilde; he tries to lob the keeper, but his intentions give him away. Lombardo, a 53rd-minute substitute for Invernizzi, dashes down the flank, beats the defence and passes the ball to Mancini. The Blucerchiati number 10 is brought down in the box and the ball runs loose. Salsano, on as a 93rd-minute substitute for Katanec, arrives and shoots, but the ball hits the post and bounces back into the keeper's arms. He cannot hold it though and, like a hawk, Vialli arrives and fires it in. After 105 minutes, it is 1–0. In the stands, the supporters go crazy.

Two minutes later, Samp double their lead: Lombardo passes the ball to Salsano in the middle, who passes it again, diagonally, to Mancini on the right. Mancio reaches the byline, looks up and puts in a perfect cross for Vialli, who meets it with a perfect header. Goal. It is 2–0.

The Goal Twins have struck, and Samp have won the title that they have been chasing for five years. 'Congratulations to the European Cup-winners' Cup winner 1990, UC Sampdoria,' reads the electronic board. Luca Pellegrini, the captain, raises the trophy and Mancini kisses it. It is party time in Gothenburg.

When the plane lands at Cristoforo Colombo airport in Genoa, an oceanic crowd is waiting. An enormous amount of people, coming to greet, hug, hold and celebrate the champions. Gothenburg is the ultimate recognition for the team built brick-by-brick by Mantovani and Bórea. It is the first and, to date, the last European title for the Blucerchiati.

Gothenburg is also where the Snow White club signs its continuity contract. Mancini proposes it to the long-time team members on the eve of the match: 'If we lose, each of you is free to go his own way. But if we bring that cup home, we must all stay and win the championship.'

We complemented each other

A conversation with Gianluca Vialli

Gothenburg, 9 May 1990. You scored twice to win the game for Sampdoria, and with three goals became the top scorer in the tournament. How do you remember that first European victory?
'That final began a year before in Berne, when we lost against Barcelona. I played with a strained muscle, as Boskov wanted me on the pitch at all costs. "When they see Luca Vialli," he said to me, "they are scared." Just as well, because they won 2–0. After that defeat, there were players like Toninho Cerezo and Beppe Dossena who doubted that we would get another chance to win in Europe. Instead, with great persistence, we managed to make our way back to another final, against an easier opponent, less prestigious than Barça. We gained experience, we grew up as a team and felt stronger. It just felt right. And the stadium in Gothenburg was packed with our supporters. We went into the final with great respect for our opponents, but we also trusted ourselves. In extra time, I scored the opening goal. It wasn't very nice: the ball bounced off the post, the keeper grabbed it but lost it again, and I came running and kicked it in. I simply took advantage of the situation and broke the deadlock. The match until then had been quite even. Then I scored again, meeting Roberto's pass, but that first goal was so important – it is possibly the most exciting one I scored in all my Sampdoria years.'

Thanks to that goal, Sampdoria's golden age began. You won the championship the following year, then reached the European Cup final a year later …

'We had already started making our own history. We really raised the bar with Vujadin Boskov. He gave us a winning frame of mind: he made us aware of our skills and made us believe we could beat anyone. He was as cunning as a Neapolitan; he was a world citizen – he spoke six or seven languages; he was great fun to be with and a great expert on human psychology. He always said the right thing at the right time. Ours was a constant progression: Coppa Italia, Uefa Super Cup, Cup-Winners' Cup, the league … we kept growing to reach the highest levels, when we were European Cup runners-up. We got closer and closer to the scudetto each year. It was almost inevitable – because of our willing-ness, our willpower, our talent, we knew we had to get there, sooner or later. We deserved it.'

Inevitable, also because the core of the team decided to stay until the title was won.

'We kept saying to one another, over and over again: we must stick together, stay focused, and work towards that scudetto. At the time, there would be frequent – not to mention pres-tigious – offers: offers that would be beneficial to the club as well as in terms of personal rewards and satisfaction. It happened to many of us. We would think about it, we would falter, we would really be tempted by those calls … then someone reminded you that it wouldn't be right to leave, that it would be unfair – maybe even a mistake – because winning a title with Samp was going to make us happier than many of our fellow footballers had ever been, gaining other achievements with better-known teams.'

These are the words of the other 'twin', the one that made

such a remarkable pair with Roberto Mancini, the one with whom few in Italian football can compare. Young Vialli made his debut with his hometown team, Cremona, at 16. He then moved to Sampdoria, where he would stay for eight years, scoring 85 goals. After that, Juventus, then Chelsea: 278 goals altogether, in a career spanning over 500 matches. He then went on to manage Chelsea and Watford, a team where the chairman is one Elton John. Vialli is now a sport consultant for Sky Italy, appearing as a pundit and talking candidly about football. He has been living in London for quite some time: it is a city he loves, and it from there that he reflects on his and Mancini's shared history, and comments on his former twin's subsequent career.

When did you first meet Roberto Mancini?
'I first met Roberto during the [Italy] Under-16 matches, but we started playing together and hanging out when Vicini capped us for the Under-21 team. I played for Cremonese; he played for Sampdoria. Mantovani had invested a lot in young, talented players such as Pari, Pellegrini, Galia, Renica. I ended up with them all in the Under-21s, and each of them persuaded me – or at least tried to – that, if I was choosing between Juventus (who were interested in me) and Sampdoria, it would make a lot more sense for me to go to Sampdoria, because those guys were already there, because of the environment, and because it was a growing team, willing to achieve great things.'

How was that eight-year relationship with Mancini?
'Well, technically, Roberto and I were very similar at the beginning. We were both modern strikers, who could do a bit of everything, who had quantity and quality. I wouldn't want to go too far, but I'd say that we both could score, and create chances for others. In that respect, we were interchangeable.

Roberto could play as a centre forward and I would move further back, or the other way round – on the opposing side, this would make the defenders' job a lot more difficult. Then he developed this wish, this skill he'd had for a long time – forever I would say – to always give the last pass, and instead I got used to being a centre forward. Roberto now says he used to make my day, that I scored all my goals because of him; I reply that it was the other way round, because I turned into great shots the completely impossible passes he would just throw forward. Let's just say we always helped each other out, a lot. We did it all without envy; we actually thought about what was good for the team. In this sense, our relationship worked really well, and that was the case on and off the pitch.'

How was your personal relationship, outside the football field?
'We were two young guys, same age, same life philosophy. Football brought us together, as well as the love for our team. We had different characters, but we complemented each other. It was fun to be together.'

What was the best moment in your relationship?
'Please,' Vialli laughs, 'can you stop calling it a relationship?' He continues, 'Once, only once in so many years, we ended up quarrelling. Our bad mood only lasted two or three days. Perhaps we were too nervous, because things at Samp weren't honey and roses all the time. Everyone thinks that our road to victory was quite light-hearted, but in reality we all swallowed some bitter stuff; we had big arguments and had our bad moments. I remember when I signed for Juventus, Roberto was waiting for me at the restaurant, together with some other dear ones … we all burst into tears, because we realised that our important adventure together – which had to do with our sport, but not only that – had come to an end.

'Maybe the best moment was celebrating the scudetto at Carlini, the other stadium in Genoa. Mancini, Lombardo, Mannini, Bonetti and I went on stage in front of thousands of fans, dressed up like the rock band Europe [of 'The Final Countdown' fame], make-up and all. Until poor Lombardo lost his wig, no one realised it was us. We sang completely out of tune. There were many other good moments, though. Unfortunately, Roberto couldn't play in the match that made us Champions of Italy: he was suspended. He could only come on to the field after the 90 minutes were up.'

And your worst memory?
'Perhaps not the worst, but the most unpleasant, was the European Cup final. Even though we had been telling each other that it was an incredible achievement just to be there, to have got to the Wembley final against Barcelona in our first season in the competition, we still had a really hard time in the changing rooms once the match was over.'

You had already signed for Juventus before playing that final. How much did that decision affect your performance, and the team's?
It did affect us, for sure. It is harder to prepare for a final under those conditions, even though it does not necessarily mean that the game is lost from the start. First of all, knowing that you've come to the end of an era – in other words, knowing that you won't get another chance – will actually make you play harder. Second, that was not the only problem: I remember that the previous Saturday we played at home against Fiorentina, and we needed a victory to secure a Uefa Cup place. So that was an important match, too. Under different circumstances, first-string players would have been left out to get some rest, but our manager just couldn't afford that. It was 30 degrees and I got cramp, so neither our heads nor our legs were really in the best condition. I should add

that we felt quite excited, playing such an important game for the first time, against an opponent like Barcelona. So apart from the final result and the fact that I missed two goals, it was still a really good game. You don't very often see such open play in a final.'

In the press the next day, the player ratings indicated that Mancini hadn't contributed much to Sampdoria's cause.
'That's not true. I remember he sent a couple of good balls my way. To tell you the truth, I am more and more convinced that it was my fault we lost that match.'

For lobbing Zubizarreta, and having to watch the ball bounce to the side of the Blaugrana net, while thousands of supporters were already starting to cheer?
'I must admit that, just before that last bounce, the ball was aiming for the post. I remember thinking, "I wonder whether it will hit the post and go in, or bounce off it and go out." When the ball hit the turf, it deviated to the left and rolled out. It wasn't my only regret in that game: when Lombardo crossed the ball in, I got there a little too late, and off balance. My shot went right over the goalpost.'

That was your last match wearing the Blucerchiati jersey. You moved to Juventus, and later to England – the same decision that Mancio made.
'I was 32, and Juventus hinted that they weren't going to renew my contract. So you wonder, where do I go from here? To another Italian team? Well, not really, I'd rather choose England. I had always loved English football, and I was quite lucky in the fact that Chelsea wanted me. So it all came naturally to me. I believe it was the same for Roberto, he must have thought that England was worth a try, he wanted to experience it himself. After a while, you start liking Italian football

less and less – you stick with it because you're addicted, but then you understand that you can live without it and there's more out there. You realise that you can have fun and live better in England, so you pack your things and go. Roberto first experienced English football when he played for Leicester; he then had a long spell [in management] at Fiorentina, Lazio and Inter Milan, which was much needed; and in the end, he probably thought that it wouldn't be at all bad to get some work in the UK. He made the right decision and he had the patience and the willingness to start afresh.'

As a football commentator, what do you think of Mancini's last couple of years with Manchester City?
'He has done an extraordinary job. Sure, it helps to have a president, an owner, who is a sheikh. Anyway, you must know how to use your money, and spend it wisely. This is the manager's summer job, or at least 50 per cent of it. The rest of it comes during the season, when you are actually managing players. Roberto is very good at spotting the players he needs, and at managing them well. These are two fundamental skills that not everyone gives him credit for. They argue about whether it is going to be 3-5-2 or 4-4-2, but tactics are only a means to achieve an aim. The difference, though, is made throughout the season, when issues come up and you must solve your problems as they arise. Roberto handled Tevez very well, and also dealt wisely with the difficulties his team experienced, when it looked like Manchester United had already won the Premier League. Mancini is a coach whose merits are not yet fully acknowledged.'

He handled Tevez all right, but it didn't work with Balotelli, did it?
'That's not true. Look, maybe Roberto went mad a few times, but in the end he got some good stuff out of Mario, with all his highs and lows. I don't know how another coach would

manage Balotelli – if another coach ever would. Mancini is
doing a good job.'

What did you think when City and United were head-to-head?
I was leaning towards Manchester United, but Roberto
and I texted each other just before the last week of the
Premiership. I believe that City deserved to win the league,
and that United still had an awfully good season. Well done
City, you were stronger.'

*Manchester City–QPR. The final minutes of the last game. What
were your thoughts, during those moments?*
'Knowing British football, I was aware that anything could
have happened, right to the end – not necessarily something
good for City. You must also remember that the Stoke v.
Bolton game ended three minutes before the one at Etihad
Stadium. The happiness of the Queens Park Rangers fans
was infectious for those on the football field, so perhaps they
stopped fighting tooth and nail – they were still fighting
of course, but not all guns blazing. Man City were creating
three goal chances every minute, so I calculated that, with
three minutes left to go, there would still be seven, eight
good chances for them to score. And that's how it went: two
went in, and it was a beautiful end to the season not only for
City fans but for neutral supporters. It was a unique experience, something that won't happen again, maybe. We hadn't
seen anything like that in the Premier League for 25 years,
not since that time when Liverpool and Arsenal played for
the title until the last second [in 1989].'

And what did you think of Mancini during those moments?
'I saw him jump, I saw him run, and stick his hands into his
pockets. So later I asked him, "Why did you have your hands
in your pockets, what were you holding? Were you worried

that something would fall on the ground?" Roberto told me why, he told me what was in his pocket and then I realised.'

So, are you going to tell us then?
'No, not really.'

So, how do you see City's future, both in Europe and in the Premier League, now that they have won this title?
'They could win the Premiership again, but we are not talking absolute and lasting supremacy, because Manchester United, Arsenal and Chelsea will always turn it into a tight race. With respect to Europe, the Champions League is Roberto's next aim. I wouldn't call it an obsession for him, but he came so close, both as a player and as a coach, and never won it. But Europe is a complicated scenario: if your legs don't work for a week you're out, while in the championship you have a whole season to show that you're the best. I also think that City need to grow before they can class themselves as favourites; they still need to rise through the ranks, just like Chelsea did in recent years. When you've paid your dues, you either win the Champions League big time – or you have fucking good luck, just like Chelsea did.'

The thing

Toninho Cerezo blows kisses to the stands as he hobbles off the football pitch. There are twenty minutes of the match remaining, and Samp's 'old man', with Boskov's blessing, departs the arena with his hands up in the air. Damiano, the tambourine-playing figure well known to Samp fans, walks round the perimeter of the field, his snow-white hair covered by a Blucerchiati cap, wearing an official jersey and various charms, spreading salt to guard against bad luck. Samp are already winning, but you never know. After Mannini's second goal, an Italian flag with the number 1 embroidered on it appears in the southern stand of the Marassi Stadium. The chanting of 'Champions, champions, champions' begins only after the third goal, scored by Vialli. No one has contravened the good luck spells – that's good. After the final whistle has sounded, Mancini carries 'the thing' onto the pitch: a huge polystyrene shield, which goes around the stadium like a giant cake, passed from hand to hand.

Gran Bar Veneto, right opposite the football stadium, has invented a Blucerchiati pizza: it is just for show, though, not for eating. Still, outside the Marassi Stadium, supporters are stuffing their faces – victory makes people hungry, and everyone feels like buying more flags, more memorabilia. There are some three or four hundred street traders, selling scarves, horns, rosettes, huge flags. They come from Naples, Palermo,

Turin, the suburbs of Milan. They sniffed out a good business opportunity, and in the hue and cry they can even get away with shouting 'Go, Napoli'. And why not?

'Fuck off, Vicini' echoes around the stadium, but only once. Then, 'If you aren't jumping, you support Genoa' many, many times, over and over again, until people are sick of it – but it brings good luck. At the end of the game, all the players join in, around the fountain in Piazza de Ferraris – but the chant is heard all over town. Another chant goes 'It is better to win one than to be presented with nine' – this is the polite version, at any rate; elsewhere, the rude version sounds something like 'Nine scudetti, I don't give a fuck, I'd rather win one and see it close up.'

Paolo Mantovani made a plea to supporters prior to the match: don't dirty monuments, don't use smoke bombs, don't invade the pitch. For 20 minutes, the hard-core supporters have repeated this message over their loudhailers, over and over again. 'Out, out,' they shout from the stands. They are not trying to get the players to come back on to the pitch; they just want those 50-odd fans, who chased the champions on the Marassi pitch, back in their seats. Surprisingly, they do eventually go back and sit down, and the players come back out in their underwear, bare-chested, for the last time. Their final lap of honour.

Thirty thousand supporters leave Marassi along Via XX Settembre; they cross Piazza de Ferraris and heads towards Sampierdarena. By car, by motorbike, by lorry: the same old merry-go-round. Battered and overcrowded Cinquecentos. Flags and giant banners hang out of the windows. The trains from Brignole to Sampierdarena – the quickest way to get around in such a madhouse – are packed. On the 2020 local train to Savona, a large pool of water gathers – the remains of a dip in the Piazza Ferrari fountain.

Mancio started it all on the football pitch: miraculously still wearing his jersey, and a cap, he gave the magnum of Champagne a good shake, and off came the cork. He soaked photographers, hardcore fans and teammates alike. Then came the turn of Mikhailichenko, the Soviet grizzly. With his extra height, he managed to get the first rows of the stands wet, too. Many were crying, included Emilio Bucci, the clubs' federation president: on the Sunday morning, in the Alcione Theatre, he had already warned, 'If later today you see us old men crying, just try to understand.'

At the beginning of the match, over a hundred metres of coloured sheets had been lifted over the southern stand using an ingenious pulley mechanism. The curtain rose at the beginning of the match: it had taken two months to prepare, but it was worth it – the effect was spectacular. On the northern side of the stadium, the Blucerchiati flag was stuck at half-mast: maybe sabotage on behalf of the Lecce supporters? Actually, no: after realising they had no hope left, and they were going to be relegated, they joined the party. Other gatecrashers came from Milan, Piacenza, Turin and Alessandria. When asked why he supports Samp, one Milan boy answered, 'Well, everyone supports Juve, Milan, Inter. No one supports Samp, they always lose.' Maybe he will need to change teams from now on.

Two gentlemen in the Porta Principe neighbourhood are discussing what happens next. 'We must find someone to replace Cerezo next year,' they say, 'but he is irreplaceable! Still, we need a really good team next year – we must win the European Cup.' In the background, music comes from a man playing an electric accordion outside a restaurant. A drunken man is dancing, the traffic stops, immigrants enjoy the scene. The playlist is typical of a football stadium: the Bersaglieri theme, Bella Ciao, Brasil, Aïda, Jesus Christ Superstar. And chart-topping Italian prog rock band the New Trolls have written a song for Sampdoria: 'Every match is a celebration, come on Doria everywhere'. Everyone sings it standing up, like a rendition of 'Happy Birthday'. And it really does look like a birthday party, until, around one in the morning, after blowing out the candles under the headquarters windows, people head home to get some sleep. They have work the following day.

A factory worker at a famous factory says, 'Italsider [the steel works] gets worse and worse, the dock is not taking off, there are no jobs for the young, Colombiadi [a Christopher Columbus-themed exposition] is the usual Italian mess, there are too many immigrants and the historic city centre is a disgrace. Football, and a scudetto, are only a sop to us, but for one Sunday, one crazy Sunday, after 67 years, we are allowed to fly high.'

'We won the league!' shouts Maurizio into a public payphone, close to losing his voice. 'I can't believe it yet, I can't believe it – tape everything, all the programs: *Domenica Sportiva*, *Pressing*, anything. I'll believe it only when I see it on TV.' He hangs up, and walks away, humming to himself. The dream has come true.

—*Il Manifesto*, 21 May 1991

It is a dream come true for a city, for a club, for a president and for the Goal Twins. It happens at 5.45pm on a Sunday in May 1991, the penultimate match day in the Serie A season. Earlier, 'the thing' landed on the Marassi Stadium after only three minutes of play, when Cerezo managed to head the opening goal from Vialli's cut-back. The ensuing goals, from Mannini and Vialli again, were simply a prologue to the celebrations that would go on for weeks.

The last championship in the region was won by Genoa in 1924. Now, 67 years on, the cradle of Italian football has again produced the champions of Italy. It is the cradle because Genoa Cricket and Football Club was founded here back in 1893: a sports society for emigrated Englishmen, which opened its footballing arm to Italian players as well in 1897, thanks to James Richardson Spensley. This year, it is the turn of the Liguria region's younger club to celebrate.

There is no questioning the title won by Samp: they really deserved it, beating the big guns of AC Milan, Juventus, Inter Milan and Napoli along the way. Only Genoa and Torino managed to steal three points (out of four) from them. Nor can there be any doubt when the final league table is consulted: 51 points (20 matches won, 11 drawn and three lost; 57 goals scored, 24 conceded). AC Milan and Inter are five points behind, while Juventus and Napoli are 14 points behind. What's more, Gianluca Vialli is the division's top goalscorer with 19 goals, ahead of Lothar Matthäus, the German playing for Inter Milan. Roberto Mancini, with 12 goals, ranks tenth in the list of goalscorers.

'How much is this scudetto worth?' Mancini is asked amid the celebrations on the pitch. 'It is worth an awful lot to all these people,' he answers. 'It is their first time. I just can't believe it.' The disbelief is understandable, as at the beginning of the season, the Gothenburg pact notwithstanding, the Italian championship seemed no more than a dream. Sampdoria were not among the favourites, at least on paper. Roberto and Gianluca were starting on the back of a bad summer – the 'magic nights' of Italia 90 were a true nightmare to them.

So the 'Goal Twins' went into the 1990/91 season really

wanting to redeem themselves, showing the world that not only could they look good and play well, but that they were more mature now as well – that their Samp would not be the usual unfinished beauty. The fallout from the tournament had perhaps triggered an even greater desire to win.

The only big news in personnel terms for the Blucerchiati was the arrival of the Ukrainian Oleksji Mikhailichenko, a star in the Soviet national team and for Dinamo Kiev. Ivano Bonetti arrived from Bologna and Marco Branca from Udinese, while Amedeo Carboni, Victor (the Spaniard) and Fausto Salsano left during the summer. Still, the hard kernel, the backbone of the team, built and refined over the years, was still there, and that's where Grandpa Vujadin took his lead from, trusting in all that the 'Twins' could do. Shortly afterwards, he would say of them, 'In the football universe, they are an exceptional pair. They have class, brains, speed. They are born to impress, to play together. There is no need for words: they understand each other straight away.'

Nevertheless, when the championship began, Vialli was out, recovering from meniscus surgery. Despite his absence though, Samp drew against both Juventus and Parma, and beat AC Milan at San Siro, thanks to a goal scored by the 'old man' Cerezo. By the time they travelled to the San Paolo Stadium on 19 November for their ninth league match, the Blucerchiati were top of the league. Vialli, by this time, had been back for a week, but many were doubting his ability to make a full recovery. Such doubts were quickly washed away: against Maradona and Careca's Napoli, Gianluca scored twice. 'His two goals are worth 20 for us,' Boskov declared. 'With this, we can assert confidently that Vialli is back. Sampdoria have matured, and can now fight Juventus, AC Milan and Inter Milan for the championship.'

Mancio was keeping up nicely with his 'twin': he had also scored twice in the Napoli game, one of these goals being immortalised in the opening credits of *Controcampo*, the sport program on Italia 1. Attilio Lombardo put a perfect cross in and 'Bobby Goal' struck a half-volley with the instep of his right foot, beating Giovanni Galli all ends up. It was a masterpiece.

Mancio now was as happy as a lark, with his football and with his life. On 13 October he became a father when Federica gave birth to their first child, Filippo. And in Bogliasco, the atmosphere was calm and serene. As Vialli later remarked, 'We have more determination, self-assurance, and concentration. We were young before, but now we are more mature and experienced. And our achievements reflect that.'

Still, exactly one week after the 4–1 win in Naples, the Blucerchiati flopped against Genoa. A potent free-kick from Branco, the Griffins' Brazilian, swung the game against Samp. Losing the derby was awful for all concerned, especially because it allowed Inter Milan to reach the Blucerchiati at the top of the table. Still, there was no despair in the dressing-room, and Boskov pumped up his boys with one of his gems: 'You guys, if you don't win the league, this Mister tells you, you are shite.'

They were not, of course, but all their commitments started to weigh heavily on them. On a neutral ground, in Bologna, on 29 November, Samp conceded the Uefa Super Cup to Arrigo Sacchi's AC Milan, who had just won their second European Cup with a win over Benfica. The score, a sharp 2–0, signed by Gullit and Rijkaard, rendered the first-leg draw at Marassi totally useless. In March, they will go on to be unexpectedly knocked out of the Cup-Winners' Cup in the quarter-finals, by Legia Warsaw.

At least things were going well in the championship. On 30 December, Sampdoria beat Giovanni Trapattoni's Inter Milan, with Mancini wrapping up the 3–1 win. But then came Torino, Samp's usual bête noir. The match ended with a defeat and a brawl: Mancini was sent off, Pagliuca was suspended for two games. Now one disastrous match followed another. Lecce, then Lazio, triumphed at Marassi – so that on 20 January, the season's midpoint, Inter Milan were confirmed 'winter champions', one point ahead of AC Milan and three points ahead of the trio of Sampdoria, Juventus and Parma.

Boskov and his boys were showered with criticism once again. However, the Grandpa from Novi Sad showed his strength by keeping a cool head. And in the second half of the championship, everything turned around. Parma, the inexperienced club from Emilia, fell behind, and Maifredi's Juventus fell apart. After Maradona's refusal to go to Moscow for a European Cup tie, Napoli also disappeared from the scene, despite being the defending champions. Only Inter Milan and AC Milan remained in contention, but Sampdoria managed to prevail in their head-to-head matches against those two opponents. On 17 February Vialli sank Juventus, and on 10 March at Marassi, Samp took their revenge on Rijkaard, Gullit and Van Basten's Milan with a 2–0 win, signed, once again, by the Goal Twins.

This marked a turning point in the championship because AC Milan fell three points behind Inter, while on the same day, Juventus fell out of the running. It was now a head-to-head race against the Black-and-Blues, a race that ended in San Siro, on 5 May, the 14th match day in the second half of the championship season.

The Blucerchiati went into the match three points ahead of the Black-and-Blues, who had no intention of throwing in the towel. Desperate to get back to the top of the table, they attacked like mad, but Gianluca Pagliuca was amazing, saving everything. Mancini was brought down by Giuseppe Bergomi and, with no penalty given by the referee, there was a confrontation between the sometime Italy teammates.

Like Solomon, the referee, Mr D'Elia, sent them both from the pitch, making it ten against ten. Vialli took advantage of a mistake by Stringara and passed to Beppe Dossena, who fired it in, the ball brushing Walter Zenga's goalpost: 1–0. But it was not over yet. A penalty was awarded to Inter Milan. Matthäus – the last person anyone would expect to miss a penalty – took the kick, but the miraculous happened and Pagliuca saved. Inter Milan continued to attack; Pagliuca kept on making saves. With 15 minutes remaining, Vialli overcame Ferri at full speed and hurdled Zenga to wrap up the 2–0 win. While 'Spiderman' Zenga complained to the referee, calling a non-existent offside, Gianluca performed celebrations to rival those of Real Madrid's extrovert Mexican Hugo Sánchez. Sampdoria had one hand on the shield but, fearing bad luck, no one would say so yet.

Only two weeks later, when Mannini has scored the second goal against Lecce, can they admit it. Until the last minute, Mancini was hoping to play in this match, but the Federal Commission turned down Sampdoria's appeal against the player's suspension. So Roberto has had to watch the game from the changing room steps, wearing jacket and cap just like any other die-hard supporter. After three minutes, he was swept away in the embraces of herds of fans. Then, half an hour into the game, all 40,000 supporters forgot about bad luck omens and started celebrating, a huge party that will continue until the final day of the championship, a week later, at the Olympic Stadium when Sampdoria play Lazio.

The party will peak weeks later, with the massive celebrations held at the Carlini Stadium – despite the club's defeat against Roma in the Coppa Italia. It is a day to be remembered: Gianni Miná, Paolo Villagio-Fantozzi, Gino Paoli, the New Trolls and the Europe impersonators are there. The happy scudetto party, as the newspapers call it, rolls on. Lombardo, the bald, rampaging winger, is wearing a wig.

Vialli turns up with his hair dyed platinum blonde, looking like Andy Warhol's depiction of Marilyn Monroe. Ivano Bonetti does the same, with an Italy shield shaved into the back of his head. Cerezo goes blonde, too, while Vierchowod wears a shield-shaped earring – as do Gianluca Pagliuca and Fausto Pari. Mannini goes over the top with three piercings in one ear: one green, one white, one red. No one needs to ask what they stand for. 'We took these oaths during the summer, in case we won the league,' Bonetti explains.

Roberto Mancini is the most sober of the lot: there is no transformation in his appearance, but he receives unanimous words of praise from the press: 'A fabulous player'; 'Together with Matthäus, the best player in the championship'; 'Consistent as he never was in the past, he has now rewarded us with spectacular goals – a world-beater.' And Gianni Brera, one of the greatest sports reporters, concludes in *La Repubblica*, 'Mancini [is] a champion who, all by himself, can set the quality of the game for his whole team.'

He gave it all for that jersey

A conversation with Marco Lanna

He comes from Genoa. He was born among the hard-core Sampdoria fans and raised in the Blucerchiati youth teams. Marco Lanna was a full-back who started playing on the wing, but showed his competence as a sweeper, too. He made his debut in the 1987/88 season, when he was only 19. Grandpa Vujadin needed him to fill gaps in the defensive line, and he was never scared to gamble on those who excelled in the youth teams. But any apprenticeship has its difficulties, especially at the beginning. 'I played first rank very early,' says Lanna, 'so I was an easy target, let's put it that way. Sometimes, rightly so. In any case, when you're young, a good telling off can be useful.'

Marco Lanna, class of 1968, was four years younger than the iconic players around whom Sampdoria revolves. He had to go through a qualifying period before he was fully accepted among them. He remembers his initiation to the club with pleasure, now that he is 44. He has just finished a spell as a sports director with Piacenza, and he is now looking around 'to see if there is anything interesting to be done in the football world.'

'I respected my teammates a lot, and older players in general,' he says of those early days. 'So at the beginning I just tried to keep my head down and work hard. I must say, though, that Mancini, Vialli, Vierchowod, Mannini and Pellegrini, welcomed me warmly right from the start; they always tried to help me out. They knew that, by doing so, they didn't just support me, but they made our team stronger. They helped me grow, both as a man and as a player.'

What was the atmosphere like in the club, the year that Samp won the league?

'It was an experience that I doubt could be repeated. Times have changed. Paolo Mantovani built that team not only by buying the most talented young players on the market, but he also chose the men, and educated them. The whole club, from the president to Paolo Bórea, from Claudio Bosotín the warehouse-keeper, to Arnuzzo – well, it was a family. Training with Boskov was a pleasure; it was real fun. The manager taught us how to handle difficulties in a serene manner … Vujadin was hardly ever angry – or maybe he just didn't show it. Still, what he conveyed to us was confidence. Thanks to him, we used to take the field serenely, looking forward to a good game. I played with other teams [Roma in Italy, Salamanca and Real Zaragoza in Spain], but I never came across such a close group of people, having fun both on and off the pitch. We were a top club, achieving aims that only a few thought we would achieve. Let's say that, after that [Cup-Winners' Cup] final in Berne, in 1989, we started a winning cycle that lasted until the 1991/92 season. Even though we lost the European Cup final against Barcelona, those five years were the best for me, with regard to my spell at Sampdoria, and to my entire football career. I believe that all our fans remember that time happily: it was a time when you would be glad to go to the football stadium; when you knew that – besides the results – you would be watching a good game. Even today, many years on, when people see us, they remember those moments with joy – not only because of our victories, but for the positive vibes of those years.'

Going back to the tellings-off: did Roberto Mancini give you many of those?

'Yes,' Lanna grins, 'he used to do that a lot. When he saw that something wasn't working during a game, he came up and told me, straight to my face. He was just trying to fix mistakes. I remember that, during a cup match, I failed to control the ball and the other team scored ... as soon as the referee blew his whistle, he came running to the defence line, shouting all sorts. I was angry at the time, but I knew he was doing it for me and for the team. It was a sort of wake-up call. For this reason, I always took his screaming as something positive. It was a cold shower, a challenge. I wanted to be a better player, in order to show him that I deserved to be with Samp. It was hard on the football field, but things were different in the dressing-room: we would discuss the game more calmly and with more ease, and this was great help for me, the young one in the club.'

What was Mancini like, seen through the eyes of a young player?

'He did everything for that jersey, and he gave it all to the team. He never gave up. He wasn't only a player, he was truly a handyman.'

What do you mean?

'I mean that he used to take care of everything that would further the image of the team and the club. He even used to check the designs for our official kit. Mancini always paid great attention to detail, something that has also come across during his career as a manager. Every move, every play – coach Roberto always has something to say about it.'

A born leader, then?

'Yes, absolutely. At the time, Sampdoria had more than one leader: Vierchowod, Mannini, Pari, Vialli. Players with a strong personality, who would drag everyone else along at difficult times. You always knew they were there for you, and that they would lend you a hand. It was enough to glance at them, and you could feel their drive, their motivation to win and do well. Among all of them, though, Roberto was the most attached to the club colours.'

Why was that?
'I think it was because of his passionate temperament. At first sight, Mancini might come across as shy and reserved, but he always puts his heart and soul in what he believes in. Also, he practically grew up in Sampdoria; president Paolo Mantovani was just like a father to him. He probably got so attached to the team and the club over the years, that he never backed down when something needed doing. He was always like that. Maybe he got it wrong sometimes, but his intentions were always good: to make himself, the team and the whole environment better.'

What did you envy him for?
'There were many things you could envy Mancini for ... he was the sort of player who could make a difference at any time. You could envy him his technical skills, his ability to always spot an unmarked teammate, to come up with stuff that would be impossible for any defender to foresee. You knew that Mancini and Vialli, up front, could create chances for goals even after 90 minutes of play. In other words, I envied his ability to be always in the right place, at the right time.'

You played against him when you were wearing the Roma jersey, from 1993 to 1997. Was he a scary opponent?
'Well, actually yes ... both him and Vialli, who at the time was playing for Juventus, used to give a lot of hassle to defenders.

Playing against former Sampdoria teammates always made me feel quite uncomfortable, because I reckon that unforgettable time in our lives joined us together. It still does. During our training, I used to mark Mancini quite often, but in a match – well, he was definitely something else. I knew he was the sort of player who could come up with a masterstroke at any time, when you least expected it, so I marked him tight – which was practically impossible for me, given that at the time, with Carletto Mazzone's Roma, we played a zonal marking system. So you either brought him down, which was hard for me, or you just had to hope he wasn't having a particularly good day.'

Were you surprised when he became a manager?
'I was at the beginning, because Mancio, as a player, never used to compromise. Then I was lucky enough to have him as a coach at Fiorentina, in 2001. I wasn't officially on their books: I was supposed to sign a contract but the club went bankrupt, so nothing came of that. Still, I was there training with him for three months, and what really surprised me was his calm, his coolness, his ability to explain football. Beyond all tactics, he was good; he'd had Eriksson as a teacher. He would explain all the tricks of the trade, even to the young ones. He taught defenders how to mark, how to anticipate; to strikers how to overcome opponents, how to move. I was quite impressed, because during my career I hardly ever found managers who would have this pedagogical approach. They perfected your technique, but they weren't teaching you anything. I think Mancini really called himself into question when he started coaching. He was different as a person, too: he wasn't shouting, screaming and complaining anymore. On the football field, he kept calm and kept a clear head, too, so that he could teach and explain stuff. That's right: he really impressed me.'

A wasted chance

Eyes red from crying, Roberto Mancini shakes hands with Lennart Johansson, the Uefa president, as he receives his consolation medal. Gianluca Vialli does not even turn up for the awards ceremony. It is Johann Cruyff's Barcelona who lift the European Cup. Sampdoria have surrendered, in the 111th minute of the game – well into extra time – to a powerful shot by Ronald Koeman.

Only a year and a day have passed since that historic first Blucerchiati championship victory. And from that great happiness in Marassi, it is a short step to great disappointment at Wembley, on 20 May 1992. Mancio is the living image of anger and sorrow. After the referee, Mr Aron Schmidhuber, blows the full-time whistle, the Sampdoria captain tries to chase him, while Domenico Arnuzzo holds him back. Mancini shouts something after the black-clothed German, who in turn writes something down in his notebook; then Roberto sits down in the middle of the pitch and bursts into tears. Neither he nor Vujadin Boskov will attend the post-match press conference – an unprecedented development for a European final.

'It was the worst evening of my life at Samp,' Mancini would later say. 'The next day it was even worse though: you realise clearly what a chance you wasted. I wanted to win so badly. That cup had always been nailed in my head, and I only managed to brush past it.'

For Mancio, and the whole of Sampdoria, that cup has become a Holy Grail. The Blucerchiati have been pursuing it since the summer of 1991. In the wake of their Serie A title win, there were a few comings and goings. The legendary captain of the team, Luca Pellegrini, one of the first purchases of the Mantovani era, left for Verona. Mancini was given the captain's armband, and Marco Lanna became the new sweeper. Mikhailichenko left, too, for Glasgow Rangers, while Marco Branca moved to Fiorentina. The new arrivals were Renato Buso, Paulo Silas (the Brazilian), Alessandro Orlando and Dario Bonetti, who came from Juventus to join his brother Ivano.

With this stronger line-up that they hoped would bring European success, Samp brought home their first trophy of the season on 24 August 1991. This was the Italian Super Cup, won against Roma, the Coppa Italia holders. With 15 minutes of the match remaining, Mancini scored from outside the box with an amazing volley, right under the Red-and-Yellow crossbar.

So they came to the European Cup qualifiers, and when the draw said Rosenborg, many among the Blucerchiati thought, well, Norway brings good luck: after all, the Cup-Winners' Cup adventure started on Scandinavian soil. In fact, their first home match ended in a 5–0 win. The away leg, though, led to a mini-crisis: in freezing cold Norway, Vialli won a penalty, Mancini scored, and Samp won the match; however, Vujadin decided to play Cerezo and leave out Beppe Dossena, as the relationship between them had become increasingly rocky (in fact, the player would move to Perugia in the middle of the season). Mantovani did not agree with the Serbian's decision, and when Samp lost against Parma the following Sunday, with neither Cerezo nor Dossena playing, he took the decision to sack Grandpa Vujadin and replace him with Liedholm, 'the Baron'. Luckily, the Goal Twins were able to intervene, as they had done on many other occasions, and persuaded the president to leave things as they were: better not to change anything, they argued, with European Cup commitments on the horizon.

In the next round of qualifiers, they faced Honvéd of Budapest, historically a prestigious club: in the 1940s and 50s, it was the club of Ferenc Puskas, József Bozsik, Zoltán Czibor and Sándor Kocsis, the footballers who transformed the modern football universe with their national team, getting as far as the World Cup final in 1954. However, by the 1990s, Honvéd no longer scared anyone. With an aggregate score of 4–3, Samp went through to the group stages.

Their Group A opponents were Red Star Belgrade, the Serbian team who had defeated Olympique Marseille in the previous year's European Cup final; Panathinaikos of Greece; and Samp's old friends the Belgians of Anderlecht. The winners would go on to play the winners of Group B, which was to be contested between Dinamo Kiev, Sparta Prague, Benfica and Barcelona.

On 1 April 1992, on a neutral ground in Sofia (there was an international blockade against Serbia and Montenegro, because of the bloody war in the Balkans), Samp played the second leg of their tie against Red Star Belgrade. In the first leg, Mancini and Vialli had struck to earn a 2–0 win, but the return game was shaping up to be a lot more complicated. First of all, it was the fifth match day for the group, and the team's previous exertions had taken their toll; secondly, Samp were playing Jugovic, Mihajlovic, Pancev, Belodedic, Savicevic and their team to top the group; and finally, the atmosphere was truly horrendous. Thirty thousand Serbian supporters had invaded the city: they besieged the hotel where Samp were staying, and they tried to attack the team coach on its way to the stadium.

The streets of Sofia were a battleground, and things were no different on the football pitch. The Serbian hard-core supporters tried to break into the changing rooms, and on the stands, and behind the gates, all manner of things was happening. The 300 Sampdoria fans dared not say a word; they hid in a corner of the stadium where they were guarded by police. So even kicking the ball around became scary. And when Mihajlovic, 20 minutes into the game, scored the opening goal with a powerful shot from way outside the box, Samp must have thought it was all over. However, Katanec arrived in the box to equalise following a goalmouth scramble, after which the Twins took care of the rest. Mancini headed the ball towards Vialli; Vasiljevic, under pressure, tried to anticipate him, but only managed to put the ball into his own net. With 15 minutes left to go, the Mancini–Vialli partnership was working wonders. Mancio passed the ball to Gianluca just outside the box, Vialli provided a chipped return pass, and Samp's number 10 beat Belodedic and the goalkeeper to score. That was it: 3–1.

To get over the final hurdle, Samp still needed a result against Panathinaikos at home. Once again, Mancini settled the score, hitting an unstoppable shot just under the crossbar to equalise at 1–1. With eight points, two more than Red Star Belgrade, who lost against Anderlecht in their final group game, Samp had qualified for the Wembley final.

Things were not going so well in the league though, with Samp only making sixth place, missing out on qualification for the Uefa Cup. In the Coppa Italia, the Blucerchiati were knocked out in the semi-final against Parma, so the game against Barcelona – the same club that had beat them in Berne three years earlier – now represented their only chance to finish the season in trophy-winning style.

The London bookmakers had made Barça the favourites, and Johann Cruyff, the Catalans' manager, was forthright about this assessment. 'Sure, the odds are for us, and I believe that's right, too,' he said. 'Being favourites means that our opponents respect us, and I can't see why being favourites would put any extra pressure on us.' Pep Guardiola, then the deep-lying playmaker for the Blaugrana, asserted, 'They have Vialli and Mancini, so what? We have Nando, Ronald and Hristo. What's the big deal? We must enter the field with determination and boldness, and without fear.'

Actually, the Spaniards must have been trying hard to keep their fear at bay, having previously experienced some crushing disappointments at this stage of the competition. In their 93 years of history, they had played two European Cup finals, and lost them both. The first was in 1961 against Benfica; the second was in 1986 against Steaua Bucarest, when they lost on penalties. After 120 minutes, the Rumanian goalkeeper Ducadam saved four of Barça's spot-kicks.

And it was not only the past they had to worry about, but the present, too: Real Madrid were top of La Liga, two points ahead of them, and the club was burdened by endless arguments between Cruyff and the president, Josep Lluis Núñez.

Fear was also weighing on the Samp side. There was less pressure on them, but still they knew that it was a unique opportunity. Vialli, sounding every inch the philosopher, said, 'He who fears beforehand is strong; he who fears in action is a loser; he who fears afterwards is mad. We are afraid, and we hope our fear is of the right kind.' The papers, meanwhile, were full of his imminent departure for Juventus. The other 'twin' chased his fears away: 'Barcelona are favourites: they are a more prestigious club and they are politically influential. But we are not scared, we know we will have chances to win and we will try to make the best of them,' he said. Vujadin Boskov was on the same page, arguing that it was Barcelona who had more to fear. 'Cruyff may sound arrogant, but it is only a strategy,' he asserted. 'In fact they have a lot of problems.'

As anticipated, there were no great surprises in the line-ups named by Vujadin and Cruyff. Barça began with

Zubizzareta, Nando, Ferrer, Koeman, Juan Carlos, Bakero, Eusebio, Guardiola, Salinas, Laudrup, Stoichkov. Samp named Pagliuca, Mannini, Bonetti, Vierchowod, Lanna, Pari, Cerezo, Katanec, Lombardo, Mancini, Vialli.

Arrigo Sacchi, the then Azzurri coach, was in the stands and offered his unbiased opinion before the game: 'These two teams have very different ideas on football, and in a final, fear usually prevails over play. In order to overcome their defensive instincts, Sampdoria will rely on Vialli and Mancini, so they will base their game on counter-attack. Barcelona will dominate ball possession, but they will need to be careful. They have players who can make a difference, such as Laudrup and Stoichkov, but we are still talking about an unpredictable final.'

The man from Fusignano was right: the outcome of the match was so uncertain that it took 111 minutes to settle it. Before then, both sides had good chances. And although Barça held the ball and dominated possession as they tend to do, Samp were troubling them with their counter-attacks. Pagliuca saved a free-kick by Koeman, but equally Zubi had to punch the ball clear from a Lombardo shot. Pagliuca was also called upon to repel a header from Stoichkov.

Both teams had their best opportunities in the second half: Julio Salinas prevailed in a scramble among many white shirts, and fired in a sharp shot; Pagliuca got a fist to it. Then, a few minutes later, the Sampdoria keeper saved a Eusebio shot with his foot. In the other direction, Lombardo on the wing crossed to Vialli in the middle but the striker, alone in front of Zubi, fired his shot just over the crossbar. Next, Stoichkov, on a solo run, hit a cross-cum-shot that – while the Catalan commentators were already cheering – bounced off a post. Vialli again lost his marker Koeman, but Zubi raised his hands high to push away his powerful right-foot shot. Then Mancini played a perfect ball to his 'twin', whose finish left the keeper helpless – but the ball went just wide, brushing the post. Vujadin's scream, together with that of the bench and 30,000 Sampdoria fans, died in their throats.

After 90 minutes, the score was still 0–0 in a Wembley Stadium painted blue and red. Extra time began. In the 111th minute of the game, Laudrup crossed the ball in to Stoichkov, just outside the box, who passed it to Eusebio. Invernizzi, on for Samp as a substitute, challenged for the ball, and both players went down. Mr Schmidhuber blew for a foul and awarded a free-kick to Barcelona. Knowing that this represented a golden chance for their blond-haired Dutchman, who had already tried to inflict some damage from a similar position in the first few minutes of the match, the Catalans rejoiced. Sampdoria's players, meanwhile, protested fiercely, but to no avail: the shot was taken and the ball went straight through the wall and into the net, beyond the reach of the diving Pagliuca.

So it is all over, and there is nothing that can be done about it. In the heat of the moment, Mancini (and not only him) takes it out on the referee – the same man, as it happens, who refereed Samp's game against Anderlecht two months previously, in which Mancio had a goal disallowed and Lombardo was booked. Invernizzi can't believe the decision made by Mr Schmidhuber for the crucial free-kick. 'He fouled me,' he would say. 'I really had to hold back not to punch the referee.' Vialli, replaced because of cramp, admits that 'life goes on, no one died, but the free-kick their goal originated from was dubious, to say the least.'

Sampdoria's goalkeeper, Pagliuca, offers his perspective: 'I'll tell you what is really sad: the goal we conceded came right at the end, when the match was almost over and in my mind I was already preparing for a penalty shoot-out. I had worked it all out; I knew everything about their penalty takers. And then came that free-kick from Koeman: beautiful, but a one-off.'

Vujadin's judgement is that 'In the first 90 minutes, we could have won 3–1. They hit the post once; we had so many chances with Vialli and Lombardo. With Gianluca's lob, I really saw the ball in. But I don't want to sound like I'm against Barcelona. They did their duty. Just like in any other battle, generals know why they lost, but there is no sense in talking about it now.' The following day, the Serbian will add, 'Good players play well in big games. I played in World Cups and Olympics; I know winners from losers. In a final, the team that makes more mistakes loses: that's what happened to us. We had more chances, and we lost. It would have been better to lose this game on penalties.' He is asked whether it is Mancini and Vialli's fault. 'I'm not saying that,' he replies, 'I'm only saying that the match was in their hands – well, in their legs. Mancini wasn't with it; Vialli was unlucky: he didn't score, and it looks like he played a mediocre match, but if he had scored, he would have looked phenomenal.' The impression is that he was expecting more from the 'Twins'. That is also the case with the press, who are hard on Mancio. 'On the field of Wembley,' they write, 'Mancini got on the ball properly only a couple of times, and apart from his brilliant opening, he almost looked out of the game. He is supposed to be the hinge around which Sampdoria revolves, but he was either failing to get involved, or else the play just passed him by. He was not really effective, either in attack or in midfield – so in short, to be totally honest, he was no use to Samp at all.'

Between the lines, and sometimes even explicitly, they hint at the end of an era. 'That's not true,' Mancini responds, 'sooner or later I'll get another chance in the European Cup. The truth is that we felt the weight of this game too much, and suffered for it.' He is hopeful about the future, too: 'I really hope we can still be all together. I am just sorry for Cerezo: he won't be playing another final again. Vialli? What about him? I don't know where things stand with him at the moment, and I am not sure whether he knows either.'

On this, the Sampdoria captain is wrong. On 22 May, on a dull afternoon, a press dispatch from Ansa reads, 'UC Sampdoria have reached an agreement for Gianluca Vialli's transfer to Juventus FC. The deal will be officially closed according to national standards. UC Sampdoria thanks Gianluca for the wonderful achievements gained together.' Vialli is traded for four players (Corini, Giampaolo, Michele Serena and Bertarelli), plus a fee of about 4 billion liras. The cost of the whole deal for the Black-and-Whites is over 30 billion.

After eight seasons, 221 appearances, 84 goals, one league championship, three Italy Cups, a European Super Cup and an Italian Super Cup, Vialli is leaving. Mantovani has honoured his promise to Juve president Gianni Agnelli, made a few years earlier. 'When I finally decide to sell Vialli or Mancini,' the Samp president had said to 'The Lawyer', 'you will have first refusal.'

Mancini, who just that morning had been talking about the possibility of another championship, is devastated by the news, and the Blucerchiati fans with him. Everyone thought that, just like on the previous occasions, either Mantovani or Vialli would eventually have spoken up and said 'Look, nothing is happening.' However, despite the supporters' and his friends' desperate attempts to call off his departure, Vialli packs his bags and leaves. 'I must do this,' the president says, while Vialli explains, 'There are feelings at stake, but also rationality. I'd rather see Samp without me, but remaining in Serie A, than us all being relegated together.' Mancini states that Sampdoria are not dying, and that they will live on even without their top goalscorer. Vialli joins in: 'They'll be a great team, even without me. They should not fear the future: Mancini will lead them to great achievements.'

On 24 May, at Marassi, Gianluca Vialli plays his last game for Sampdoria, against his former team Cremonese. It is eight years since his first appearance in the Blucerchiati jersey, on 16 September 1984, against the same opposition. On his right arm is the captain's armband – a kind offer from his 'twin' Mancini. And after 51 minutes, he scores his farewell goal. He goes around the football pitch for over a minute, to say his goodbyes. Everyone is standing and clapping for their number 9. 'When you leave, you will realise what being loved means,' reads a huge banner made by the Tito Cucchiaroni fan club.

After 71 minutes, Fausto Pari – who received the captain's armband upon Vialli's substitution – scores the penalty that makes it 2–1, before he too says goodbye after nine long years. And they are not the only ones. Toninho Cerezo appeared on the pitch prior to the game with his wife and four kids, to take his leave of the supporters.

Vujadin Boskov, the manager who led the Blucerchiati to the top, says, 'I grew fond of this city and these people, who have given me a lot in the past six years.' And even though Marco Lanna and Gianluca Pagliuca deny that a chapter has been closed, the best part of it, sadly, is over.

As good as gold

A conversation with Fausto Pari

'After the European Cup final, after the awards ceremony, I threw my medal into the 30,000 Samp supporters. Then, on the Saturday, when we were carrying out a final training session for our last match against Cremonese at the Marassi Stadium, this guy comes up to me and says, "Here is your medal; I'm giving it back, but you must let me have an official jersey." "I don't want it, I hate that medal," I answered. He froze on the spot, he really did. "Well, if you change your mind, here is my phone number," he said. My wife took it, and it was her who did the swap. I still don't know where that medal is, but I suppose my wife does.'

This is Fausto Pari, Sampdoria's former number 4, and latterly – until last June – sporting director at Modena. He reflects on his darkest moment wearing a Blucerchiati jersey.

'"Dark" is the correct word,' he says, 'but only with regard to the final result. Otherwise, getting to Wembley on our first attempt, playing against a great club like Barcelona, was incredibly rewarding. Unfortunately, we started losing that final way before then.'

Why was that?
'Because I had signed for Napoli three days before that; Vialli had already been sold to Juventus; Cerezo was going to stop playing altogether. Boskov was leaving and Eriksson was going to be the new Samp manager. All I am saying is

that, perhaps, because of all of these reasons relating to the transfer market, we weren't calm enough to face up to such a challenge, even though it was a game that either team could have won on the pitch. It ended during extra time, with that damned free-kick: the referee awarded it to them when it should have been given to us instead. That free-kick cancelled the dream that all of us believed in.'

Why were so many departures announced before such an important match?
'Maybe president Mantovani, who was aware of his health conditions – who knew he wasn't feeling well at all – wanted to leave behind a healthy and leaner club. If those transfers hadn't been announced and we had won the European Cup, no one – as it had happened before – no one would have left, and that loop wouldn't have closed.'

That European Cup final was your next-to-last match wearing a Blucerchiati jersey. You played against Cremonese, then you left, after nine years in total.
'That's right. I arrived at Sampdoria from Parma in the summer of 1983.'

Mancini had been bought just the year before. What was the Boy like?
'Roberto was Mister Billion Dollar, because of the fee that Mantovani had paid to Bologna for him. During those first years, he really didn't get along with coach Bersellini, and there were too many arguments. When I got there, I lived with him for a year, in a lovely flat with a garden, on via Fabio Filzi, in Quinto di Nervi. He was quite shy and reserved: good as gold – too good really – so sometimes people would simply take advantage of that. On the football pitch, he really changed: that jersey motivated him and gave him a real boost. He was so in love with those colours, that

he sometimes went over the top with his remarks and his rebukes to teammates, or in his arguments with opponents and referees. The fact that he felt part of the club project made him rather short-tempered. Then, as the years went by, he matured a lot and he got over that. However, he also had a great quality: once things were over, they were over for good. The match ended, the training session finished, everyone had a shower and washed it all off. It was as if nothing had ever happened.'

What was the club, the atmosphere, like at that time?
'It was great, thanks to the one who made it all happen – in a word, president Mantovani. He was the heart and soul of the project, we were his arm. His idea was to buy the best Italian players around, under the age of 21, and to build a great team with them. He followed that guiding principle back then. We were close friends, both on and off the pitch: when we arrived in Genoa we were almost all single; we always had dinner together, seven or eight of us. We were like brothers, and we took on to the pitch this willingness to help our teammates, to stand by one another, to fight together. We created this joint effort, this great big family, and Mantovani was like a father to us all.'

The father had his favourite son: Roberto Mancini …
'Roberto came to Sampdoria when he was really young; it was understandable that Mantovani had a soft spot for him. I should say, though, that the president loved us all dearly – but when we deserved a good beating, he took care of that too, just like a real father. He made us grow up and gave us a great opportunity, both professionally and in economic terms.'

Let's go over those years again, good and bad times alike.
'Good times were more frequent than hard times. As I

said, we were growing all the time. We started by winning the Coppa Italia in 1985, our first trophy, when Bersellini was our manager and Souness and Francis were still with us. Graeme really made a difference to our team. He was a European champion, the standard-bearer for Liverpool, and he gave us that winning frame of mind that we did not yet have. He was a great character, and a good buddy – outstanding, in every respect. Francis was great, too, but he had a problem: he got injured very often. However, he showed his great skills when he was playing, and he never gave up.'

The real turning point, though, came with Vujadin …
'That's right. He was our main turning point, because Boskov encouraged us, he gave us responsibilities and always gave us the opportunity to use our skills. He came from great clubs, and really made us step up in class. In his mind, Samp was a competitive team – almost invincible – and we proved him right: in the European tournaments, we always got to the final stages.'

How much did Mancini learn from Boskov?
'He helped him mature fully. Just like he did with the rest of us.'

What was this 'mature' Mancini like, on the football pitch and in the dressing-room?
'Roberto was important, really important, because he was the most talented player in our team. He could come up with some amazing stuff, like that volleyed goal against Napoli in the year we won the championship. Only a great champion, with technical skills to match, could manage something like that. In 1991, when Luca Pellegrini left, he inherited the captain's armband, but even without the accessories, everyone held him in high esteem and listened to him carefully.

He would pass a lot of his strength on to others on the field. He had a direct line to Mantovani, even though it was three or four of the established ones, Vierchowod, Vialli and I, who acted as a liaison with the management.'

Seen from another midfielder's point of view, what were the 'Goal Twins' like?
'A real beauty. They complemented each other perfectly. It was pure class, with added strength. One preferred passing, the other one scoring. And Roberto always helped whoever played alongside him to score, very much so. He was a true passing player, the best of all time. Roberto Baggio, whom Roberto was compared to so many times, was a lot better at scoring; he relied on [service from] his teammates to do that, though, while Mancio liked his teammates to score instead.'

Ifs and buts get us nowhere, but let us try anyway: if Mancini had followed Vialli's example and signed for a big club (Juventus, Inter Milan, AC Milan), would he have achieved more?
'It is hard to tell, because Roberto has many qualities and one peculiarity (I wouldn't call it a fault): being quite intro-verted, he wanted – and still wants – to be the centre of atten-tion. That's how it was for him in Sampdoria. In our national team, he always achieved less than his skills enabled him to, because he felt like he was just one of many.'

And what do you think of Mancini the manager, seen from the outside, and his victories with Fiorentina, Lazio, Inter Milan and now Manchester City?
'If I'd been told years ago, at the end of Roberto's playing career, that he would become the manager that he has in fact become, I wouldn't have believed it. When asked about his future prospects, I would have said that he couldn't sit on a bench because of his introvert disposition and his fiery

temper; because of his relationship with his teammates and his rowdy arguments with press and referees alike. And I wasn't the only one holding that opinion. Still, he proved all of us wrong. He has been great, and has really improved over time. He went to Inter Milan, who hadn't been winning for years, and achieved what he achieved. He left Italy and he is doing great things at City. Not everyone could win the league like that, after 44 years. He is clearly becoming a global football star. I am glad about that, and I feel so happy for him. What he has achieved – and what is yet to come – is only good news because, for me, talking about Roberto is like talking about my brother.'

The long goodbye

Where does the end begin? When does the thread that ties Mancini to Sampdoria begin to fray? Maybe the day after their Wembley defeat, or maybe a few days afterwards, when his 'twin' Vialli moves to Juventus, breaking their blood oath. Or perhaps it is when Paolo Mantovani passes away: nothing will be the same again. Or else it is when one too many referees has worn him out, and he can't take it anymore. When the big clubs say they want him at all costs. When Enrico Mantovani, son and heir to Paolo, won't let him go to Inter Milan and he feels like he is held hostage by Samp. Perhaps, after all, Mancini's is just a long goodbye, like one in a love story, which burns out little by little and drags on for years before one party or the other plucks up the courage to call the whole thing off. Mancio's story with Sampdoria lasts five more seasons, before the big breakup.

Everything changes in the year 1992/93, following the departures of Vialli, Pari, Cerezo and Boskov. Other players leave too: Alessandro Orlando, Silas, Dario Bonetti, Zanutta and Breda all depart the club. New players arrive: in addition to the four footballers who joined Samp as part of the Vialli deal, Jugovic, Walker, Sacchetti and Bucchioni all join the Blucerchiati. Enrico Chiesa also returns following a loan spell with Teramo. On the bench sits Sven-Göran Eriksson, the professorial-looking Swede who is returning to Italy after three years with Benfica. Apparently, Mancio was involved in the managerial selection process, even going along to the

160

meeting between the Swede and Paolo Mantovani in Monte Carlo, and giving his consent.

In any case, it is a new Sampdoria that begins the 1992/93 league championship. Of the historic core, Vierchowod, Mannini, Pagliuca, Lombardo, Lanna and Invernizzi remain – and, of course, Mancio: the perfect captain, reflecting the club colours and representing the team. What's more, he becomes the symbol of the club: he discusses transfer moves with the president; he acts like an assistant manager helping the newly arrived Eriksson to understand how the team works; he has dinner with the fans, designs the kit, buys Sampdoria memberships for children and gives them away for free; he plans photo shoots for Christmas cards. It is hard to tell where Sampdoria ends and where Mancini begins. 'He was either a player supporting his team, or a supporter playing for them. He planned and felt the match like a supporter would, he just didn't accept it when he couldn't play,' remembers Amedeo Baldari, Samp doctor for 28 years. 'I saw him play with a raging fever, injured or just generally not in the best condition. He just wanted to be there, even when he wasn't 100 per cent.'

However, even though Mancio is doing his best, the team – with its new zonal marking system, introduced at the request of the Swedish professor – does not take off. At the beginning of September, they are out of the Coppa Italia, defeated by Cesena. And at the end of the season, they are out of Europe too, missing out on sixth place in the league by a single point. The new purchases, Buso and Bertarelli, are not scoring, possibly because they don't mix in very well in the dressing-room. Des Walker, the England defender, bought from Nottingham Forest for £1.5 million, does not fit into Eriksson's pattern of play, and has been making the opposition look good in attack, so that he will come to represent the proverbial lemon to many Samp supporters.

Gianluca Pagliuca, with four games to go till the end of the championship, crashes his Porsche Carrera 4 into an artic on the Genoa–Livorno motorway: by some miracle, he is saved, but his collarbone is fractured, so that's the end of the season for him.

In the midst of such disasters, it is, by contrast, quite a good year for Mancini. On 13 September 1992, his second son, Andrea, is born, and as far as football is concerned, there is nothing to be said: he scores 15 goals, his personal record. But this Vialli-less Samp doesn't really appeal to the playmaker. On 5 May, on the eve of the match against Pescara, just short of his 300th game in a Blucerchiati jersey, he comes across as unsure about his future. After training, he throws out a cryptic sentence: 'I could leave, really. It is not written anywhere that I have to play with Samp forever. I signed a contract till 1995, but things may also change, with two years left to go.' The press are astonished and various theories are advanced: Mancini wants to check out the transfer market; he wants to make the president understand that he must invest more in the team to make it stronger ... who knows?

And where, may we ask, would the captain go? To Roma, is the answer, where Vujadin has settled, although Mancio says that this preference has nothing to do with the Serbian manager. He expressed an interest in the Red-and-Yellows some time before.

At first sight, it looks like the champion is merely going through an uncertain spell; however, when the transfer market opens in June 1993, his plans are confirmed within the first few weeks. Pages and pages are devoted to the subject in the sporting press. Everyone is talking about Mancini and Pagliuca's possible transfer to Roma, worth 20–30 billion lira, plus Giuseppe Giannini, the Red-and-Yellow sweeper who would happily move to Genoa after 13 seasons in Rome.

But all of this is easier said than done: after Mancini has taken a look at both the departures list (Lanna, Chiesa, Buso, Walker, Corini and Zanini) and the list of new arrivals (only Fausto Salsano), he asks Mantovani to let him go to Roma. The answer is a loud 'fuck off'.

A few weeks later, Mancio receives three phone calls. It is the president, informing him of his new purchases, Bubu Evani, Ruud Gullit and David Platt. Once again, daddy Paolo listened to his gem and promptly went from a saving-it-all attitude to a spend-it-lavishly one. Three billion to AC Milan, plus two directly to Gullit for a two-year contract. The Dutchman, who has won everything there is to win with the Red-and-Blacks, says he chose Genoa because of the sea, because the atmosphere in Sampdoria is good and there is not the same expectations as at Milan. With Mr Dreadlocks comes David Platt. He has no future at Juventus, and he doesn't want to go back to England, so he chooses Samp. The 'Goal Twins' have much to do with his arrival: it is Gianluca Vialli – now wearing black and white – who suggests that he goes to Genoa. Mancio, meanwhile, has been keeping an eye on him for quite some time, since Platt wore the Bari jersey and played against him. Roberto likes him a lot. They don't know each other, but the Sampdoria skipper gets hold of his phone number and calls him up in January 1992, asking him to come and play for Samp. Mancini doesn't give up, either: every two weeks, he gives Platt a ring. In the end he wins him over, and the same happens with Mantovani, who is persuaded to pay £5 million for the English midfielder, even though the player who was on the president's shopping list that summer was actually Parma's Marco Osio.

Still, the captain's wishes are fulfilled. At the beginning of the 1993/94 season, Sampdoria present themselves as a pol-ished, well-equipped and shiny piece of machinery. Mancini is back to his usual happy, confident self. Within a few weeks,

Platt becomes his perfect partner, and a true friend. Gullit, who came in as a playmaker, partners Mancio up front, and it looks like the good times are returning. This strike partnership yields 27 goals (15 for the Dutchman, 12 for Mancini), and Roberto remarks that 'Ruud is awesome: a great champion. I haven't met many others like him.' He is on the same wavelength with Salsano and Jugovic, and Lombardo won't stop running up and down the wing.

The results show: in their first league match, Sampdoria defeat Napoli at San Paolo, and the following Sunday they beat Piacenza in a home game, with Mancini scoring a penalty. It is 5 September 1993, and Paolo Mantovani is sitting in the stands with his daughter Federica. He seems to be doing well, just like in the summer, when he spoke in front of 10,000 Sampdoria fans to introduce the new team, and he said, 'Mancini? Something must happen, for him not to be playing with Sampdoria anymore: either he quits, or I do.' These are his famous last words, as he feels faint at the end of the game against Piacenza. He leaves the football stadium staggering, his family propping him up. Four days later, he is admitted to the Galliera hospital in Genoa. Mancini and his teammates think it will be the usual check-up – he has had many before. But it is not so. On 14 October 1993, at 11.40am, Paolo Mantovani's heart stops beating. Carlo Novara, the family chauffeur, calls the players. In the dugout at the Bogliasco training ground, Mancini cries as he hugs Enrico and Federica, the president's son and daughter. He has only a few words for the press: 'It is the saddest day, and the greatest pain in my life.'

The funeral is on Saturday 16 October, in the church of Santa Teresa del Bambin Gesù, in Albaro, the Genoa neighbourhood where Mantovani lived when he arrived from Rome, forty years earlier. A jazz band from New Orleans is playing; floods of people are bidding farewell to the coffin;

the pallbearers are Enrico Mantovani, Mancini, Vialli, Pagliuca, Mannini, Vierchowod and Lombardo.

On the dedication page of his autobiography, *Io, Mancini*, Roberto would include the words 'Dear president, I will thank you forever for treating me like your fifth child, and for paying me the best compliment I have ever received in my entire life, when you said that you wished that one of my children would be just like me. Thanks for understanding me better than anybody else, when you were so great and I was so small. And as you said that you weren't having fun if I wasn't playing, well, I hope you will be having fun up there, watching me play, for a long time to come.'

The day after the funeral, Samp are playing at home against Roma. But it is as if there is no match to play for the overwrought Blucerchiati players. Still, from that day onwards, they want to dedicate a trophy to their late president. They do not make it to the top of the league: despite a good season, they finish third, six points behind the new Italian champions, AC Milan. However, Sampdoria do make it to the final of the Coppa Italia. And in Marassi, on 20 April 1994, they beat Ancona 6–1. Mancini is not playing: he pulled his thigh the previous Sunday against Inter Milan. Wearing his scarf and cap like a hard-core fan, he sits in the stands and watches his team claim their fourth Coppa Italia, the first trophy of the Enrico Mantovani era.

In the summer, the new president overhauls the squad, getting rid of Gullit, Katanec, Amoruso, Dall'Igna and Bucchioni. He trades Pagliuca for Walter Zenga, the Inter Milan keeper, and from Inter he also gets Riccardo Ferri. Maspero, Melli and Mihajlovic are the other arrivals. At the end of August, Gullit's AC Milan (the Dutchman is back in the Red-and-Black jersey, but only for a few months; he will return to Sampdoria in the spring) deny Samp the Italian Super Cup.

Europe becomes the team's new aim, after two years' absence. Mancini is out for four matches, suspended for his comments to the referee in the European Cup final at Wembley. He will make his European return in March, against Porto in the quarter-finals, a two-legged match that ends in penalty kicks. Sampdoria prevail and, for the fourth time, will contest a European semi-final.

The match is against Arsenal, on 20 April 1995, and it is decided on penalties once more. However, the London team defeat the Blucerchiati at Marassi. They are out of the Cup-Winners' Cup, and out of Europe. They also lose the derby against Genoa in the league, and ultimately finish the season in eighth place – which means they will be limited to Italian football in the following campaign. Mancini fumes, and continues to do so over summer, as Enrico Mantovani, in order to balance the books, sells Lombardo, Jugovic and Vierchowod to Juventus, Platt to Arsenal, Gullit to Chelsea, Serena to Fiorentina, Maspero to Cremonese, Melli to Parma and Buso to Napoli. His only purchases of note are Christian Karembeu and Clarence Seedorf.

So we come to 5 November 1995: Sampdoria are playing Inter Milan at Marassi. After 32 minutes, Seedorf puts Mancini through with a diagonal ball, Bianchi misses his pass and Mancini is alone, facing his former teammate Pagliuca. He hurdles him and goes down. The referee, Marcello Nicchi, does not award a penalty: instead, Mancini gets a yellow card for diving. Mancio walks back to the middle of the pitch, turns towards the stand where Mantovani is sitting, takes off his captain's armband and shouts something. He wants to be replaced. His teammates and coach all try to stop him. Mancini stays on the field for two more minutes, during which time he covers the fourth official with insults, knocks down Inter's Paul Ince, and insults Mr Nicchi until he is sent off.

Gianluca Pagliuca will say: 'I led him away because I was afraid he'd be banned for life. He could have eaten the referee alive. That penalty: what about it? I didn't feel any contact, so I could say it was not a foul. Of course, that's my opinion; Roberto's will be different, but that doesn't matter – what really shocked me was how he took it. I'd never seen him like that.' Eriksson says, 'It was my mistake, I needed to replace him when he lost his head. But it is always hard to replace the player who is supposed to make a difference in your favour. What will happen next, I don't know. The sporting judiciary will decide.' Mancio, it is determined, will be out for five matches; this is later reduced to four.

What is happening to Samp's captain? His nerves are on edge for personal reasons: he is furious because he had to stay in Genoa while everyone else left; because Samp are not considered a major, influential club; because he hasn't been getting along with Enrico Mantovani for quite a while; because he has begun the season playing up front, in accordance with Eriksson's wishes, and not as a midfielder as he would have wanted. In Bogliasco, Mancio will admit his mistake: 'The responsibility is solely mine. I apologise to everyone: to Samp supporters, whom I love dearly; to the crowd, especially to children, whom I ask not to take me as an example; to my teammates, to my club and to my manager, who has been taking the blame for too many things that are not under his control.' No reference is made to Mr Nicchi, the referee, who has sent a peace offering from Arezzo, where he lives. 'No problems with Mancini,' are his words. 'I am willing to go for dinner with him! I'll tell you what, we'll bring our families, too. I think highly of him, as a player and as a man. It looks like he is going through a rough patch, nothing to do with football, though. I would go back to Genoa and referee Samp anytime, with Mancini playing, too.' His invitation is politely returned to sender, with a joke: 'I'm on a diet.'

Mancini badly wants to leave Italy, maybe for Arsenal, where his friend David Platt can put a word in. Samp's planned short break in England – two away games against Arsenal and Middlesbrough, from 9–12 November, may just give him the chance to firm up his plans. However, Inter Milan intervene, as Massimo Moratti wants him at all costs. The two of them meet in Tortona before Mancini flies out to London. Over a nice steak, the Black-and-Blues president outlines his projects and offers every possible incentive, from monetary to footballing ones. Even though he doesn't want to play in Italy anymore, Mancini is on the verge of accepting this tempting proposal. Mantovani junior agrees: he will not stand in the way; he rather sees the trade as a way out for a character who is starting to cause trouble to the club.

Roberto thinks about it, and after 48 long hours of talking to his friends and teammates, and listening to pleas for him to stay with the team, he decides not to go. 'It wasn't an easy decision to make,' he would explain later. 'If I had chosen to leave, I would have gone to Inter Milan alone. My love for Sampdoria and the gratitude I owe to the Mantovani family have stopped me. I could have left many other times, but I was never so close. I never reasoned as a footballer, nor as a professional – otherwise, I would never have turned down such a good offer. It is an opportunity you don't easily get at 31. I don't regret it, even if Inter Milan are on their way to becoming one of the strongest teams in Europe. I have made my mind up, and I am going to help my club – so far, I have only been a burden. Sure, time goes by and it is hard to get used to it: almost all my old teammates left; our challenges are not the same as before. Moratti's offer – an amazing person – flatters and encourages me. I can still play three seasons big style. And I can play them here, in Genoa.'

When the team return from their little English tour, he finds 5,000 supporters at the Cristoforo Colombo airport,

Above: A young Roberto Mancini (front row, second right, wearing number 9) quickly showed star quality while playing for his home-town team during the 1970s.

Below: Mancini was only 16 years old when he got his first taste of top-flight Italian football, playing for Bologna in the early 1980s. He soon became the star of the team.

Above: Mancini (front row, second left) joined Sampdoria in 1982 and stayed at the club for 15 years. Trevor Francis and Liam Brady (back row, centre) were also there.

Below: England international David Platt also played with Mancini at Sampdoria. They became room-mates and friends, before joining up again at Manchester City.

Above: Having retired from playing, Mancini cut his teeth as an assistant to Sven-Goran Eriksson (right) at Roman side Lazio in 2000. The Swede was a major influence on Mancini.

Above: Mancini restarted his playing career with an unlikely move to Leicester City in 2001. Although his stay was a short one, it gave him a clear insight into English football.

Left: After returning to Italy, Mancini proved himself as a coach at Inter with three successive Serie A titles. Here, he embraces goalkeeper Julio Cesar after the second win in 2007.

Below: Installed as the new Manchester City manager in 2009, Mancini walked into a storm caused by the sacking of predecessor Mark Hughes, but soon won over the City fans.

Above: Mancini had already managed the mercurial Mario Balotelli at Inter before bringing him to City in 2010. Their relationship has been more father-son than manager-player.

Right: Carlos Tevez was already at City when Mancini became manager. The pair rowed over Tevez's apparent refusal to come on as a substitute during a Champions League match against Bayern Munich in 2011.

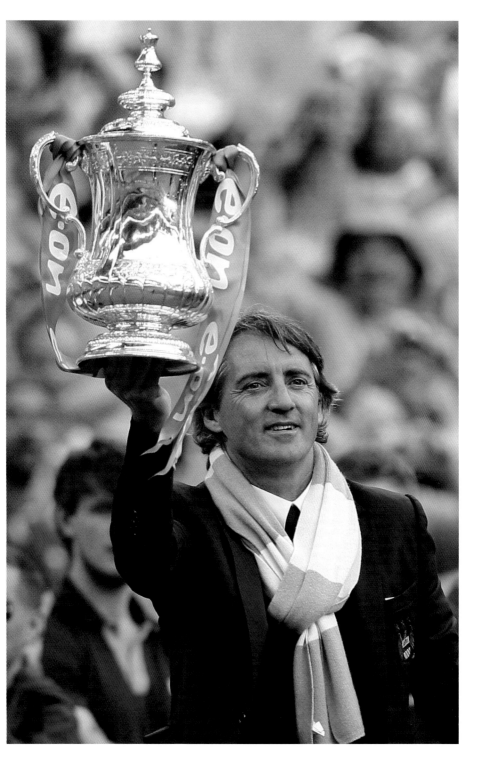

Above: Mancini shows off the FA Cup at Wembley after his team had ended the Blues' 35-year trophy drought, by beating Stoke City 1–0 in the final in May 2011.

Above: Mancini and triumphant City skipper Vincent Kompany soak up the adulation of the Blue masses as they parade the Premier League trophy around Manchester in May 2012.

ready to welcome him home and say 'thank you for not leaving'. At the end of the season, Samp are eighth in the league and qualify for Europe. Mancio speaks with Mantovani; he tells him he wants to go to England. He is looking for a good offer, but he can't find it, so he ends up renewing his contract at Samp, from 1998 to 2001.

Three months later, everything changes: Moratti is back, again offering him a Black-and-Blue jersey, and this time Roberto has no doubts. With this Samp, he has very few chances to win, while with Inter Milan everything could be different. This time though, it is Mantovani who stands in the way. One year earlier, he was more than willing to get rid of his number 10; now, he is worried that, without his captain, the whole team could fall to pieces.

The news of the Inter Milan offer filters into the public domain. On 15 October, at Marassi, in the game against Piacenza, the crowd gives Mancio a ten-minute standing ovation. No one wants Sampdoria's standard-bearer to leave.

The Mancini affair causes an uproar, and the expected departure of Karembeu for Barcelona adds to it. The situation becomes intolerable and the president announces that he is resigning – then he changes his mind. In the meantime, Mancini has made his decision. He talks about it with the manager, with Mannini, with Salsano. They all understand his reasons. It is no betrayal: he only wants to play at his best for the last years of his football career. Everything seems to be working out all right: Mantovani seems about to give up; but in the end he denies permission to leave. 'Your contract is until 2001,' he says. 'You must stay.' And Mancini, prisoner of his jersey, starts again with Samp for the 1996/97 season. Chiesa has left and Montella has arrived in his place. Juan Sebastián Verón – nicknamed La Brujita, 'The Little Witch' – arrives from Argentina.

At the halfway point of the season, Sampdoria are second in the league. The Blucerchiati again seem like championship contenders; the Samp supporters start believing that nothing is impossible for the 'crazy and beautiful' gang, as Eriksson calls them.

For Mancio it is a second youth. 'Why are you all so surprised?' he asks, speaking to *La Gazzetta dello Sport* 'I have been playing like this for years. My age? What about it? If one is in good health, age is not a problem ... Linford Christie won the World 100m title at 35; and I feel like I am 25, really. The truth is, every year we are back to discussing the same things, again and again. When someone's results are better than his previous ones, you conclude that that's his best season, forgetting all the good stuff he did in the past. I don't see that many differences between my current championship and the previous seasons. I have been playing like this since Boskov, more or less. This is no special season.'

It might not be special, but Samp's dream seems to have come alive again, despite all the negativity surrounding the club in the autumn. They are aiming for Europe, but some harbour dreams of something more. By the end they have dropped to sixth place, 12 points behind champions Juventus, but that still means entry into the Uefa Cup tournament. With 60 goals, Samp have the most prolific attack in the division. The Mancini–Montella partnership has turned out well, with the new arrival scoring 22 goals and Mancio totalling 14.

This will be Bobby Goal's last record with Samp, though. The first rumours reporting the number 10's imminent departure surfaced at the end of January: apparently, he had had dinner with Sergio Cragnotti, the Lazio president, and everything was decided. Mancini denied it. 'At the moment, I am staying,' he said, 'that's my only option. I belong to Samp.' At the beginning of March, though, things were starting to look clearer. Eriksson had been released from his contract with Blackburn Rovers, whom he was supposed to join in the summer, and he was now about to sign for Lazio instead. As well as the Swedish manager, Cragnotti wanted Mancini, Bórea, Verón, Mihajlovic and the masseur Viganó. 'I am not going to comment on that,' was Mancio's response to the hungry press in Bogliasco.

The issue was on everyone's lips until 30 May; then Mancini summoned the press for a 7pm gathering in the Nervi hotel room where the Blucerchiati usually met. 'I'll be quick,' he begins. 'I just wanted to say that I'll be playing my last match wearing my Sampdoria jersey on Sunday.' Acknowledgements followed: to the Mantovani family; to Paolo, the president; to all those who stood by him; to the directors who were not there anymore. A special thanks went out to his supporters: 'I don't know if there has ever been a player more loved by his club. You always stood by me, even when I made mistakes. But I always did it in good faith, that's what I'm like. So a big thank you to all those who supported me, and also to those who didn't. To all the managers who coached me; to my teammates, from my first year up to now. If I mentioned each and every one I would never finish, so I will just pay my compliments to the boys, who this year gave a lot more than what was expected of them.' Then he handed over to Mannini, saying, 'I was honoured to be the Sampdoria captain for so many years, and I am now happy to leave the captain's armband to Moreno, who has always given so much to the club.' More tributes: 'I am so happy to have played with so many champions. I will stick to recent ones and mention Mihajlovic, who is among the best players in the world, and Veron, who will most likely be so in the near future. Also, Karembeu, Laigle … everyone.' And again: 'I am in love with Samp; they will be in my heart forever – I am not just saying that; my love for this club will never end. And I'll stop here, before I sound pathetic.'

Then came the questions: 'So where are you heading to?' 'I don't really know,' replied Mancini, 'I haven't signed any contracts yet.' He was asked whether he could see himself playing against Sampdoria, in the future. 'I haven't been able to think about this coming Sunday yet,' he responded, 'let alone consider what happens next.' 'Are you expecting Samp to retire the number 10 shirt now?' was another question. 'It would be a great honour, but the decision is Enrico Mantovani's,' answered Mancio. He was also asked why he had made the announcement with two days to go until the final game of the season. 'I wanted to wait,' he said, 'but in the end I thought, the sooner the better. I am not being sarcastic – I owe it all to Samp, to the Mantovani family, to its son and daughter who always loved me dearly. Perhaps I won less than I could have, but the love I felt is worth more than victories. My only regret is the European Cup. It is really hard to say goodbye, but I have made my decision and I hope that those who love me will respect it. When did I decide, you ask? One, two months ago, I can't remember and it doesn't matter.' Someone asked when his next team will be made known. 'I don't know, I haven't signed anything yet,' he reiterated, 'and I am leaving for the US with Samp next week. Will I come back as a coach? Well, you never know in life.'

Sunday, 1 June. At Marassi, Samp play Fiorentina. There is nothing riding on the outcome. Everyone has come to say farewell to their standard-bearer, the champion who is leaving. A long, really long walk around the football pitch, while the rain pours down. In his hand is a bag with ten number 10 jerseys, the ones he has worn in his long career with Sampdoria. He throws them into the four sectors of the stands. His 15 years with the club end here, without the farewell goal he has been pursuing in a flooded Marassi; denied by Mareggini, the Fiorentina keeper.

So ends this chapter, 424 league appearances and 133 goals – no one has worn the Blucerchiati jersey for so long, nor scored so many. On 2 June, Mancini signs a preliminary contract with Lazio: three years and 2,800 million liras, net, per season. His decision was made at the beginning of May. Inter Milan came back again, but Mancio had already given his word to Cragnotti. He will leave for the US with Samp, before linking up with the White-and-Blues from 15 July. There is, though, one last gesture towards his former club: on 16 July, the day when the Blucerchiati players officially meet up for pre-season, a page appears in *Il Secolo XIX*, the most widely read newspaper in the whole Liguria region. A special page, paid for and designed by Mancini. In block capitals, it reads, 'Best wishes, dear Samp. You will always be in my heart.' Above this are the names and nicknames of all his former teammates. Below are those of all the club's other employees, attendants, masseurs and warehousemen. At the bottom is an inscription to all his supporters, and an autograph, together with his shirt number: the number 10.

He needed to be loved

A conversation with Moreno Mannini

When Mancini left Samp for Lazio, you chose to stay, and signed a three-year contract. How was that goodbye?
'It wasn't good, let me tell you. Things needn't have been handled like that. Roberto had a clash with Enrico Mantovani, who was the president back then, and that's when his idea to leave came up. And right at that very moment, Sergio Cragnotti's Lazio made him a very, very good offer. The two things came together: a good offer from a good club, as Lazio was at the time, and the need for a change of air.'

Who didn't handle the situation well enough? Enrico Mantovani, or Mancini?
'Both of them, actually. Roberto and Enrico both had strong personalities: they were different, but alike in many respects. When they made a decision, it was difficult to get them to change it. I believe that departure could and should have been handled differently, in PR terms. Roberto was 32 already. Although they had their arguments, the issue should have been between them, because Mancini was a true standard-bearer for Samp.'

Still, a transfer had been on the agenda for quite some time: Arsenal, Inter, Blackburn ...
'You heard about these because, in Enrico Mantovani's

last years at Sampdoria, there was always friction between him and Roberto. When Paolo Mantovani was there, you wouldn't hear about this stuff, because they would be played down straight away. The president would invite you over to Villa Sant'Ilario for dinner, and everything would be worked out; we would agree on the money without going through agents. He was like a father to us: he handled us as if we were his most cherished possession; he treated us as if we were his sons. And we were proud to have someone like him: good, charismatic, strong, powerful, and skilled. That's the reason why we all stayed with the club for so many years, and no one really considered moving, even though it would have meant earning more and going to a better club.'

Was Mancini his favourite son?
'He surely was, because he was the first to arrive when he was still a boy. Mantovani saw a promising talent in him – the footballer who could lead Sampdoria to win the championship one day, that was his dream. Roberto earned the president's respect and Mantovani helped him grow, with love and affection.'

Moreno Mannini was a full-back also capable of playing further forwards, and the player who inherited the captain's armband from Roberto Mancini. He was born in Imola, a little town in the province of Bologna; it was there that he ended his football career, and it is there that he lives today, working as an estate agent and managing sports businesses. He clocked up 377 appearances in a Blucerchiati jersey, scoring seven goals; then, when he left, he joined his friend David Platt for a stint of ten or so games at Nottingham Forest. But let us start by going back to 1984, the year he came to Genoa from Forlì.

Mancini had just turned 20, back then ...
'He was, and he still is, a very charismatic player and man. We used to listen to him because at the time, if things weren't done the way he wanted, he would go mad. Although he was young, he could always get a place in the team, even when competing with important players like Trevor Francis or Gianluca Vialli. He has always been an influential man.'

Even more so with Vujadin Boskov?
'Unlike other managers, Boskov understood Roberto straight away. He understood that Mancio just wanted to be loved, and he could make him feel that love; he made him feel stronger. So Roberto would reciprocate on the football pitch.'

Mancini, Vialli, Vierchowod, Pari and you – were you all managers on the field?
'I wouldn't say that. Vujadin had us believing that we could all influence his decisions, but in the end we always did what he said. He wasn't obsessed with tactics and patterns: he knew he had a strong team. He used to say, "Go out there and have fun." I remember that, on Sunday mornings, before our match, he used to gather us in the meeting room and he would stand in front of the blackboard. "We are playing Roma today," he would say. "Right, Pietro, Moreno: don't let the opponents' attack touch that ball. You just pass to Toninho. You, Toninho, simply kick it forwards – Vialli and Mancini will score anyway." And they would – they would really score all the time.'

What were the 'Goal Twins' like?
'Oh man ... they were truly exceptional. We were lucky they played on our side.'

And Mancini?

'Roberto was an attacking midfielder, and he made many a teammate's fortune: from Vialli – who became top goalscorer – to Gullit, Chiesa, Montella, Vieri. Whoever played with him scored heaps of goals, mainly because Roberto was such a generous player. His main satisfaction was in helping his teammates score. I remember one match; it must have been Sampdoria versus Como. Roberto cut through the opponents' defence, including the keeper, and then, one step away from the line, instead of kicking the ball in, he waited for Gianluca, passed the ball to him and let him score. If I remember correctly, the two of them had had an argument over some trivial matter, and they hadn't been talking for a few days. That pass was Roberto's way of getting Gianluca to make peace with him.'

A memory of Mancini off the football pitch?

'I have so many, we could be here talking for days. Roberto and I shared a room for seven, eight years, during training camps and away matches … I don't know how he put up with me, because I never slept. I would turn the telly off at three in the morning, whereas he would curl up on his bunk bed and be asleep at half ten.'

Would you have imagined him as a coach, back then?

'Considering how intense he got on the football pitch, I never thought he could become a manager. He had the technique, all right, he always knew what he was supposed to do; but he was unable to communicate with other players. I remember wondering how he would speak to his team each day. A manager must give players instructions, but also advice. He must motivate them. And he couldn't do that with us. Still, Mancini got better and better, and now he's brilliant at communicating, too. With us, he would shout, and that was that.

Some people would take it personally, and they would come to blows. It happened with Francis once; we had to step in so that no one would get hurt. It happened with Pagliuca, after a match in Ascoli. It happened with Vierchowod. Roberto could be really irritating at times. He thought that everyone always had to do what he thought was right. But, remember, not everyone is Roberto Mancini, so not everyone managed the things that came so easily and so naturally to him. So, he thought you were getting it wrong, or you were not trying hard enough, or you were not concentrating – and he used to go ballistic. In the end, us oldies, since we knew what he was like, we used to say to him, "Yeah, okay Roberto, you're right," and just carry on. But some people, as I said, would take offence and it could get really personal, and come to blows. The good part is that, once the match was over, it was all over for Roberto, too. He had forgotten absolutely everything. No hard feelings, no grudges.'

How were things with the referees?
'Roberto used to make the odd scene with the referees … but it has to be said, they paid their dues with him. It really drove him crazy when they were not fair, so as soon as they got something wrong, he would jump down their throat. It was their conceit that drove Roberto up the wall. Some referees weren't very competent and they would punish you if you dared to complain. Still, Roberto was full of respect for those referees who were very professional and had good people skills; those who knew how to talk to players and who would also know when to show a yellow card and when to let it go, because it wasn't right to keep going at a player who was already mad.'

Right, referees: in the 2011/12 season, Mancini was heavily criticised because he demanded a red card for Maynor Figueroa, for handling the ball during the match between Wigan Athletic and Manchester City.

'Roberto has become a little more rational, more composed and thoughtful in that respect. But he always has that sparkle in him, ready to explode.'

Rome, a beautiful end

'Rome is always beautiful, but it is mostly the Olympic Stadium that fascinates me, like some kind of magic. Every time I have played there, it has always been a great match. It is the best football stadium in the world.' On Mancini's first day of pre-season training with Lazio, in Formello, the footballer faces many questions about his ideas on the capital and what he hopes to achieve in the White-and-Blue jersey. 'Either the championship or the Uefa Cup,' is his response to the latter, 'these are my plans for now.'

Lazio haven't won the league for 23 years. The last time was in the 1973/74 season with the Maestrelli gang: Pino Wilson, Luciano Re Cecconi, Mario Frustalupi, Giorgio Chinaglia and manager Tommaso Maestrelli. Since that success, the club from Rome has experienced only dark years of scandals, rotten bets and relegations to Serie B. However, Sergio Cragnotti, a Roman financier, has brought it back to the fore, taking over SS Lazio from former president Gianmarco Calleri for 25 billion lira in 1992 and investing billions more to build a team that can challenge for the top honours. They finished second in the championship in 1995, and third in 1996, but Cragnotti wants the scudetto really badly, and it is for this miracle that he has turned to Eriksson and Mancini.

'Lazio are a great club,' says their new number 10, 'they have great players, but you must have team spirit, in order to win the championship. We had that at Samp. We were close and we helped each other out. If we can recreate that something, that sensation, that shiver that runs up your spine and makes you give it all, not only to the team, but to your teammate, too, then the problem is solved.' Mancio is persuaded that, just like the early Samp, Lazio lack only a winning frame of mind, a history of success. 'But if we start winning,' he says, 'everything will become easier; you grow inside your mind and the environment around you does, too.' This is what he is here for.

At 33, Roberto Mancini does not need to prove himself anymore. He could have ended his career on a quiet note, watching his bank account grow. But that is not what he has done: he has decided to put himself at stake, to have fun with a football between his feet again, to score goals and to create goals for others. And he still wants to win. He really does.

In Formello, his new teammates welcome him warmly. Beppe Signori, the captain, who has already scored 105 goals wearing the White-and-Blue jersey, is confident that 'Mancini will be our Ronaldo.' Signori says, 'He will help us raise the bar, he will be a key player in our club. Only a few footballers in the world can match his passing skills – that pass that creates the best possible opportunity for the striker to score. And I'm not just saying that because I like the man; the figures speak for themselves: Vialli, Chiesa, Montella, are all strikers who made it into the top goalscorers' chart with Samp.'

Mancio totally fulfils these expectations. It is sufficient to look at his first 100 days with Lazio. Six assists, with five different players benefiting, and a goal scored in the first match of the Serie A season, against Napoli. Sure, the White-and-Blues' game is not yet wholly convincing, but these things takes time. 'Give us a little more time, and we'll show you what we can do,' says the new number 10. 'I can assure you, after a while, all Eriksson's teams start playing by heart, and we shall have a lot of fun then.'

For Lazio, the fun starts in the 109th Rome derby on 2 November 1997: a night game at the Olympic Stadium. Zdenek Zeman's Roma are going strong, with a young Francesco Totti in their ranks, and after eight minutes Lazio are reduced to ten men when Favalli is sent off. However, the Red-and-Yellows do not press home their numerical advantage, and, at the start of the second half, Casiraghi gets the ball and passes it to Mancini, who slips past Servidei and Tommasi and finishes with a right-footed shot into the top corner, impossible for Konsel to save. Ten minutes later it happens again: Mancio breaks away and crosses to Casiraghi, who puts it away with a volley, right in the corner. The game ends 3–1 to Lazio.

'Thank you, thank you!' shouts Cragnotti in the changing rooms, beaming. 'What a memorable night; you were phenomenal; this is a team that can win the championship!' Mancini's stunning performance, capped with a goal, is repeated again two months later, on 6 January 1998. Lazio are again playing their neighbours, this time in the Coppa Italia and Mancini wraps up the 4–1 victory for the White-and-Blues, scoring with a lovely lobbed finish.

So Mancio has managed to win over the Olympic Stadium that he always held in such high esteem. He fits in well with Lazio, and he has become a leader. It is harder for him to adapt to the city life, where everything seems so big, brash and chaotic. He found a place to live in only a few days: a big villa swathed in greenery, for his sons and Federica. For his part, he is leading a fairly secluded life in Formello, he only sometimes goes out for dinner or to the cinema with his new friends: Orsi, Casiraghi, Marcolin, De Mita.

One week after the derby, Mancini has a date with nostalgia. On 9 November, Lazio are playing at home against his Sampdoria. 'I really don't know what it will be like, playing against Samp,' says Roberto. 'I really believe I won't be able to figure out what's going on for a few minutes. That Blucerchiati jersey is almost like a second skin to me. I will never manage to take it off.'

When Eriksson is asked how Mancini will play against his former team, he answers, 'Like he always does. And even if he didn't do that, he is always a world-beater, one of those who – as the Argentinians say – you can do whatever you want to stop him playing, but in 90 minutes he will fool you at least twice.' The manager is right. Mancini beats Balleri with a feint, and the player connects with his right leg: the referee awards a penalty kick and, only 25 minutes into the game, Lazio are ahead. Mancini does not want to twist the knife, so does not take the penalty himself. During the rest of the game he pulls three or four breathtaking masterstrokes, as his feelings take a backseat to his professionalism. The final result is 3–0 to Lazio.

The return match is on 14 March, when Lazio travel to Genoa. Mancini meets his friends again, and he also meets Beppe Signori, the Lazio captain who had welcomed him so warmly, but who then, following many controversies, asked for and was given a transfer to Samp in November, after Eriksson had confined him to the bench. A curious story of intertwined destinies. On Samp, Mancio calls for a news blackout. Vujadin Boskov, the Serbian, who is sitting again on the Samp bench, comments that 'Many flags have fallen in football, but Mancini's heart is still here with us.'

Half an hour before the match starts, Mancini walks out on to the pitch before everyone else. He receives a never-ending round of applause, picks up a bunch of flowers thrown from the stands. He reads a banner saying, 'We remember you like this: a champion.' With ten minutes of the game remaining, Eriksson allows him to parade. Mancio does not celebrate any of Lazio's goals. At the end of the match (4–0 for the White-and-Blues), he takes off the Blucerchiati scarf he is wearing and waves it for a long time, standing behind the goal. 'It was nice,' he says afterwards, in a faint voice. 'Was I feeling emotional? Of course I was, very. It would be strange if I hadn't felt that way.'

The result in Marassi means that Lazio are now undefeated in 14 matches, but no one wants to mention the championship just yet, although deep down, everyone is hoping. Juventus are still ahead of them though. 'In the final leg, the Black-and-Whites have tradition on their side, their history, their awareness of being strong in every aspect,' says Mancini. 'We have many commitments here with Lazio, but we mustn't plan too much.'

On 5 April at the Olympic Stadium, Juve's Pippo Inzaghi – with one of his usual goals – crushes the White-and-Blues' dreams. Lazio lose the year's crunch match, the one that could have confirmed them as the Italian champions-elect. In such cases, the repercussions can be devastating. Mancini tries to keep everybody calm. 'This defeat must not influence us,' he says. 'I have a lot of trust in our team as one that is able to prove its character even at hard times.'

Now a week will define Lazio's whole season: on 29 April they play AC Milan in the Coppa Italia final at their home ground, the Olympic Stadium; then on 6 May, at Parc de Princes in Paris, they will contest the Uefa Cup final against Inter Milan. Of the latter, Mancini says that, for Lazio, 'Such a final happens once in a lifetime, once … a century. This is why this match is so exceptional to us. Ronaldo, the best in the world, will be there, against our Nesta. It will be a tremendous fight, but there will be other players on the pitch who could prove decisive. Does the fact that Inter Milan are still playing for the championship go to our advantage, you ask? It doesn't, really, because in a one-off final like this, no one is ahead, just like in a derby. Actually, we risk getting to Paris lower on energy, because we are playing AC Milan for the Coppa Italia the weekend before. Now, it is important for us to concentrate, in order to get to the end, and get there well. It would be awful to end up empty-handed on the night of May 6th.'

They won't be empty-handed. Lazio win the Coppa Italia against Fabio Capello and Paolo Maldini's AC Milan. It is the second time that the White-and-Blues have won the trophy, but the first time was in 1958, when the team was coached by Fulvio Bernardini. It is our number 10's fifth Coppa Italia.

Mancini failed to sparkle in the first half, as did the rest of his team, constrained by the Red-and-Blacks who were intent on retaining their 1–0 advantage from the first leg. Moreover, in the second half, Lazio went a goal down, but then 'Bobby Pass' started knocking great balls here, there and everywhere, and the team as a whole managed to get angry enough to overturn the deficit: from 0–1 down, they win 3–1.

So they have reached their first aim, and they fly to Paris. Lazio are coming into the final having won seven and drawn three of their matches in the competition (including home and away legs). They defeated, in order: Vitoria Guimares, Rotor Volgograd, Rapid Vienna, Auxerre, and Atlético Madrid. However, past achievements don't count in Paris: it is Inter Milan who laugh last, and who raise the cup to the sky. The final, which looked so well balanced, isn't really so. After just four minutes, Iván Zamorano finds Luca Marcheggiani's net, and in the second half Javier Zanetti scores with a rocket. It is 2–0. Ronaldo, 'the Phenomenon', then scores the third goal to seal the win for Inter.

The following day, Mancini is not yet over his anger. He looks for an excuse. 'Unfortunately, we were very tired when we got to the final,' he says. 'But after 50-odd matches, it is understandable. Personally, I hope to play 30–35 matches next season, having a rest from time to time, playing as a pure striker. This year, I made this sacrifice, running around a lot, propping up the midfield, and that was the right thing to do, as Lazio needed that from me.'

The Paris final notwithstanding, Mancini is happy about his first season in Rome and he feels 'proud after having brought Lazio back to victory in a tournament where they had been missing for too many years.' 'Together with Juve and Inter Milan,' he adds, 'we dominated the season. Our supporters should be proud of their team – a team that will play a leading role next year. I am sure that Cragnotti is building an even stronger line-up, and our fans can rest easy in the knowledge that there will be more finals to play, and to win. I have in me the willingness to play more of them, to cancel our defeat against Inter Milan. Such a date is not very far off, given that we could play Juventus for the Italian Super Cup right at the start of next season.'

On 29 August 1998, by a 2–1 scoreline, Lazio beat Juventus to win their first trophy of what will be an unforgettable season. In the build up to the campaign, there has been a juicy exchange of opinions between president Cragnotti and Mancini. The hot topic had to do with loans and purchases. Incoming were Igor Protti, Marcelo Salas, Dejan Stankovic, Fernando Couto, Sergio Conceiçao, Christian Vieri and, for a fee of 30 billion, plus a 6 billion signing-on fee, Barcelona's 'Little Buddha', Ivan de la Peña. Mancini was not happy. 'Unfortunately, the team has changed, and everything has become more difficult,' he said. 'A lot of footballers playing in key positions have changed. The newcomers are good, but they have different skills. For the time being, we only have a group of good players – excellent maybe – but it takes a lot of work to turn that into a team.' Cragnotti's forthright response was, 'Mancini can think whatever he likes, but he must remember that Lazio lost almost all of their final ten games last season. And he was in that team. So it was necessary to make changes, to motivate the group. The team needed renovation.'

The renovation works out in the end, with Mancini, who is irreplaceable for Eriksson, on board. On 13 December 1998, again, against Samp, Mancio makes his 500th appearance in Serie A – an achievement that only a few players have reached. Many former teammates congratulate him for this, but it is not the party he had imagined – he hears a comment from Enrico Mantovani that he could have gladly done without. The Samp president, appearing on a talk show for a local TV station, calls Roberto 'a spoilt child, who always needed things to go his way, otherwise he would lose his temper.' 'Our relationship,' he says, 'went down the drain when I started treating him as a grown up person. It was impossible for me to keep treating him like my father used to, it was a father-son relationship with one-off results. He demanded certain players, a half-billion coach, things that we just couldn't afford. I couldn't have given him what he asked for, even if I had wanted to. I only needed to give: he would have taken it all, and stayed. I expected more gratitude from Roberto, especially towards my family.'

The 'spoilt child' would like to respond publicly, but he sticks to the press blackout called. Perhaps he would rather avoid a head-to-head match (the team from Genoa is flirting with relegation to Serie B), which ends 5–2 to Lazio. But it is another former player who sinks Samp that day: Siniša Mihajlovic, with three goals from free-kicks.

'Mancini is a genius, Parma bows to him,' writes the *Corriere della sera* on 18 January 1999. And it is not the only newspaper to devote its headlines to Mancio. 'The man with the golden heel' and 'God's heel' are the recurrent expressions. What happened? It's simple: Lazio's number 10 has pulled a new trick out of his hat, a back-heeled shot. In an away game at Parma, 23 minutes into the second half,

Mihajlovic takes a corner; Mancini is first to it but has his back to goal, so he lifts his leg and makes perfect contact with his heel, striking the ball cleanly and powerfully past Gianluigi Buffon, who can only stare in wonder and admiration. It is a goal for the history books, the papers write, and on and on they go about Mr Heel.

It is not the first time Mancini has scored or passed the ball with a back-heel. Earlier in his second season with Lazio, on 29 November against Roma, he scored his first goal of the sort. And Mancini's memory book is full of such masterstrokes, carrying his signature. 'I used to hit the ball with the heel of my foot, even as a boy,' he remembers, 'but many coaches told me off for that. If I was doing it in an advanced midfield area, we would be subject to counter-attack. I am more careful now.' He even goes so far as to say that 'With the heel or the front of the foot, it doesn't make much difference to me.' Roberto continues, 'Do I train for certain masterstrokes, you ask? I don't, actually, it all comes naturally to me. I usually come up with about 10–15 of them during a training session, though.'

Mancini readily admits, though, that the back-heeled goal against Parma is his best one. In fact, he contends that 'It is among the top five in football history.' Aesthetics aside, that goal earns his team a victory, which brings the White-and-Blues up to the second place in the league.

On 21 February, the team, beats Mircea Lucescu's Inter Milan at the Olympic Stadium. With front-runners Fiorentina drawing against Roma the same day, Lazio are now top of the league, and set fair. From then on, in less than a month, they build up a seven-point lead over AC Milan in second place. A head-to-head match between the White-and-Blues and the Red-and-Blacks, held at the Olympic Stadium on 3 April, ends in a 0–0 draw.

Lazio are now six points ahead, with only seven matches

left till the end of the championship. Worryingly though, they are starting to look a little worn out. 'It is those who chase us who are worn out,' replies Mancini. Still, the signs of decline are obvious: their recent results have amounted to two defeats and three draws. They haven't won a league match since the end of March. And on Sunday 25 April, there is only one point between the top two teams.

Lazio's next opponents are, strangely enough, Eriksson, Mancini, Lombardo and Mihajlovic's former team: Sampdoria. Bobo Vieri scores to seal the win, and the Blucerchiati already see Serie B coming, while Lazio are on their own at the top of the league. However, on Saturday 16 May, AC Milan overtake them, winning against Empoli while Lazio stand still (they draw 1–1 against Giovanni Trapattoni's Fiorentina).

AC Milan: 67 points; SS Lazio: 66 points. The final outcome will be determined only on the last day of the championship season, 23 May. At the Olympic Stadium, Marcelo Salas scores both Lazio's goals in a win over Parma, but Alberto Zaccheroni's AC Milan defeat Perugia, and so win the league by one point. There is no miracle; the die was cast in Florence. Lazio are sad, bitter and disappointed. However, their season will go down as a great one, thanks in no small part to their success in the European Cup-Winners' Cup, which they won a few days earlier, on 19 May, beating Mallorca in the final in Birmingham. Having fallen at the final hurdle in their European adventure the previous season, this time they have gone one better. It is the first European trophy in the club's history, won in a match that could not be called beautiful, but was certainly exciting. Mancini was feeding the strikers, but sometimes his skills were not enough against the Spaniards' efforts. Christian Vieri was the real hero of the match, scoring the first goal and creating the second one with a beautiful shot that the goalkeeper saved but could not hold: Pavel Nedved reacted and scored with a half-volley after 81 minutes to seal the score at 2–1.

So the season ends, and with it, Mancini's playing career – or so it seems. At 35, he is supposed to move from the pitch to a desk, where he will replace Julio Velasco, the former volleyball coach who is now Lazio's general director. Sergio Cragnotti's offer is quite tempting for Mancio, who at first seems to be considering it. He asks for 20 days to think about it, but in the end he refuses – the football pitch is calling him, still. He prefers to play, even coming off the bench, rather than being part of the club management. More, even, than a second scudetto, he really wants to win that European Cup – now the Champions League – that he's been chasing ever since it escaped from under his nose at Wembley. 'It would be nice,' he admits, 'if I could finish my career achieving that aim, cancelling out that negative, even if some time later.'

Watching the European Super Cup match on 27 August 1999, it looks like the foundations to do well are all in place. In Monte Carlo, Lazio beat European champions Manchester United with a goal by Marcelo Salas. Sir Alex Ferguson will have to do without that trophy, which is still missing from his collection. And Mancio, in his senior career, as the papers write, demonstrates that he is still a great champion. However, on 20 January 2000, Roberto Mancini announces, 'I will stop playing football; I will become a manager.' He explains, 'I have made this decision because I don't feel like moving to another team and starting again from scratch. I don't like sitting on the side-lines; playing is important for me, and this year, as I haven't played very much, I am still not feeling the best. I would really love to be Eriksson's assistant, but he already has his technical team working with him.'

Two months go by, and his hope becomes reality. At 3pm, on 30 March, the day before the Juventus–Lazio match, a note appears on Lazio's website announcing that 'The president Sergio Cragnotti, during his visit to Formello for the morning training session, has informed the whole first-team squad that Roberto Mancini has officially joined the club's technical staff. Although he will still be active as a player, Roberto will be working alongside the technical staff under the direction of the manager, Sven-Göran Eriksson, starting from today.' In essence, Mancini has been promoted to Eriksson's assistant.

In Formello, Roberto trains wearing the technical team tracksuit, and in Turin, against Juventus, he sits in the stands like a tactical observer. This way, Cragnotti thinks he can fulfil Mancio's desire to help the Swede in a hectic end-of-season spell, but the first target – the Champions League which Roberto wanted so badly – soon fades away. Mancini has the satisfaction of beating his 'twin' Gianluca Vialli's Chelsea at Stamford Bridge, but Lazio can't take the next step; they don't make it through the quarter-finals. On 18 April, at the Olympic Stadium, the lovely goal scored by La Brujita Verón is not enough to catch up with Valencia, who scored five in the first leg at Mestalla.

With the championship also now seeming out of reach, it looks like the White-and-Blues will end the season with nothing to show for it. By the 30th round of league fix-tures, Carlo Ancelotti's Juventus are still five points ahead of Lazio, but two weeks later, on 30 April, they are beaten by Verona and the gap closes to two points. Mancini plays in the penultimate league match against Bologna, and the White-and-Blues win 3–2. Juve overcome Parma 1–0, so everything will be decided on a high-octane final day of the championship on 7 May. Lazio are playing at home against Reggina, while Juventus are playing an away game against Carletto Mazzone's Perugia.

Eriksson's team, featuring Mancini, only needs the first half to get into a winning position, the goals coming from

Inzaghi and Verón. Thereafter, everyone is glued to their radios to find out what Juventus are doing: the score is dead-locked at 0–0. At the end of the first half, a violent thunder-storm hits Perugia. The pitch is like a swamp; even the locker rooms are flooded. At the Olympic Stadium, the second half starts ten minutes late: everyone is waiting for the Perugia match to start, but the pitch is unplayable. The game gets going in Rome. Cholo Simeone scores a third for Lazio, but somehow it almost doesn't seem to matter. Everyone is just waiting to hear from Perugia, where the referee Pierluigi Collina, instead of calling the match off, makes the teams play.

The match in Rome ends, while at the Renato Curi the second half is just starting. Alessandro Calori puts his team ahead, and the Olympic Stadium roars. The supporters invade the pitch, waiting for more news. Juve can't find an equaliser. Collina needs only to blow his whistle, which he does at 6.04pm, and Lazio win the championship for the sec-ond time in their history.

The White-and-Blue party starts here, and it won't stop for weeks, as Lazio just can't seem to get enough. On 18 May, in Milan, they draw 0–0 against Inter in the second leg of the Coppa Italia final. The first-leg match at the Olympic Stadium had ended 2–1, so Lazio achieve a historic double victory: the scudetto and the Coppa Italia. Roberto Mancini ends his playing career as a winner. Someone tries to per-suade him to carry on playing, but he says that 'it is better to leave now, with a shield embroidered on my jersey.'

Mancini has played 136 games for Lazio, scoring 24 goals. This means that, all in all, since 1981 when he made his Bologna debut at just 16, he has made 734 appearances and scored 204 goals. Many will regret the departure of our number 10, a playmaker who has often been compared to Roberto Baggio, who had Michel Platini as a role model and

Francesco Totti as an heir. A footballer who was perhaps mis-understood in the national team, but who was able to lead traditionally less successful clubs to victory, to turn players into a team, and a team into an enterprise. The stylish mid-fielder, capable of improbable strokes of genius, has decided to leave, and the football world is missing him already.

Roberto doesn't look back, focusing instead on the future. 'Now I just want to be a manager,' he says. 'I will start in July, attending the preparatory course in Coverciano. Dreams, you say? Maybe, but Lazio are my reality right now, and who knows, perhaps one day I could coach them.' Talking about Eriksson, he adds, 'Sven is almost 60, and might not manage to run around for that much longer. Maybe he could be a technical director.'

Sven carries on, however. Mancini is to be his assistant in the season 2000/01. Nevertheless, the pairing won't last. For Eriksson, the victory in the Italian Super Cup on 8 September 2000, 4–3 against Inter Milan, will be his last trophy with the Rome club. The news will become official at the end of October, after various rumours and indiscre-tions: the Swedish Professor will leave Lazio at the end of the season to manage the England national team. Roberto Mancini looks like the perfect candidate to succeed him. Many observers put him top of the list, the man with the best chance. The only problem is his lack of experience.

'I don't know if I am going to be Lazio's new manager, it is not up to me to say. Ask Cragnotti,' Mancio will say. He is asked what his decision would be, if he was in Cragnotti's shoes. 'Well, if I were the Lazio president, I would employ me! But I'm not asking.' Being an assistant does not appeal to him anymore. 'Another manager would bring with him someone he trusts,' he says. 'I am in this position because of all the gratitude shown to me.' The situation is uncertain until 9 January 2001, when Sven-Göran Eriksson officially resigns. 'I spoke to the players, and realised a shock was necessary,' the Swede says. Just before midday, Roberto Mancini enters the press room and puts the matter to bed. 'I thank everyone for these wonderful four years,' he says. 'I will play and celebrate with Lazio, then leave.'

That night, Lazio plays a friendly match against China at the Olympic Stadium. It is the closing party for the club's centenary. A strange occasion, which turns into a series of goodbyes: to the Swedish manager, and to his playmaker-turned-assistant Mancio. Talking about his decision to follow Eriksson out of the door, he says, 'With my decision, I am simply taking responsibility [for the team's recent poor form]. I was Eriksson's closest assistant, and if things didn't turn out too well, it is my fault, too. I am so sorry, because I have spent beautiful, unforgettable years here. But in football, as well as in life, people come and go, and maybe they come back again. Who knows.'

Mancini does not want to be an interim coach: he wants to manage the team, and he does not want to play second fiddle to anyone – not even to Lazio vice-president Dino Zoff, who makes himself available to take over the poorly performing team. Of his plans for the immediate future, Mancini says little: 'I have no offers at the moment. Let's wait and see.'

Football is his life

A conversation with Sven-Göran Eriksson

'Mancini has always been really, really important to me. He was the first player I wanted to take to Lazio with me. Sergio Cragnotti thought he was a bit too old for that, but in the end we took him anyway. And what good luck that was! Mancini turned out to be fundamental for the White-and-Blues. He brought a winning attitude with him, just like Mihajlovic and Verón did – the other two players we got from Sampdoria. He found himself in a good team, and always did his best. In three years together, we won seven trophies. The happiest moment? Without doubt, the championship we won in 2000. We could have won it the previous year, but we missed it by just one point. The Lazio people had been waiting for that for a very long time.'

The Swedish 'professor' has not forgotten how to speak Italian. He speaks it like he always did, with the same inflection, dropping in the odd word in Spanish or Portuguese here and there. He has 30-odd years as a manager behind him. He has travelled the world, from Portugal to England, from Italy to Mexico, from the Ivory Coast to Sweden. And, who knows, maybe one of these days he will pack his suitcase again and go and sit in yet another dugout. The former England manager (2001–2006), who also coached Manchester City (2007–2008) and Leicester City (2010–2011), is the only person to achieve domestic doubles – winning the championship and the national cup in the same year – in three different countries: Sweden, Portugal and Italy. In these three countries, he totalled five championships and ten other cups and super cups.

His Italian adventure began in 1984, when he was coach of Roma. Straight away, he noticed a young guy called Mancini, playing with Sampdoria. Brazilian Paulo Roberto Falcao, the Red-and-Yellows midfielder, told him he should buy him. And he did try, but Paolo Mantovani wouldn't let his darling go. So the meeting between Sven-Göran Eriksson and Roberto Mancini was put off until the 1992/93 season, when the Swede replaced Vujadin Boskov as the new Sampdoria manager.

'We won the Coppa Italia, we finished third in the championship and we did quite well in the Cup-Winners' Cup,' remembers Eriksson from his home in Sweden. He also remembers how much Paolo Mantovani, the president, used to love Mancio. 'When we played an away match, he used to call me and ask whether Roberto would play. Only if I confirmed that he would, he came and watched his team.'

What was Mancini like, as a footballer?
'He was phenomenal, fantastic, a great player. He was fast, he could make that final pass, he could score … he was very intelligent as a player. He had an incredible vision for the game. He saw things before everybody else did – almost before they happened.'

And he was a nightmare for his teammates.
Eriksson laughs. 'He was a really peculiar guy. On the football pitch, he had quite a strong temper. If he saw that his teammates weren't doing things right, if they messed things up or simply weren't doing their best, he would go mad, he went berserk, because he thought that they could do better, that they could do more. He never took it out on the

opponents, only on his teammates. Nevertheless, he never did it for himself – he was doing it for the sake of the team. He always wanted to put on a show, and he always wanted to win. Roberto is a perfectionist, in everything he does.'

And he often lost his temper with the referees as well …
'Yes, that's right, that was awful. When he thought he had suffered some injustice, he couldn't control himself. That also happened when he believed a referee had something against him.'

30 March 2000. Mancini becomes your assistant at Lazio.
'That was only for a short period of time. However, knowing him for a long time as I did, I had no doubts he would become a great manager.'

What made you feel so sure?
'Because Roberto loves football, he lives for football, football is his life. He had always shown an interest in coaching, since he was a player. He was interested in the preparatory skills, the training, the team layout, the patterns of play, the defence and attack patterns …'

Mancini always points to you as his mentor. What did you teach him?
'I am not sure about that. As a player, Roberto had many managers: Sacchi, Boskov, Vicini, Burgnich … I suppose he learned a little bit from each one of them, he probably took something from one, something else from another.'

What about his being calm and cool during a match, something that the English admire about him: did he get that from you?
'Well, perhaps he did learn that from me after all. He took that from a Swedish model.'

Apart from being a role model for Mancini, you were also his patron, promoting his cause on English soil: first, when you wanted to take him with you to Blackburn; then putting his name forward for Leicester City; and finally, suggesting he should go to Notts County.

'That's right. I spoke about it with Peter Taylor, and he really liked the thought of Roberto going to play in Leicester. I did it because Roberto was always talking about England, about English football. I thought that must have been his dream, playing in England.'

How was that dream born?

'I believe he must have always liked English football, I don't know why, but he was always discussing it with his teammates. And when Lazio were not playing, or in any case as often as he had the chance, he watched all the Premier League matches that he could catch on TV.'

You coached Manchester City yourself. What was the atmosphere like in that club?

'Manchester City has almost always been United's little brother. Then the new owners decided that it was not going to be the case any more. They wanted the situation to end. They now want City to become the older brother, and they are doing well at that. When I used to be the manager, the club didn't have all this money; it is all different now. In other words, it is a completely different story: they have the resources to purchase, more or less, anything and anyone they want.'

How has Mancini worked at City, in the past years?

'Really well. The successes he has achieved so far prove that: FA Cup, Premier League, Community Shield. To be quite honest, I don't see any other team in the Premier League that can measure up to City. Without doubt, they are the strongest football team in the English Premiership.'

And in Europe? What chance do City have in Europe?
'I am persuaded they can put up a good challenge to Real Madrid and Barcelona, which are undoubtedly the best teams – at least on paper, that is.'

What are the best skills of Mancini the manager, in your opinion?
'Roberto fully knows football, he thinks football. And he can handle a group. I reckon he must have learned that in Italy, especially at Inter Milan – a team with many great champions, many nationalities and strong personalities. That's right, I believe the Milan stage to have been fundamental to him.'

Do you think he handled the Tévez and Balotelli affairs well?
'Men like that are not easy to handle, but they are great players, and results are what count in the end. They won the Premier League, and that's the end of it.'

Roberto Mancini – a friend?
'I don't speak to him every day, but we do talk a couple of times a month. He is very respectful, he still calls me "Mister". I have told him many times to address me less formally, like I do with him, but he won't have it.'

What are his qualities, as a person?
'Roberto has always been very generous to everyone. I still remember, when he was the Sampdoria captain, he used to buy dinner for the whole team once a week, at Piedigrotta, a restaurant in Genoa. He is a very strong man, and deep down, a simple man, too. I know his mum and dad, they raised him well. Roberto has a deep affection for his family. Besides football, that's his greatest passion.'

The Ledge

To England on 11 January, back to Italy on 12 February. Just over a month; five matches, played only in part – but he remembers it all fondly, and even more so those who watched him play. After all, he was nicknamed 'The Legend', or 'The Ledge' for short.

It was Sven-Göran Eriksson who mentioned Mancio to Leicester City manager Peter Taylor. The incoming England manager, who was due to start his new job on 28 February, met Taylor after watching Leicester lose to Ipswich Town. While chatting away, the Swede mentioned Mancini's name, and promoted his former assistant at Lazio by labelling him as 'pure genius'.

'Sven told me that Mancini is a fantastic professional and that he would be ideal to come here and do the job of adding experience to our attack.' Taylor would later recall. So he didn't think twice about it, as he needed someone to help his strikers develop. Ade Akinbiyi, Trevor Benjamin, Richard Cresswell – all were still a bit green. The former Samp and Lazio player, who ended his playing career the previous summer, sounded like Taylor's best bet. For the Filbert Street boss, the fact that Mancio was 36 was not a problem. 'I am looking for his football knowledge, not his legs,' said Taylor. 'There will be enough young legs around him to do the running, so that should be all right.' More important would be the impression Mancini made, and there were to be no worries on that front.

The idea was to see how things went for about a month, and then sign a contract until the end of the season. The deal was closed and announced officially on 17 January 2001. Robbie Mancini was a footballer again, at Leicester City. Photos show him standing by the club crest, longish hair and stubble; he smiles while pointing at the fox on the club crest. Further photos show him standing next to Taylor, and finally holding his new blue jersey, with the number 10 on the back.

When asked about the details of the deal, and how much the Italian would be earning, the Leicester City manager answered, 'Robbie's got enough money. He hasn't come here for the money. He has come here to do well. If he had been unemployed for five years and living in a one-bedroom flat in Rome, I would be nervous thinking he was just coming here for the money. But he probably has 500 one-bedroom flats in Rome.'

Something else was bothering the British press: the Football Association. The theory went that this deal made all three parties happy – meaning, in order, Leicester, because they got a striker who could master a football and who could educate Taylor's young cubs; then Mancini, because he would keep fit, he would experience English football in the flesh and he would learn the language while waiting for a coaching job to come up, in Italy or in England; and last but not least, Eriksson and the FA, who would have another pair of eyes to select players for the national team. This suggestion was not to Taylor's taste. 'I just want to clarify that Robbie is not here as a coach or a scout for Sven,' he said. 'Robbie wouldn't be coming here as a player, if you think he was going out four or five nights a week scouting. He is here working for Leicester City. This move has nothing to do with the FA.' Still, he pointed out that he had nothing against the possibility of Eriksson and Mancini meeting, and talking about the way Tony Adams or Paul Scholes was playing. It could be good for England, Taylor said: 'It's another voice looking at things.'

Mancini insisted on this issue, as well. He did not want to be seen as the England manager's spy. 'I can go out for dinner with Eriksson in London but I am not here to look at players for him,' he explained. And he added that he was very happy about his choice. 'It can be a great experience for me,' he said. His friend Gianluca Vialli had already recommended England, and told him that the Foxes are a good team who do a lot of running.

Mancio's arrival in Filbert Street throws the club into a turmoil, and elicits some funny jokes. Everyone is curious to meet the Italian star, or as they call him, The Legend. 'Muzzy Izzet [the Foxes' Turkish midfielder] said he would move out of his mansion, let Robbie move in there and he would go and live in a caravan,' says Peter Taylor, adding, 'Everyone now wants an 'o' at the end of their name: Savagio, Izzetio and all that.' Robbie Savage, the Wales midfielder, now working for the BBC, remembers, 'I was quite close to manager Peter Taylor and he told me Roberto Mancini was coming to help us out. But when Roberto walked through the door, I still couldn't believe it, because I was used to watching him on Italian football on TV. To just get changed in the same dressing-room as him was an unbelievable feeling and an honour, as he was a huge name.'

During his first training session on British soil, Mancio makes a good impression on both his coach and his new teammates. He is in good physical shape, he fits in well with the group and he has understood his role well. He also demonstrates that he knows of some of the Foxes' players already. In any case, he takes his work home with him: videos of the last matches, photos of first-XI and squad players so that he can memorise them. He has settled with his family in a hotel in Leicester city centre.

The English language is not his thing, even though he is studying hard; his new friends help him out with that. For instance, Savage recalls, 'I have been the new guy at clubs and it can be difficult – let alone when you can't speak the language. So I said to Robbie that I would take him out. I introduced him to all my friends, who helped him learn English as well, and I think Roberto liked me because I was different. We both had long hair and I used to dive on him in training and mess about with him. I made him feel at home by taking the mick out of him. We even roomed together on away trips and I fondly remember he introduced me to pasta.' It is something that the Welshman won't forget; the subject will arise again in interviews he gives about Mancini as Man City manager.

Savage, just like everyone else at Leicester, is impressed by Mancio's behaviour. He is 'cool, well mannered', and above all he is not showing off: he does not look down on people, even though he is the talented one and the famous one. His talent is obvious in training, when one watches him control the ball perfectly, or sees his back-heels, his free-kicks and his spectacular goals. So much so that the group, usually not particularly soft on newcomers, pauses in order to applaud the Legend. Taylor's mouth hangs open. 'You won't believe what this guy can do,' he says.

His debut is scheduled for Saturday 20 January in a Premier League match against Arsenal. David Platt, who is managing Nottingham Forest, and Gianluca Vialli, who is attending a coaching course in the Midlands, have taught him the basics of the language that he will need to get by during the course of a game – things like 'man on' and 'time'. He will use these during the match against Arsene Wenger's team, but unfortunately Leicester are soon reduced to ten men after Matthew Jones receives two yellow cards in 39 minutes. So Mancini must play a covering role, in a position that is not his. He plays for 73 minutes, before being replaced by Ade Akinbiyi. All in all it is a good debut; he pairs well with Dean Sturridge, and the result is decent (0–0, in spite of heaps of chances created for Henry and Wiltord).

On 27 January, at Villa Park, Leicester play Aston Villa in the second round of the FA Cup. Mancini plays 72 minutes, before being replaced by Cresswell, and watches from the bench as Arnar Gunnlau scores the goal that secures a 2–1 victory for the Foxes. On 31 January comes Mancio's first defeat in the Premier League, away at Southampton – Dan Petrescu scores just before the end of the game. Mancini had a good chance himself, six minutes into the second half, for what would have been his first goal for Leicester, but his shot from close range was saved by Jones.

On 3 February, another Premier League match: the Foxes face Claudio Ranieri and Gianfranco Zola's Chelsea. Naturally, Mancini is asked about his Italian opponents. 'Ranieri has a reputation of being a good manager who makes the players play well,' he replies. Of the players, he says, 'I know all the Chelsea players – I know Gianfranco Zola better than the others because we have played together. I would like to do as well as Zola has, here in England, but the situation is different. Zola was much younger when he came, while I have been successful before.'

The match ends 2–1 to Leicester. With much self-abnegation, Taylor's team have managed to upset the odds and defeat one of the strongest teams in the competition, bringing to an end a run of five league matches without a win. Mancini played his best match so far, but he is still not shining at his brightest. As Taylor rightly points out, it will take another month before he is in top shape.

Mancini likes English football. 'It is very different from

Italian,' he says, 'it's more physical and matches are always very open. People talk about the speed of English games, but in Italy referees blow their whistles very often so you cannot build up speed. In England, referees wave play on, and so it becomes faster.'

On 10 February at Goodison Park, Mancini starts on the bench but comes on for Jones at half-time. Leicester, by then, are two goals down, and Everton seem to be controlling the match. However, in the second half everything changes. Sturridge scores to give the Foxes hope, and Mancini takes control, using his best passing skills. It is a pity that Eadie cannot do more with the beautiful pass that takes him behind the Everton defence. The Merseysiders hold on for a 2–1 win, and this proves to be the last match for Mancio on British soil.

The following week, Leicester gives him permission to return to Italy. The official line is that 'he must sort out family problems', but rumour has it that there is a coaching job at Fiorentina waiting for him. Anyway, in Leicester, everyone is expecting him back for Saturday's FA Cup match against Bristol City. However, on the night of 14 February, Taylor receives a call from Roberto, who apologises and tells him that he can't make it back in time for the match. He still hopes he can continue playing with Leicester, though.

'It was obviously a big blow,' Taylor would admit afterwards, 'because we were expecting him to be playing on the Saturday. It was an important match. But sometimes these things happen when you bring someone in from abroad.' The matter is expected to be cleared up speedily; a Leicester spokesman announces, 'Roberto has kept us fully informed of his situation and is staying in Italy for some extra time. We plan to talk to him early next week.'

The matter will indeed be cleared up, but Roberto Mancini has already taken a different path: he is leaving

Leicester for Florence. Still, he won't forget that month. 'It was a very good experience for me – short, but enjoyable,' he will say, years later, when he returns to Leicester as manager of Manchester City. 'The Leicester fans were wonderful to me and the players were very respectful and friendly, too. I'd like to thank everyone connected with the club and particularly the supporters for making my time with them so happy.'

But, for now, Florence beckons.

A season of living dangerously

'It happened on a very cold Saturday; it was snowing right up to the Tuscan borders. I didn't have Mancini's phone number, so I rang Gianluca Vialli instead, over in England. He gave me Roberto's number, and I called him. He was in Cortina. Four hours later, he was in Florence.'

So speaks Mario Sconcerti, former Fiorentina vice-president, bringing recalling the day in February 2001 when he decided to offer Mancio the role of coach for the Purples.

'The Emperor' Fatih Terim, the Turkish manager who had come to Florence from Galatasaray the previous summer, had good instincts and had seemed to be getting the team to play the right way, yet results had left much to be desired. Up and down the team went, like a yo-yo. They went out of the Uefa Cup tournament straight away, against the Austrians of Tyrol Innsbruck, and in Serie A they went from an astounding victory (4–0) over AC Milan to what would go down in history as a notoriously bad match against Perugia. So, on 19 January, Terim announced that he would leave at the end of the season, citing reservations about the future direction of the club.

Speculation mounted regarding the manager's future plans, and in the meantime, Fiorentina – apart from nego-tiating the early rounds of the Coppa Italia – just seemed unable to get it right. In the championship, they were on a miserable run of three defeats and three draws. The club was in free-fall. Vittorio Cecchi Gori, the president, had been on the verge of sacking the Turkish manager on no fewer than three occasions before the final straw came at last on Saturday 24 February.

'The home match against Brescia ended with a hard-earned 2–2 draw,' recalls Sconcerti. 'Roberto Baggio sunk us with two goals, and in the changing rooms there was a heated argument, quite an unpleasant one, between the president and the manager. At that point, I was told to find another manager, quickly. I immediately thought of Mancini.'

But why him? He had no prior experience, other than assisting Eriksson. Sconcerti, a great sports journalist, who nowadays writes for the *Corriere della Sera*, answers without hesitation, 'That rumour [that Mancini would be joining the Purples as coach] had been going around all summer, but nothing came out of it. At that moment, we needed to replace Terim with someone who had a strong personality, just as strong as the Turk. Mancini was a different sort of person, although just as charismatic. We were persuaded he had what it took to fill the gap and overcome that difficult stage.'

It was 1am when, after battling snow, ice and a distance of hundreds of miles, Mancini arrived in a hotel in Florence, where he met up with Cecchi Gori and Sconcerti. The three of them quickly came to an agreement. Mancini really wanted to become a coach, he had always said that, and he was ready to handle this hot potato. However, the news had to be kept confidential, until the bureaucratic aspects were resolved; as before Mancio could sit on the Purples bench, he needed to overcome one last obstacle. The Italian Federation of Football has a rule that the same manager cannot work for two different clubs in the same season. And Mancini, up to 9 January that year, had been Eriksson's assistant at Lazio, so he would need special dispensation. At Fiorentina, everyone felt that this could be achieved without much hassle, and acted as tactfully as possible.

On Monday 26 February, Mario Sconcerti reported to Coverciano, where the Federation has its technical headquarters, to attend a meeting with Azeglio Vicini, the former national team coach and president of Assoallenatori, and to test the water.

'That one was actually a meeting among coaches, discussing tactical and latest issues,' remembers Sconcerti. 'Suddenly, this journalist, Giorgio Tosatti, who was a colleague of mine and was chairing the assembly, comes up and says, "All right, let's talk about Mancini and Fiorentina now." I raised my hand and, when I was allowed to speak, I said to them, "How dare you speak like that! You are doing serious damage to me." Then I approached Vicini and told him that he could have shown a little more discretion, at least. He answered that I knew how things worked in the football world – it was impossible to keep a secret. Still, the dispensation would come, in the end.'

In the meantime, news of Mancini coaching the Purples went around in the blink of an eye, and at 5pm, Terim, together with his staff and general director Giancarlo Antognoni – a true icon of Italian football – handed in his notice. At 7.30pm, the Fiorentina vice-president was forced to officially announce the signing of a new manager. There were endless arguments between new and old directors, while the supporters threatened mass demonstrations, demanding the resignations of the president and the club's management. The situation was about to blow up.

'All this mess does not worry me,' Mancini says from Coverciano, where he is attending a coaching course. Waiting for the verdict, he adds, 'If I get my cake, I'll obviously eat it. But they can't talk about a future job for me at Fiorentina, because nothing is official as yet; I wouldn't want to say anything inappropriate.' For the time being, he speaks only to Luciano Chiarugi, who is temporarily managing the team. At the beginning of March comes the decision by the Federation Technical Sector: rules are rules. No manager can sign with more than one team per season. Therefore, it is a definite no.

'At that point I started to worry,' recalls Sconcerti, 'and I told Mancini, "Roberto, I must also look elsewhere, I can't risk it." So I called Ottavio Bianchi [who used to coach Napoli and Inter Milan], who would later become Fiorentina technical director.'

While looking for a solution, Sconcerti keeps fighting against the Federation and the Olympic Committee. His argument is that Mancini was only an assistant at Lazio, so he does not fall under the rule preventing a manager from coaching two clubs in the same season. In the end, this argument will prevail: in fact, Giovanni Petrucci, FIGC special commissioner and president of the Olympic Committee, overturns the verdict expressed by his own technical committee. 'The rule forbidding managers to coach two teams in the same league,' he declares, 'does not apply to assistant managers.'

Azeglio Vicini resigns from his job as vice-president of the Football Federation technical team in protest. He says that the Mancini affair is a scandal. Carletto Mazzone, the Brescia team manager, adds, 'Vicini here and Vicini there … it is Petrucci who should resign! He broke a rule that he was supposed to make others respect.' Most coaches in Serie A share this opinion, although no one has anything against the former Sampdoria and Lazio number 10. As Renzo Ulivieri says, 'This has nothing to do with Mancini as a person. I wish him all the best as a manager – an even better career than the one he had as a player – but no one can ignore that the basic rules of our organisation have been trampled upon, and a bad precedent has been set. Democracy is dead.'

Naturally, Roberto Mancini is asked for his thoughts on the matter. 'All this squabble happened because it was me we were talking about, and I must thank Vicini for this,' he says. 'My case is completely different from others. First of all, we are not talking about a dispensation, but about an interpretation of the rule; and secondly I add that a decision has been made, and it must be respected. There is no point in going on about it for ages.'

So it is a yes after all; he can sit on the Fiorentina bench without further ado. This means he can finally be introduced to the town as the new manager. At 7pm on 8 March 2001, at the club's headquarters, he begins like this: 'It is true, I have never managed a team before, but I am sure that my 20 years' experience as a player will help, and so will the club and the supporters.' He is calm, modest, a little excited and dressed smartly, as usual. He admits that 'the difficult part will be from Sunday onwards. Luckily, I have good and enthusiastic players like Rui Costa and Chiesa. I know I am taking Terim's place, a coach who was very much loved. I hope this can be the case with me, too.' He doesn't commit himself to how the team will play: 'It wouldn't be right to arrive and change everything out of the blue. I haven't got time for that, for a start. My philosophy will be to go out there and try and win, playing well and making the supporters have fun. But we shouldn't look at the league position right now; we just need to move upwards.' He doesn't offer much about himself, although he says, 'I have always jumped a stage. I was playing in Serie A when I was 16; now I come to an important club as a manager straight away. Back then, I was totally irresponsible. Now I feel more mature and confident. And I will also be more tactful.' Mancini's contract ties him to Fiorentina until June 2002, on a yearly wage approaching a billion and a half lira.

His first match is a home game against Bari, which the Purples lose 2–1 after a last-minute goal by Antonio Cassano. Mancini has to watch it from the stands. However, he is on the bench on Sunday 11 March for the game against Perugia. Serse Cosmi, the Griffins' manager, does not hide the fact that he prefers facing Mancini the manager, rather than Mancini the player. Of the former Samp and Lazio star, he says, 'On the football pitch, he would surely give us a lot of hassle – but as a manager, he is still at the beginning of a career which is completely new to him, and differs from what he is used to as a player.'

This is true, but Mancio's destiny is predetermined. A designer clothing range to which he put his name used the phrase 'Born to be number 10.' Now, just substitute the word 'manager' for 'number 10'. That's right: this new job fits him like a glove. Roberto Mancini faces his debut with a very British countenance, spotless blue suit, rebellious hair, thin smile, as he walks among the photographers. Later, during the match at the Renato Curi Stadium, he never sits down; he is always one step away from the white line – that white chalk line which separates the past from the present, his old life as a footballer from the one he now has as a manager. Variously folding his arms across his chest or making moderate and light gestures, the new coach has style. As a playmaker, he used to organise the team and he dreamt of being a manager: it was not on a whim that he studied to pass the first, entry-level, management qualification in April 1997, when he was still Sampdoria's captain. His demeanour and behaviour on the sidelines are impeccable: he takes after his patron, Sven-Göran Eriksson. Just like Sven, Mancio does not get flustered, not even when Fiorentina are two goals down at the end of the first half. He celebrates, in moderation, with his arms up in the air, only when Lassisi equalises. When it is all over and he faces the press, he thanks his players first. 'They were great,' he says. 'This team has got character.' And he defends his technical choices.

'Mancini always appeared very much in control right from the start, and he was very confident,' recalls Sconcerti. 'The group followed him, but you know, with Manuel Rui Costa, our number 10, things weren't exactly great. You know how it can be: two imaginative players, both very skilled, take time to get to know each other. I spoke to Rui, a wonderful person really, and the matter was cleared up. We came out of that campaign well, a nice mid-table ranking in the league championship and a victory in the Coppa Italia. It was the Purples' last trophy.'

Before that final, a big party is thrown for Roberto in Genoa, on 7 May: Mancio Day. It is for him to say farewell to football, as a player. At the Luigi Ferraris Stadium, Sampdoria's scudetto-winning team of 1991 face the Lazio side that were league winners in 2000. Many are the former players who attend: from Pagliuca to Vierchowod, Gianluca Vialli to Toninho Cerezo. Thirty thousand people are there, cheering for Bobby Goal. Mancio does not manage to score on this occasion, but he makes good passes to two very special number 10s: his sons Filippo and Andrea. On the bench, Vujadin Boskov and Sven-Göran Eriksson are making sure that the celebrations run smoothly.

Cup final day comes: 13 June 2001. Fiorentina are playing Parma, coached by Renzo Ulivieri, Mancini's former coach at Sampdoria. The first leg of the tie had ended 1–0 to the Purples, at the Tardini Stadium. Now, in the second leg, at the Artemio Franchi Stadium in Florence, Parma take the lead with a goal by Milosevic, but Nuno Gomes equalises to make Fiorentina the overall winners. It is Roberto's seventh Italy Cup, albeit his first as a manager. There is no doubt about it: he is a cup specialist.

The great merit he showed on this occasion was the ability to change his tactics on the run, even though they had been already implemented. Mancini had set his team up to defend their first-leg lead, ensuring they would be difficult to break down, while having Enrico Chiesa on his own up front, playing high, to occupy the Parma defence. After Fiorentina conceded the goal, in the second half Mancini played a different team: more balanced, with more of an attacking threat, and Nuno Gomes rewarded his decision with the goal that brought them overall victory.

'This showed that Mancini was, and still is, a winner,' comments Mario Sconcerti. 'All his history, as a player and as a man, is a winning one. Not only that: I must admit that Roberto, in my opinion, has also got quite an intuition for politics. He knows how to move, he can be extremely practical, modest, but he can come up with pure genius a moment afterwards.' Just a few days later, Sconcerti will leave the club, before it goes bankrupt.

The verdict is finalised by Co.Vi.Soc (the federal committee in charge of reviewing the balances of football clubs), in a letter delivered on 14 June to the Purples' headquarters. In order to balance the budget and be enrolled in the championship for 2001/02, Fiorentina must find, by 12 July, over 100 billion lira. The fans let loose against the president Cecchi Gori. The shareholders cannot come to an agreement regarding the recapitalisation, and the Court of Florence files a proceeding for bankruptcy in the name of Fiorentina Football. Rumours spread about Mancini's possible departure, which he denies. 'I never even considered that,' he says, adding, 'I will carry on with my plan.'

But his plan is affected significantly when his most valuable players leave for Milan: Francesco Toldo and Manuel Rui Costa, to the Black-and-Blues and the Red-and-Blacks respectively. It is not long since Mancio – on the back of a restaurant menu, over dinner with Sconcerti – jotted down a possible winning team, considering all the variables, replacements and so on needed to win the championship. But it was all just an illusion: instead the young Purple manager ends up with a weakened team, his club having turned into a selling club in the summer transfer market.

The bad news continues into the new season. Enrico Chiesa, the team's top scorer in recent years, is injured after only five matches. In short, Mancio ends up living a nightmare, and it is one he is compelled to face alone. The club is largely absent. There is more talk about courts, budgets and foreclosures than there is about football. At the beginning of December, after their umpteenth defeat, this time in a home game against Piacenza, Fiorentina sit second-bottom of the league. The ghost of relegation is palpable, and Roberto seems ready to hand in his notice. However, Luciano Luna, the club's chief administrator, reaffirms the club's trust in him and argues that 'letting Mancini go would not be the right course of action at the moment.' Still, fans start questioning his work. During the match against Juventus, a banner reads, 'Mancini, brother, you have been nominated' – a clear invitation to leave. Then there are chants and protests that resound all through the week, so that the manager is forced to get a minder.

On 6 January, the day of the Epiphany, after conceding three goals to Perugia in the match that brings up the midpoint of the championship season, Mancini hands in his resignation to Cecchi Gori. 'I am the first one to blame,' he admits. 'I shall speak to the president, but it is impossible to carry on this way.' The fans, having had enough, spent the game shouting their anger to the players, and some twenty-odd hard-core supporters targeted the manager's dugout, hitting and kicking the Plexiglas right behind his bench. It all ended with Mancini being escorted from the pitch by police, with officers charging and deploying tear gas, and fans burning rubbish bins.

The following day, Vittorio Cecchi Gori refuses Mancini's resignation, agreeing instead to give him what he has been asking for for a while now: a few extra players, with whom he is convinced he can save the team from relegation to Serie B. Leonardo Dominaci, the Mayor of Florence, comments on the Purple story and writes off the whole back-and-forth surrounding Mancini's resignation as 'a big show'. Put off by the bad publicity, the leaders of the Fiesole, the stand behind the goal, openly blame the manager for the team's poor performances, for its defence being the worst in the division, for being knocked out of every cup tournament and for totalling 11 defeats out of 17 matches.

Supporters clubs make clear that they cannot keep their most troublesome members under control anymore. On the night of Thursday 10 January, those 'troublesome members' make an appearance. Mancini is on his way back from Rome, where he had a meeting with Cecchi Gori. Four shady guys have been waiting for him, four hard-core men between the ages of 33 and 50, already known to the police. They encircle him, they threaten him, they insult him. 'You don't know shit' and 'You will be the ruin of the club' are the nicest phrases he hears. They demand that he leaves, once and for all.

Roberto has had enough. 'I was attacked in front of my own house, even though only verbally,' he writes in a press dispatch. 'Despite the fact that it was only words, I was told that these aggressions could degenerate. The fear of something like this happening to my wife and sons has persuaded me that my job in Florence ends here.'

So this is goodbye. 'This is how Mancini's story with the Purples ended,' remembers Sconcerti, 'and it was even worse after that, without him. The club went bankrupt and was relegated as a matter of course to Serie C2. Only the charges Mancini had pressed against those thugs – and the ones they pressed against him – stayed. The trials expired after quite some time, so nothing came out of those either. It was a rotten season, for the club of the Lily and for Roberto.'

Number one

A conversation with Enrico Chiesa

'If I hadn't got injured, things would have worked out differently, Roberto wouldn't have left Fiorentina. I scored five goals in the first few matches, then, against Venezia, I tore the ligaments in my knee, and my season ended there. After that, Mancini was missing his first-choice striker, and it is hard to get results without a striker.'

So speaks Enrico Chiesa, now 41. Back then, in the first years of the 21st century, he was – together with Rui Costa – the most representative player of ACF Fiorentina. Chiesa was much beloved by Fabio Capello, who described him as a cross between Gigi Riva and Paolo Rossi. He always partnered great champions: Roberto Mancini at Sampdoria, Hernan Crespo at Parma, Gabriel Batistuta at Fiorentina, Tore Andre Flo at Siena. And he scored no fewer than 178 goals. 'I began as a midfielder,' he says, 'then, when I was 19 and playing in division C2, at Teramo, Luigi Delneri played me as an inside forward. And when I started scoring, I realised that this was much better than being a midfielder.'

For quite some time, Chiesa has been back with his former club, Sampdoria, coaching the youth team. He has gone back 'home' to where his football career began, and where he met Mancio.

'I was still playing with the Academy team, and I would sometimes be called up to join the first team, sometimes just for training. Mancini, Vialli, Mannini, Cerezo were there …

since then, Roberto has stood by me all the way throughout my career, first as a teammate, then as a manager. At Samp, in the 1995/96 season, Eriksson did not want to have any fixed forward partnership, so he invented the Mancini–Chiesa pairing. Roberto was an extraordinary player, he could play different positions: attacking midfielder, inside forward, centre forward, midfielder. That year, the manager played him as a centre forward, so the opposition defences worried about Roberto, and I became the surprise of the championship: I scored 22 goals. Five years later, I ran into Mancio again at Fiorentina, then at Lazio.'

Let's go back to Florence, and that difficult season.
'I think Roberto quite enjoyed being there at first, even though it was a very difficult situation. We won the Coppa Italia against Buffon, Cannavaro and Thuram's Parma. For the Purples, it was their first trophy after many years. And it didn't come for free, either! The atmosphere was good – relaxed. It was a nice group, we were building foundations for the future. Then, in the summer, everything started to fall apart, from the money to the club and, in the end, the football itself. They didn't want to sell me, and during the following season, after my injury, it was even worse. Roberto had had enough. We spoke about it: he just didn't want to go through certain episodes again, and he couldn't see a way out.'

What did you think of him at Lazio?
'He was fine; he was on his normal behaviour; he always held the same ideas. Sure, he changed slightly, but that was because he was coaching a big club. The environment was different, too, and he was under a lot of pressure. My only regret is that I came to Lazio after being out for a whole season, due to my injury. I still wasn't at my best, and I couldn't

give Roberto what he wanted from me. I am so sorry, because I went there because he wanted me there.'

How was Mancini the manager?
'Roberto is a very competent manager. He is very demanding but also lets you be. In the football world, some teammates never stop giving you advice on the pitch; they try and run the team. You can tell they have the makings of a manager, but they don't necessarily become one. Roberto did, though, growing little by little. I believe he owes a lot to Eriksson, a restrained, quiet coach who paved the way for him at Lazio. That's where Mancini the manager was born. He has great qualities, and resorted to them all the way. But he still had to fight to earn a place, to become one of the best. Because it is not easy to be a manager: it is not the same as being a footballer and giving everyone advice.'

Talking about that, how does the teammate-to-teammate relationship differ from the manager–player one?
'It was much better to interact with Mancini the manager. We chatted away, I let it all out, we discussed things calmly – this was also because we'd known each other for years. As a player, on the other hand, he was a real pain. I always said that to his face. During training he was all right: always positive with young ones. Maybe he would say to me, 'Enrico, try a bit harder,' but that was it. However, on the Sunday, on the football pitch, he was another person: he was hot-blooded – he really changed. That was because Roberto really felt the match, he couldn't just step back and let it all happen. He always had to act, and to give 100 per cent, and he needed to take it out on his teammates. It was a nightmare for those who happened to be near him – "Stay here", "Go there", "Do this" and "Do that" – good heavens! It was an ongoing torture. But that's the way he is: it was his way of living football.

More than giving you advice, he was trying to give you a boost. The year we played together, I used to score quite a bit – it was fine by me. But if by any chance I got one shot wrong ... well, that was it.'

Was he more laid-back as a manager?
'After some matches, he would come into the dressing-room and have a go at me and the team, in a really bad way. Tables were flying. But he was in a different role, and on different behaviour. At times, all managers are like that. I had Carlo Ancelotti as a coach, too: he was a really quiet guy, but sometimes he would just turn into a hyena. As a manager and as a player, Mancini always wanted to do what was right for the team, and he wanted to win really badly. And when you want that, you go far.'

Let's talk about Mancio's ideas about football.
'He is not the kind of guy who has fixed ideas or unchangeable tactics. Roberto always starts by building his defence, which is a back four, but this can change according to the situation. At Fiorentina, he could play a 4-4-1-1 or a 4-5-1, depending on whether Rui Costa was playing or not. With Lazio, he would usually prefer a 4-4-2, but we sometimes played as a 4-2-4, with Bernardo Corradi, Claudio Lopez, Simone Inzaghi and I playing up front. There's no point in calling him a "defence first" manager: it depends on how the match goes, whether you have to hold on to a lead or chase the game. I would also add that great managers, those who win and who go on for years; those who become number ones – like Roberto, or Mourinho, for example – they continuously bring themselves up to date. They are not tied down to tactics, ideas or formations which maybe were popular twenty years earlier. They evolve, because football changes, and players do, too. Because it is players who make

the system: you may have your preferences, but in the end it all depends on who you've got in your team. On paper, you can plan a nice 4-4-2 formation, but what do you do if you haven't got the wingers? This is another thing: Mancini has always been good at choosing the right players. He has always tried to take his own people with him, wherever he is coaching: his players, his staff – people he trusts. That's quite normal, because you always work best with those you know. Maybe not all clubs can meet your requests, but as soon as he could, Roberto asked for those he trusted most: Mihajlovic, Stankovic, Lombardo. These are the people who can really help you out on the pitch.'

How do you see him at Manchester City?
'I see him doing well, very well. Last season, he won the Premier League with an incredible comeback and an unforgettable final match. He beat United and Sir Alex Ferguson, which is no small thing. But Roberto knows his stuff, and when he believes in something, he's ready to take the risk, and he is capable of going against everything and everyone. I always say that there is only one Mourinho, and there is only one Mancini.'

Challenges

A Messiah or simply a scapegoat? For the Lazio fans, there is no doubt about it: their former number 10's return as coach means the Messiah is coming, the one who will lift them up again, who will redeem the club after a dim season, put some order into the dressing-room and face up to Fabio Capello's Roma. Persuaded that Mancio will become their new patron saint, they turn up in numbers – 3,000 altogether – to celebrate his first appearance in Formello, on 10 May 2002. As soon as they learn about his signing, they jam up his website with hundreds and hundreds of messages.

The media, however, don't share their excitement: in the manager from Jesi, they see a scapegoat for a club that has been going through serious financial difficulties and that has been alienating its own supporters for months. Roberto Mancini, not yet 38, does not agree. He is persuaded that he is coaching a very strong team. He is confident about the future and he is sure that Sergio Cragnotti won't sell his most valuable assets in order to balance the budget. The two came to an agreement at the end of April, in the president's villa in Montepulciano. A two-year contract, for one billion lira per year.

Roberto is Lazio's fourth manager within 15 months. He comes to replace Alberto Zaccheroni, who took the team to a sixth-placed league finish, missing out on Champions League qualification. Cragnotti would have preferred a more experienced manager – in fact he made a tentative approach to Eriksson, but the Swede politely refused, preferring to stay with the England national team. So it is Eriksson's protégé Mancini who is put in charge of the team on 9 May.

Mancio is not promising anything, but he is convinced that this is the right season for a comeback. In a dignified manner, he lays down a challenge to the big clubs from the north. To some, this might look like conceit, or even a provocation by Mancini the rebel, since the two brightest stars in the Lazio firmament were sold during the summer: the captain, Alessandro Nesta, to AC Milan; and top goalscorer Hernan Crespo, to Inter. The reality is quite different, though: Lazio shine brightly, playing enjoyable football and winning matches. They only stumble against Chievo, on 15 September, in their first Serie A game; thereafter, they start building an incredible sequence of results. They go 16 consecutive matches unbeaten in the league, Coppa Italia and the Uefa Cup competitions. Their seven away wins are a club record. Lazio's defence, even without Nesta, is among the best in the championship; their attack, even without Crespo, scores goals by the bucketload. At the mid-point of the championship, they total 36 points – one more that Eriksson's Lazio had had the year they went on to win the championship. This puts them joint second in the league, together with Inter Milan. The leaders – and 'Winter Champions' – are AC Milan, with 39 points. It looks like big clubs from the north really are within reach (Juventus have already been overhauled, for now). And let us not forget Roma, Lazio's eternal rivals, 13 points behind them. Mancini's Lazio is a big surprise indeed, especially considering the huge financial hardships and internal upheaval that the club is going through.

On 13 January 2001, Sergio Cragnotti is forced to resign the club presidency by the bank consortium, headed by Capitalia, because of a huge hole in the budget, of over €100 million. After eleven years, the financier from Rome does not own the club anymore. The same banks enact a plan to rescue the team, firstly paying all the wages owed to the players (€16 million altogether), thereby avoiding their departure free of charge, as Lazio have been officially brought into default. Luca Baraldi is called in from Parma, and given the task of fixing the club budget. Roberto Mancini joins the board of directors, acting as a link between past, present and future.

What to do then, in such a difficult situation? Just like he did in the past, he must motivate his players, striking the right chords in their souls. He must find leaders in the dressing-room, who can work together with him. He must build a close group, one that will stick together through hardships, where everyone is important and no one feels left out. In a word, he must reshape the environment, just like he has done before.

Tactically, he sets the team up to be a quick-breaking side who, with just a few precise, direct passes, can travel the length of the pitch and create scoring opportunities – like Arsene Wenger's Arsenal or Luigi Delneri's Chievo. Before each game, his message is 'Guys, we're running the show here. And don't forget: have fun.' And the players do have fun, and so does the crowd.

In the Uefa Cup, Lazio get to the semi-finals, where they are defeated by the eventual winners of the competition, José Mourinho's Porto. After the first leg ends 4–1 to the Portuguese team, Mancini's men are unable to turn it around in the second leg. Once they are out of Europe, Lazio turn to the championship. Mancini plays it cool. 'The championship?' he says, 'What about it? We mustn't think of who is ahead of us, nor of who is behind. We are racing against ourselves. Up to now, our greatest strength has been this: going out on to the pitch aiming to win. We are makers of our own destiny, and we must remember that nothing is going to come for free. We only have what we have earned for ourselves so far; we never cheated and we have always been competitive against the great clubs. However, in football, two matches can be enough to change a whole season. I don't know if we are going to win the championship, but if we carry on like this, we will surely be there, until the very end.'

As a matter of fact, Lazio do not win the championship, but they rank fourth and so achieve the main target for the club: access to the pre-qualifying rounds of the Champions League. 'It is a fair end, although we deserved a lot more' is Mancio's analysis. 'Our regrets grow because of the penalties we missed, the goals we conceded in injury time, and more broadly because of other faults on our side, but we still showed we were no less than those who ranked above us in the league.'

'Their result is truly a miracle, taking into account how the team has changed and what happened on a broader level,' says Baraldi, the club's managing director. 'The credit goes to Mancini.' The newspaper *Corriere della Sera* declare Mancini Lazio's key man, over and above any of the players, giving him a 9 in their ratings and commenting, 'His team management was a work of art; he relaunched players who seemed over and done with. The most enjoyable football in Serie A.'

Mancini prefers to give all the credit to his players. 'I am proud of what the guys did, how they interpreted the championship, despite all its difficulties,' he says. 'And my gratitude is extended to our fans, who have always stood by us.' Those fans naturally don't want their manager to leave, although apparently Inter Milan remain interested in Mancio, just like when he was a player. Around 1,500 of the White-and-Blues supporters turn up in Formello on 22 May 2003 to cheer the team and persuade Mancini to stay. A banner reads, 'Our jerseys are wet with blood and sweat ... thank you, Mancini club.'

'I will do all I can to make him stay,' swears Luca Baraldi, who is handling the recapitalisation of the White-and-Blues, not an easy job, given the club's numerous debts and the few buyers. The managing director's plan is to offer Mancini a contract until 2008, €2.5 million per year, and total freedom in his transfer dealings. The manager says, 'I love it here in Rome, and so does my family. I really like the people, I fit in rather well, and if the club behind me is a strong one, and backs up my technical plans, I am ready to stay.' He wants guarantees on the transfer market though; he wants to be sure that he will not lose Stankovic and Stam. He wants to manage a team capable of winning.

In the end, Mancini gets all the assurances he has been asking for and signs his new contract. On 2 July, the team arrives in Porto Cervo, Sardinia, for the first part of a training camp which will then continue in Vigo di Fassa, Trentino. Stankovic is still there (though he will be sold to Inter Milan in January), as is Stam. Lazio's first action of the new season takes place on 13 August, in a Champions League qualifier against Benfica. The game ends 3–1 to Lazio, and on 27 August, on neutral ground in Oporto, the White-and-Blues seal their qualification with a 0–1 scoreline in the second leg. So Lazio are through to the first group stage. 'Without this result, nothing we did last season would have mattered,' the coach comments. 'We feel really proud of this achievement, it was really important for us to get here.'

On the eve of the first league game of the season, Mancini takes an even bolder stance, saying, 'This scudetto is Lazio's, followed by Inter Milan and AC Milan.' And, talking about his team, he adds, 'I have great players. Important men have left, but they were replaced just fine. In order to win, you must want it; only if you are persuaded of your own goals,

can you reach them. We have a good chance in all the tournaments we are taking part in.'

However, the only trophy Lazio will gain is the Coppa Italia.
In the Champions League, they are drawn in Group G, with
Sparta Prague, Beşiktaş and Chelsea, and on 9 December
they are out of the competition after two bad defeats against
Claudio Ranieri's Blues. In the league, their dreams fade
until, by the end, they rank only sixth. 'Considering their
play, Lazio deserved a better ranking,' opines Mancini. 'But
it is also true that, when you make a lot of mistakes, you end
up paying for them. Unfortunately, some seasons just work
out wrong, and this is one of them.'

After the frustration of the league season, on 12 May 2004
it is time for happiness, as Lazio draw with Juventus in Turin.
On the back of their first-leg win at the Olympic Stadium,
the 2–2 result secures them their fourth Coppa Italia title. It
is Mancini's second trophy of the kind as a manager, and the
eighth of his footballing career. The White-and-Blues supporters sing his name loud. He waves at the stand behind the
goal, and afterwards, in the press room, he admits, 'This is
a special victory, after two difficult years for the club, for us,
for our fans and for Sergio Cragnotti, who is going through
a rough time. At moments like these, results make us feel a
little happier and help us face up to the difficulties in a better way.'

He denies that this might be his last appearance on the
White-and-Blue bench, although practically everyone is now
talking about his move to Inter Milan. Both Real Madrid and
Tottenham made quite tempting offers, but in the end he
said yes to Massimo Moratti, the president who wanted him
way back, when he was still playing.

Run, and never stop

A conversation with Andrea Mancini

Not much hair, imposing figure, green T-shirt. From pitch-side, the coach demands more intensity. The wiry striker with messy locks and a yellow bib slips away and gets the ball, but one of his mates calls offside.

On the city council's Vittorio Del Curto football pitch in Fano, in the province of Pesaro e Urbino, Alma Juventus 1906 is training. There is only one month left before the end of the regional second division championship. The team's aim is to avoid relegation. Karel Zeman, 35, son of Zdenek (who trained the miraculous Foggia, Lazio, Napoli, Pescara, Red Star Belgrade and now Roma) is the coach who took over the team a couple of weeks ago. Andrea Mancini, 19, son of Roberto, is the centre forward who arrived at the end of January 2012 from Manchester City. Two of a kind: for both of them, playing football runs in the family. A great marketing coup, isn't it?

'Don't even mention that,' says Claudio Gabellini, the president of Alma Juventus Fano. 'Several factors fell together. On the one hand, I had a good connection with the Mancini family, which is from Jesi, in the Marche region. Andrea wanted to come back to Italy to get more experience of first-team football, and we agreed on a loan until June. Choosing Zeman was a specific decision: I knew the man, and I liked him a lot. He's proactive, harsh but fair and tactically strong. I think he's very good. Just like his dad, you say? Well, possibly better.'

And Andrea? Is he better than his father? 'You see, Roberto was playing in Serie A when he was only 16. Andrea might be suffering from this comparison. He needs to cut his teeth. He is still inexperienced.'

The 'presi' dashes off, the training session over. Karel hands the team over to the fitness coach for stretching in the middle of the pitch, under an unmerciful sun. Ten minutes later, and the players are off to the showers. Andrea kicks off his white trainers, his name embroidered on them in gold letters. He stares at them. Then, sitting in the shade in the tiny dugout opposite the green artificial turf, he allows himself to talk about his life and his famous father.

Andrea was born in Genova on 13 September 1992, when his father was the standard-bearer for Sampdoria. He supports Lazio, however. 'When my dad wore the Sampdoria shirt, I was too young to realise what was going on. I started attending football matches when I was five, and at that time he was playing for Lazio. Then, when he was coaching the white and blue team, I followed him. I fell in love with the supporters, and those colours stayed in my heart for ever.'

The passion for football does run in the family. It was shared by his father and his grandfather before him, a living football bible. 'My grandfather has been watching football for 60 years. He is the real expert, and he is always free with advice. And tellings-off, too,' adds Andrea, who, like his brother Filippo, two years his elder, made football his chosen career. Filippo trains with the City reserve team, waiting for an opportunity with another club. Andrea grew up in the junior football teams of Inter Milan and Monza; then, just like his dad, he moved to the junior team in Bologna.

He came to the city of the Two Towers in the summer of 2009, and the following year he played in the Viareggio tournament – 'a great experience, there were teams from all over the world.' In September 2010, he flew to Manchester to join his father's City team. Other than a short loan spell with Oldham Athletic, where he went with Luca Scapuzzi, another young player from the City youth team, in November 2011, he stayed in Manchester until his adventure with Alma Juventus.

Why here, only a stone's throw from Jesi, where your father was born and your grandparents still live?
'I chose Fano because it has a history behind it. It is a reliable club, which provided me with a valuable and solid future perspective. I knew it would help me grow, and that's why I came here from City, on six months' loan. That meant saying no to other offers, too, offers from other teams playing in the Greek, English and Portuguese top flights – not convincing enough, though. There is a new coach here now, Karel. He is young, very competent, you can tell he's got ideas and he knows how to put them across to the team. He is changing the players' mentality. You must keep your head down and work hard, and in the end, we'll take stock.'

Where did you learn to play football: from your father, with Inter Milan, Bologna, City, or here?
'Everywhere, more or less. I always had coaches teaching me an awful lot. I could also say that it helped me that I was older when I came to Manchester City, because it meant I had the chance to train with the first team. This is something that helped me grow – when you are training with champions like Agüero, De Jong, Balotelli, Yaya Touré, David Silva, you just live and learn.'

Who impressed you most in the City team?

Young Andrea thinks about it. 'It is hard to name one person. They are all great players. Take David Silva, for example. He could be up for the Ballon d'Or. He's a fantastic player, and his masterstrokes – well, I have seen them even in training sessions, you would never believe how that guy does it. He's from another planet. He's on the same level as Xavi and Iniesta. But if I really had to pick a player from Man City, I would say Tévez.'

The one who was questioning your father's judgement, who was waging war against the club for months.

'Yes, but when El Apache takes the field, he is really impressive with his strength, technique and commitment.'

And what about your father? What did you learn from him?

'Back-heels.'

So you really scored a goal like Roberto Mancini's, in that famous Parma v. Lazio game?

Andrea jokes about this, and laughs it off. 'No, I didn't … still, my dad taught me so much. He has been coaching for years, and he cares about me deeply – this is the reason why he has always given me good advice, telling me where and how I can become a better player. I believe I have learned a lot from him, just like the players who were under his management have. This is because I was always one of the players on the pitch, and never his son.'

The best advice?

'Run, and never stop. Always give 110 per cent on the field, because football is about physicality and running. And if you want to play at a certain level, you really must put in the effort. Technical skills and talent are not enough. This is what my dad and my grandfather keep telling me.'

Just how hard is it to be Roberto Mancini's son, in the world of football?
'It was hard, at the beginning. When I was a boy and I started to play, I was always compared to him – and he is one of the best players and strikers ever ... this wasn't good for me, because I'm Andrea, and he's Roberto Mancini, two different people. Little by little, I got used to it. Now what people say goes in one ear, and out of the other.'

Is your father, for you, an example to follow?
'Of course he is. For all he has done and for all he has achieved, both as a player and as a coach. However, [as far as role models go] I also appreciate Antonio Cassano very much.'

For his one-liners?
'No, for the way he plays! In my opinion, he is technically one of the strongest players in the world. He's got style to spare, and he's got the body to match. Low centre of gravity, strong legs, good reading of the game, both imagination and genius. I can see myself in him, a little.'

So, what are the main qualities for a second striker or a centre forward?
'The last forward pass and kicking a goal.'

And Roberto Mancini's main qualities, as the Manchester City coach? Your opinion as a footballer, not as his son – that goes without saying.
'To be quite honest, I think he did a good job at the Citizens. In three years, he took the team to levels that could not

even be imagined until recently. Don't forget that, before Mansour bin Zayd Al Nahyan stepped in, City were a team halfway down the Premier League, and they hadn't won any trophies for years and years. Sure, there has been a lot of money put into the project, a lot of great players brought in, but it's not easy to create a good team, even with great names. It takes time, and my dad is succeeding.'

The dawn of a new era

The longest engagement in Italian football (as Giacinto Facchetti, the Inter Milan president, describes it) ends at 9pm on 7 July 2004. Roberto Mancini finally consents, signing a contract which ties him to the Black-and-Blues for three years. Such is the natural conclusion of a courtship which started years ago, when Mancio was a young promise at Bologna, and was nearly consummated in 1995 and 1996, when the Samp captain planned to leave Genoa and was enticed by Massimo Moratti's promises.

Inter's approaches have been even more insistent in 2003 and 2004. Now the accompanying drama, which has carried on throughout the spring and summer, is finally at an end. For the last few weeks, since 16 June, the commotion has been at crescendo level. After accepting Alberto Zaccheroni's resignation, Inter Milan officially announced the arrival of their new manager, but it would take weeks for the whole matter to be settled. Lazio had no intention of letting the coach from Jesi go, as he had signed with the White-and-Blues until 2008. It took an endless number of meetings and discussions before the parties came to an agreement, which includes (or so the press says) the loan of four Black-and-Blues players to Lazio: Mohamed Kallon, Daniele Adani, Alessandro Potenza and Abdullah Isah Eliakwu. The club from Milan denies that this is part of the agreement, but either way, in the end, Mancini is officially released from his obligations with Lazio.

On 8 July a very tanned Roberto can oversee his first

Black-and-Blues training session, at Pinetina. In the morning, he wears a white t-shirt emblazoned with the team sponsor's logo, and black shorts; in the afternoon, for the official introduction to the press, a grey suit, crisp white shirt and a dark tie. He smiles for the cameras, greets everyone, shakes hands with Facchetti – who breaks the ice, telling everyone about their 'engagement' – then Roberto takes the floor. His first thought is for Lazio: he offers 'A big thank you and a hug, for all they did for me.' 'I was sorry to leave,' he says, 'but sometimes our paths in life lead us in different directions. I am also sorry for those supporters who feel betrayed; this is not what has happened. I hope things work out for them all in the future.'

Moving on from his recent past to the present, he says, 'Being here, coaching Inter Milan, is the ideal situation for me. We are talking about one of the most important clubs in the world, with a great hunger for victory – just like me.' Despite this though, the Black-and-Blues haven't won anything at all for the last 15 years. To those pointing out this fact to him, Mancini replies, 'Like all managers, I am ambitious. I am here to win, and I'll do what it takes to get there. It is wrong to say that Inter Milan must win, because they haven't been doing so for many years. In order to win, Inter Milan must play well, and deserve whatever title they will achieve. You win by playing: so I would like Inter Milan to enjoy playing; if they do, their supporters will have a good time, too. Playing football is the best thing in the world, and there are so many good players here.' He does not fail to mention them: he is happy to meet Vieri, Stankovic and Verón again – the latter on a loan from Chelsea. He says that not many clubs can rely on so many champions, and compliments the club on its vast list of players.

In the summer, the playing roster is augmented by Giuseppe Favalli and Sinisa Mihajlovic, who join from Lazio;

Argentinians Nicolas Burdisso and Esteban Cambiasso, Dutchman Edgar Davids and Zé Maria, the Brazilian. Mancini has a smashing team on his hands; he has players he knows well – or at least players he asked for or recommended to the club – and he can count on a trustworthy technical team, including his masseur, Sergio Viganó. 'Now,' he concludes, 'we can only hope things turn out for the best.'

They are starting from a position of immense promise, so that Moratti, on the eve of the new season, admits that he is rather happy. 'We have a manager I believe in, 100 per cent,' he says. 'In these first months' work he has demonstrated skills that I did not imagine he had: method, diligence, knowledge, a solid and straightforward game plan. I can say that, with him, we are at the dawn of a new era. And for once, I start the season without the obsession of winning right away, even though we all know that we must do all that we can to get results.'

A draw in their first league game against Chievo is followed by several more – too many, really. In the Champions League, on the other hand, things are going well. In the qualifiers, in August, the Black-and-Blues knock out FC Basel, with Adriano – the 'Emperor' – in top form. Things continue to go well in the group stage, wherein they defeat Werder Bremen, Anderlecht and Valencia without many problems. Indeed, at Mestalla on 20 October, the score is almost embarrassing: 5–1 to the Black-and-Blues.

Four days later comes the 'Madonnina' derby (this epithet being derived from the statue of the Virgin Mary on top of Milan's Dome), the first in Mancini's life. It is very different from what he has been used to with Samp and Lazio. 'In Genoa and Rome, the derby was considered the most important day of the year,' the manager says. 'That changed with time, more or less. But in Milan the two clubs facing each other have already won many scudetti, and all sorts of trophies. It is an important match, but it is not an end in itself.'

Roberto tries to dampen the initial euphoria. 'In the Champions League tournament,' he says, 'we are achieving beautiful and important victories, and that makes us work better. But we still have a lot to do; we need time, and we cannot glorify one result only.' How does he see the match? 'Inter Milan will need to play calmly, knowing they have the potential and, if they do things properly, they can get some satisfaction out of it. We must really trust ourselves. This is our first truly big challenge in the championship – but we are just at the beginning, and I don't think we could call this match decisive.'

Decisive it might not be, but Inter haven't defeated AC Milan for 963 days, since 3 March 2002. In the intervening period, the Black-and-Blues have totalled four defeats out of four in the league and draws in either leg of a Champions League semi-final, at the end of which their neighbours went through on away goals. It proves to be no different this time, either. It is a good game, a lot of fun, quite spectacular and with many chances to score – but in the end, the score is 0–0. AC Milan are a sound team; Inter are still under construction. The challenge will not end here.

Two weeks later, Lazio arrive at the Meazza Stadium. When Mancini takes the pitch, the Lazio fans are not very welcoming. The chanting is awful, and there are two banners which are not easily forgotten: 'No forgiveness for those who betray' reads one; the other is '2003–2004, the Mancini plan: coaching Inter Milan for the Champions League.' The accusation is that their former coach deliberately played the wrong line-up in a game against Brescia, which could have secured Lazio a place in the European competition. The accusation is returned to sender in disbelief and indignation. The divorce from his old club left some scars, not only among supporters but also with the White-and-Blues management. Claudio Lotito, the new president, wants €5 million from Mancini as compensation for breaking his contract. The answer is, 'I am no moneybox.' The game, which ends 1–1, is a bad-tempered affair and Mancini takes it out on the referee. 'Shame on you. You can only referee Milan and Juve,' he shouts, earning himself a two-match suspension and a €2,500 fine. Same old Mancio.

Draws seem to be becoming the Black-and-Blues' trademark; they will ultimately register 18 of them in the league, as many as their victories. There are also two defeats though: one in the away game against Messina, the other at San Siro, on 27 February, in the return match against Carlo Ancelotti's AC Milan.

The Red-and-Blacks, in fact, are an opponent not only in Serie A but in the Champions League quarter-finals, too. This fixture, on 12 April 2005, descends into some of the worst scenes you could possibly expect see in a football stadium. AC Milan, with a 2–0 lead from the first leg, are also ahead on the night, through Shevchenko. Mancini tries everything to save the tie, and in the second half, Inter have the ball in the net through Cambiasso – but the German referee, Marcus Merk, disallows it. The crowd kicks up a rumpus. All sorts of things are thrown on to the field from the stand behind the goal: bottles, lighters, coins, flares. Dida, the AC Milan keeper, is hit on the shoulder by a Bengala light and goes down. The referee does what he can to enable the match to continue, but he has to send both teams to the changing rooms in order to have the pitch cleaned. The match is resumed, for a time, but since the northern stand will not stop throwing things, it later has to be called off for good; AC Milan are adjudged the winners.

'We are sorry about how it ended,' comments Mancini, on the spur of the moment. 'Do we risk a long disqualification?

Well, I can't say anything other than we're sorry. We'll see about the rest.' The Uefa verdict comes, without delay: Inter Milan must play four European games behind closed doors. 'It is an awful lot,' reflects the manager, 'the club loses out, and so do those supporters who have nothing to do with this. Things like this shouldn't happen, but they do. We are filled with deep regret, because football should be fun, regardless of the fact that one can win or lose. Only a few made a mistake, and we will have to deal with the consequences.' Mancini has one more point to make: 'There was only one thing I didn't like: every time something like this happens, everyone turns into a moralist. But not much has been done to prevent these incidents, only words. Something more could, and should, have been done.'

Once the unfortunate chapter of the Champions League is closed, attention turns to the league championship. In the end, Inter Milan rank third, with 72 points, while Fabio Capello's Juventus are top of the league with 86 points and AC Milan finish second. The following year, it will all be wiped out by the 'Calciopoli' scandal: Juventus will be relegated to Serie B and stripped of their title (which will not be assigned for that season).

Before all that, though, there is the cup. On 15 June 2005, the Black-and-Blues defeat Roma at San Siro with a score of 1–0 (following a 2–0 win in the first leg), and after a 23-year absence, the Coppa Italia returns to the Inter trophy room. It is party time at the Meazza Stadium, where the crowd also has the added bonus of being able to boo Adriano Galliani, AC Milan president and also president of Serie A. Their Red-and-Black counterparts lost the Champions League final on penalties, against Liverpool, after six minutes of pure madness.

Mancini is happy to have kept his promise; that is, taking one trophy home – even though it is neither the league championship nor the Champions League. His personal tally of Italy Cups is beginning to look phenomenal: he won six as a player, now he has three as a manager. In the stands, Massimo Moratti is all smiles: it is the second trophy for the club since he took charge. 'This Coppa Italia,' he will later say, 'is a reward for Mancini's hard work, which was important to give more confidence and self-assurance to our players. It is as if a spell has been broken, now we can look to higher ground in the future.'

His words prove to be prophetic. The following season, Mancini's second with the Black-and-Blues, starts in the same way the previous campaign ended – with a trophy. This time it is the Italian Super Cup. The club haven't won this title since 1989 but at the Delle Alpi Stadium in Turin, in the pouring rain, Juan Sebastián Veron scores the only goal of the game in the first half of extra time. It is Mancio's first Super Cup as a manager, to add to the two he won as a player, with Samp and Lazio.

There is also the added bonus of beating Fabio Capello, the Black-and-White coach he has never been on great terms with. The two men don't think much of one another and have never taken the trouble to hide it. The papers talk about their verbal exchanges, on and off the pitch ('rude', 'arrogant' and 'big-headed' are some of the terms bandied about). They have been arguing since Roberto started playing and Capello started coaching, and they have continued now that both are in management. Their early head-to-heads were when Mancini was in charge of Fiorentina and then Lazio, while Capello was with Roma; now Capello is managing Juventus and Mancini is with Inter Milan. 'We don't like each other, there is no point in denying that,' they admit. They are too different – or maybe too similar, wanting to win at all costs. 'We are from different generations,' Mancio concludes politely.

Their struggle for supremacy continues, after the Super Cup, into the league championship. The Black-and-Whites hit the ground running, and they are off. Inter Milan, who made good signings in the summer transfer market, bringing in Luis Figo, Walter Samuel and Santiago Solari from Real Madrid, plus David Pizarro and Julio Cesar, cannot keep up. And by the end of January, Roberto Mancini doesn't believe his side will be able to catch the runaway leaders. He says it for luck, but he will be proved correct. Juventus are sailing away, and no one can put salt on their tail.

Things go better for the Black-and-Blues in the Champions League, but only until they reach the Madrigal Stadium. It is 4 April 2006 and Inter are playing in the quarter-finals against the Spanish team of Villarreal. The Milan team have a 2–1 lead from the first leg but on the night they cannot get their act together; they have no legs, no head and no character. They flunk their main examination and they are knocked out of Europe by the team known as the 'Yellow Submarine', a provincial club coached by Manuel Pellegrini. A goal by Rodolfo Arruabarrena, Villarreal's Argentinian defender, seals the historic disaster. Mancini is shattered. He really believed in this cause and has given his all to Inter Milan, putting the same passion into this adventure as he had into Sampdoria's quest for the scudetto, all those years ago.

He was always fronting up, never hiding behind excuses. His choices were brave: he bet on good football and good men, some of whom nevertheless failed to deliver what was expected of them when it came to the Madrigal challenge – starting with Adriano, the 'Emperor'. Someone even suggests that, maybe, someone in the dressing-room is against Mancio. Roberto, however, does not shirk his responsibility, and apologises. 'I believe it can happen, that you lose a match,' he says, 'but this time it happened in the worst way possible – we did not play at all.'

His disappointment and anger deepen a few days later. At the Malpensa airport, a group of Inter's hard-core supporters are waiting for the team to return following a trip to Ascoli for a league match. Their faces concealed by scarves, they clap ironically inside the terminal; then, outside, comes the assault: Cristiano Zanetti is hit on the back of the head. 'End the violence,' cries Giacinto Facchetti, while Mancini, dispirited, considers leaving again, going abroad. 'Nowadays, in Italy,' he says, 'you just cannot go and watch a football match, and return home feeling upset because you lost, without thinking up something else to do. I am a manager because I love this sport very much, and it is passion that carries me forwards. But everything is getting more and more difficult here. After what happened at Malpensa, my decision to leave the country is only getting nearer.'

The protests are not over, though. On 14 April, the day of the 249th Milan derby, hard-core supporters boycott the game. Their motivation has been made public during the previous week, after the aggression towards the players. A representative for the *curva nord* (northern stand) explained, 'We don't want the whole stand to get the blame for the actions of a few mavericks.' The whole stand is sealed off with duct tape; there is only a huge banner, bearing the message 'We are not here, because you never have been.' And below, 'It is OK to lose, but not to lose one's dignity.' AC Milan supporters add insult to injury with their chanting. There are chants for the president: 'Moratti is leaving? I'll buy a couple of trash bins from him'; there are chants for the manager: 'Mancini stays, the club in disarray'; and there are chants for the players: 'Villar-real-ise our dreams.'

AC Milan leave San Siro with a smile, having won 1–0. Inter, meanwhile, can wave goodbye to the top of the championship – and even the runner-up slot – as well as the Champions League. Only the Coppa Italy is left for Mancini, who duly claims the trophy, for the second consecutive year, on 11 May, with a 3–1 win over Roma. Still, this time victory doesn't taste the same as it did twelve months before. It is a small consolation, given the bigger prizes that Mancini and Moratti had set their sights on – such as the league title, which instead goes to Juventus for the 29th time.

Roberto does not know if his marriage to Inter Milan is destined to last. 'Quite frankly, I have no idea of what will or won't happen,' Mancio says. 'I did my job; I did everything the best way I could. Some things went well, some didn't, but honestly I believe I did a good job. I have a contract for another year, but contracts don't matter much. It is Moratti's call.'

After the Villarreal game and the defeat in the derby, the president is considering a change of direction. He would like to see Fabio Capello, or who knows, perhaps José Mourinho in the Inter Milan dugout. However, after the Coppa Italia final, and Juve's victory in the championship, he thinks twice. To Sky television, he says, 'I think we will walk the same road as before.' He chooses continuity, and confirms that Mancini will remain his man.

Roberto, though, will have a few worries to face up to. There is Adriano, the goalscorer who hasn't actually been scoring for quite some time, and whose form and attitude have been a real cause for concern; then there is Verón, who has never got along with the Brazilian; there are also other tensions between groups: the Argentinians form a clique, as do the former Lazio players. So first of all, he must reconcile the dressing-room, following the disappointments that have derailed it.

In the meantime, the Calciopoli scandal is uncovered with much sensation, and everything is up for grabs again. It transpires that directors of various football clubs have been having conversations with officials at the Italian Football

Federation, the National League of Professionals and the Italian Referees Association, trying – successfully – to influence referee appointments, so that they get referees deemed 'favourable' for their matches. Mancini comments that 'now it is only time to cry and be ashamed. All that is coming out is truly awful, not only in my opinion, but also for all football fans. It is the worst thing that ever happened in the international world of football. I am gobsmacked.'

The scandal swamps everything and everyone within a few days. Franco Carraro resigns the presidency of the Italian Football Federation; Serie A president Adriano Galliani, Juventus general manager Luciano Moggi, and Juventus chairman Antonio Giraudo also resign their posts.

And so we come to 26 July 2006. After the first penalties are handed out to Juventus (stripped of their 2005 and 2006 Serie A titles and relegated to Serie B), Fiorentina (30 points deducted from their 2005/06 points total and a 19-point deduction for 2006/07, later reduced to 15), Lazio (30 points deducted from their 2005/06 points total and an 11-point deduction for 2006/07, later reduced to three), AC Milan (30 points deducted from their 2005/06 tally and a 15-point deduction for 2006/07, later reduced to eight) and Reggina (a 15-point deduction for 2006/07, later reduced to 11), FIGC officially appoints Inter Milan champions of Italy.

The team hears the news on the coach while on their way to the Druso Stadium in Bozen, where they are competing for the Sud Tirolen Cup. Before the match, Roberto Mancini comments on the Federation's decision. 'Regardless of how we got here,' he says, 'this is the dutiful acknowledgement given to those who do things the right way. We always played fairly, and it is only right that the honest ones win.'

Great charisma

A conversation with Javier Zanetti

In the Inter Milan headquarters, his desk and a door plate bearing his name are ready. A career as a club director awaits him, but the captain has no intention of giving up playing. At 35, he is still running around as he did in 1995, when he followed Juan Valentín Angelillo's advice to come to Italy to meet the Black-and-Blues management team, on the Terrazza Martini in Milan. He comes from the outskirts of Buenos Aires, from Club Atlético Banfield, and he was one of the group of young players known as the 'Passarella Boys', after coach Daniel Passarella who brought them into his international set-up.

Therefore, when he arrives at the court of Massimo Moratti, the papers write him off in a few scanty lines: a tough defender, who apparently knows how to handle a ball properly. Nothing more than that. Seventeen years later though, Javier Zanetti is the symbol of the club, the record-man when it comes to Inter Milan trophies (he has won 16) and appearances (he has made 796). He is the longest-playing footballer and the foreign player totalling most Serie A appearances (572). He is also one of the fairest players: there has never been any talk about a misplaced action on his behalf; never have the team or the club gone through any trouble because of him. Even at the worst times (and Inter Milan have had a few of those in the last 17 years), Zanetti – nicknamed Pupi or El Tractor by the Black-and-Blues supporters – has always been able to measure up to the task. In his very long football career, there has never been one single flaw.

He began as a defender, but he soon turned into a jack of all trades, capable of playing every position other than goalkeeper. He faced Mancini the player in Serie A, and in cup final. Playing under Mancini the manager, he made 189 appearances. Mancio played him in most matches, improving his goal threat and turning him into a defensive midfielder. Together they won two Italy Cups, two Italian Super Cups and three Serie A league titles. At Inter Milan's headquarters, after his training and a physiotherapy session (he is recovering from one of the few injuries he has suffered in his career), Zanetti, a quiet and shy man, with a gentle Argentinian twang, talks about his former coach.

For five years, from 1995 to 2000, Mancini was your opponent on the football pitch.
'He was one of those players who can surprise you any time, because he can always come up with something different, something that you can't predict. I remember when he played with Sampdoria. He was the club standard-bearer, and every time we were facing the Blucerchiati, we in defence knew we had to be careful, because he was going to cause us some trouble; he would surely be dangerous within the 90 minutes of play. On the pitch, he was unquestionably a leader, but he had quite a fiery temper. I will never forget that time we played them [in November 1995]: Mancini jumped over our keeper, who was Pagliuca at the time, and went down in the penalty box. He asked for a penalty, got a yellow card for diving instead, and he ended up insulting everyone. He was suspended and paid dearly for his actions. It was my first year in Italy, and that episode struck me. But it was, and it still is, his way of living football – with a passion.'

*The 1998 Uefa Cup and the 2000 Coppa Italia – two finals
against Mancini and Lazio. Which one do you remember more
vividly?*

'Of course I'd rather remember the Uefa Cup final in 1998,
at Parc des Princes in Paris, because we were lucky enough
to win, and because I scored our second goal. That was also
my first trophy with Inter Milan. The other final, which we
lost 2–1, was extremely difficult, because – I will say it again
– Mancini as a player was out of this world.'

What do you mean by that?

'He was extremely precise and accurate. Such skills allowed
him, on the one hand, to take up the right position on the
field; on the other hand, he could always find space to play
the ball into, to overcome the opponents' defence and to
create a scoring chance for his teammates. In a word, he
had a vision for the game, and the skill to turn it into an end
product. His many goals scored in the championship show
that.'

From an opponent to a manager, as the Inter Milan coach …

'As a manager, his thinking is clear. He always believes in
what he is doing, right to the end; he really does. He always
knows what is best for the team. And he does an excellent
job. In a typical week together, we used to train quite hard,
both physically and on a tactical level, and his advice before
going on to the pitch was really useful and extremely precise.
He could tell beforehand what was going to happen during
the match, and if he had to take action, he would do so at
the right time. As the Inter Milan manager, he was a winner.'

What is the trait of his that you remember best?

'Undoubtedly, his great charisma and his ability to put across
his idea of football.'

So what is his idea of football, exactly? Offence first? Defence first? Overly defensive?

'Not really, I don't think so! Mancini does not get into the game with the intention to sit back, he strikes an interesting compromise between a good defence, a constant attacking threat and, most of all, always retaining ball possession.'

What was your happiest moment in those four years when Mancini was managing Inter Milan?

'Winning the championships, especially the first time. It was a very emotional moment, because Inter Milan hadn't won the league since 1988/89. And it also marked the start of other important victories.'

And the most difficult one?

'March 2008, without doubt, when we got knocked out of the Champions League by Liverpool. That match started an inward-turning phase for the whole team, and it practically put an end to Mancini's time as manager at Inter Milan. Two months later, he was relieved of his duties.'

During your long career, you had some great managers. Let us try to make a few comparisons – for example, between Mancini and Mourinho.

'They are very different, clearly. They both have a strong personality, but their way of looking at football is completely different. For Mou, possession and defence are fundamental, and his tactics are based entirely upon the opponents' game. What's more, the Portuguese has a very different way of relating to the team.'

How about Mancini and Rafa Benitez, a manager who was quite successful in England, at Liverpool?

'Unfortunately, we had very little time with Benitez. He never had the entire team available to him, because of injuries – still, we won the Italian Super Cup with him, and the Club World Cup.'

Name one manager you had in the Argentina national team who reminds you of Mancini.
'I would say Daniel Passarella, the Selección captain when they were World Champions in 1978. He was the Argentinian who was at Inter Milan before me, and he was my manager during the 1998 World Cup. He has strong charisma, just like Mancini.'

How do you see Mancini today, at Manchester City?
'Really well. Since he arrived, he has managed to set up a good team. The head-to-head challenge with United was exciting: two great managers and two great line-ups. Mancini's merit was that he never gave up, even when winning the league seemed impossible.'

And what do you think of the two players you know so well, Carlos Tévez and Mario Balotelli, both of whom have caused a few problems for Mancini?
'There's no question, El Apache is a great player and he proved it when he came back and scored a hat trick, giving his all for the team. Mario is a great champion: it shows on the football pitch; he can create chances out of nowhere. Still, off the pitch, he has yet to find his bearings. I really appreciated the fact that he apologised for the mistakes he made in the past, but he must realise that, if he doesn't get himself sorted out, he could jeopardise his career forever.'

To win and to amaze

About his first years at Inter Milan, Roberto Mancini says, 'We have positively laid the basis for our work, now it is time to wrap things up in the best possible way.' And at the beginning of the season, in an interview with *La Repubblica*, he describes how he thinks about football. 'I am drawn to those elements that can make the team unpredictable,' he says. 'Something that corresponds to the leaps of imagination of a world-beater, who comes up with a surprising shot, catching his opponent off-guard, putting on a real exciting show. I believe this to be the essence of football, although nowadays it is more and more difficult to talk about these things. We have lost the pleasure of fun, fantasy and technical skills. Results are the only thing that matter: you win, therefore you are good – it doesn't matter how you got there. But I want to win and to amaze. Maybe it will be hard, but I have to try, especially with a team like Inter Milan.'

Mancini tries, and succeeds. He starts by winning the Italian Super Cup, on 26 August 2006, against Roma (the Black-and-Blues coming from behind to win 4–3 in extra time), and ends with the league title, Inter's 15th. The numbers are impressive: 97 points, 30 wins, 7 draws and only 1 defeat out of 38 matches. A sequence of 17 straight victories, 15 wins away from home, a record 22-point lead over the runners-up, the title confirmed with five games still to play (just like Valentino Mazzola's great Torino team of 1947/48, and Fulvio Bernardini's Fiorentina in 1955/56). Numbers and records matter, of course, but they don't tell the full story of an unforgettable season and a scudetto that had remained elusive – apart from the one handed to them in disappointing circumstances and after the event the year before – for the last 18 years.

The years of bitterness and disappointment had seen Inter Milan labelled as the eternal losers, but all that is wiped away on 22 April 2007, at the Artemio Franchi Stadium. On a hot Sunday, the Black-and-Blues defeat Siena 2–1 with two goals by Marco Materazzi. Everyone wears a shirt with the number 15 on it, and 'Champions' written above that. While the party goes on in the changing rooms, and everyone is cheering and chanting 'we won without stealing' and 'Giacinto, one of us' (in memory of president Facchetti, who passed away, aged 64, in September 2006), Mancini sits to one side, reasoning over the meaning of this first league title he has won as a manager. With this title, he goes down in Inter's history, side by side with Helenio Herrera, 'The Magician'; the Argentinian also won the championship in his third year with the club.

'It is a well-deserved victory, and an enormous excitement,' says the manager. 'The team played extraordinarily during the whole championship. We suffered at times, but we showed our character. Palermo and Roma were as good as us, for a long time but we pulled away from them in November and December and that made a real difference in the end. We showed our worth by winning 17 matches in a row. The turning point? Our first derby: we dominated and won. And winning the title with five games to go is just extraordinary.' He is asked for a dedication, and responds, 'Our success goes out to Giacinto, first of all, who is the symbol of our triumph. I really regret him not being with us today. And, of course, this scudetto is dedicated to all our supporters. In this moment, my thought also goes back to all those managers and players who were at Inter Milan and did not win, out of "bad luck", to use a euphemism.' Mancini is proud of what he has achieved, at a club where the expectation is always so great. 'My victories with Samp and Lazio are something that make me stick in the fans' memory. But Inter Milan ... well, this was a real challenge.' A challenge, he adds, that he is determined to keep rising to: 'If we do things properly, we could aim at higher goals. I am a manager because I enjoy watching good football, and watching my team play well. But it is hard to coach Inter Milan: you can get hurt, and you must listen to a lot of rubbish from a lot of people.'

An enthusiastic Massimo Moratti announces, live on TV, that the marriage with Mancini is confirmed to continue: there is a new four-year contract, with an option on the fifth year. He is very pleased with the manager that he wanted so badly. 'Mancini had an iron grip,' he says, 'he understood his men, and worked well.' Despite disappointment in the Coppa Italia (Inter's 2–1 win in the second leg was not enough to overturn the crushing 6–2 scoreline of the first leg), the season ends on the highest of high notes.

But it has not all been honey and roses for Mancini, nor for Italian football as a whole. Sure, Inter Milan pitched up to the starting line for the 2006/07 championship as one of the favourites. They had made a series of important purchases (Patrick Vieira, Hernan Crespo, Zlatan Ibrahimovic, Fabio Grosso, Maicon, Maxwell) and what's more, Juventus were stuck in Serie B, while AC Milan, Fiorentina, Lazio and Reggina had all suffered their respective points deductions. Still, it would surely take time for such a cosmopolitan Inter (Marco Materazzi would often find himself the only Italian in the team) to gel.

They could have been distracted in January, when the British press started talking about Mancini leaving for Chelsea. His replacement would be José Mourinho, they said. The rumours, however, were denied without having any real impact on the Black-and-Blues' momentum.

What did stop them, and all of Italian football, was a murder. On 2 February 2007, at the end of the Sicilian derby between Catania and Palermo, during confrontations between hard-core supporters and the police, Filippo Raciti, a 38-year-old police chief inspector with two children, was killed. Federcalcio indefinitely suspended the championships of all divisions, and cancelled an Italian national team match as well. However, the embargo only lasted for nine days, with the championships resuming on 11 February – but for any stadiums that did not comply with the government's new anti-violence regulations, matches would have to be played behind closed doors.

'This is not football. It would be better to stop here and whoever is first is the winner, just like in the Grand Prix. Then we can start again in September, when things have sorted themselves out.' These were Roberto Mancini's words after Inter Milan's win in a match played behind closed doors in Verona. 'I agreed that we couldn't go back to playing straight away, because what happened in Catania is unthinkable. Some kids won't see their daddy again, because of one, two or maybe ten idiots. But such things have happened before; still, in Italy, we always get there late. I repeat: the solution is not banning the crowd from stadiums altogether. Players go on to the football pitch to enjoy, but to amuse people as well.'

Little by little though, all the stadiums complied with the new regulations, allowing the enjoyment to resume, and likewise Inter Milan's extraordinary run of success. The only flaw, for the Black-and-Blues, was their defeat against Roma, on 18 April, at San Siro. Nevertheless, what is done is done, and the party was postponed for only a few more days.

Everything was running smoothly in Italy for the Black-and-Blues, but the same could not be said of their

European campaign. The battleship Inter Milan sank during the last-16 round of the Champions League. Again, the torpedoes were fired by the Spanish: Valencia this time, with David Villa and David Silva scoring the crucial away goals in a 2–2 draw at San Siro, to ensure the progress of their team.

So Europe is a test that the Mancini gang keeps failing; the European Cup has not sat on the Black-and-Blues' shelf since the 1960s, when Herrera was managing the team and Angelo Moratti was the president.

Massimo Moratti cannot explicitly admit that the Champions League has become their priority – 'because otherwise it may end like this year, when I must pretend that it's all right.' But it is what he wants and what he has had in mind when making high-profile signings. After spending almost €600 million across 12 seasons, he is surely entitled to expect his team to be challenging for that European crown. Still, he invests once more in the summer of 2007, although less lavishly than in previous years. So here are the new signings: the Rumanian defender Christian Chivu and the Honduran striker David Suazo. And let us not forget – although he doesn't come from the transfer market, but from the Black-and-Blues youth set-up – Mario Balotelli. The youngster has won the championship with the Academy team, and now Mancini has called him up for the first team squad.

So, there is a stronger line-up, but the Champions League challenge, in the Black-and-Blues' centenary year, ends just where it did the year before: at the last 16. This time, it is Rafa Benitéz's Liverpool that knocks Inter Milan out. On 19 February, the first leg is played at Anfield. After 30 minutes, Materazzi is sent off after receiving two yellow cards, for two fouls on Fernando Torres. Then, with five minutes remaining, when a 0–0 draw looks quite appealing, comes Dirk Kuyt's goal. And after 90 minutes, Steven Gerrard hits a venomous curling shot to make sure that the Reds have something to celebrate. It is Inter Milan's second defeat in 30 matches that season. They will need a remarkable come-back in the second leg at the Meazza Stadium if they are to go through.

The day before the return match, after a floodlit evening training session in Appiano, there is a screening of a black and white movie. It is a recording of the European Cup semi-final second leg match of 12 May 1965. At San Siro, a great Inter Milan line-up faces Bill Shankly's Liverpool, who defeated them 3–1 in the first leg. A recovery to get through to the final seems almost impossible, but Corso and his team-mates succeed with a 3–0 win. It is a historical precedent that the Black-and-Blues can aspire to recreate.

On the eve of the Inter Milan–Liverpool match, 2008 edition, Roberto Mancini tells it as he sees it. 'At Anfield,' he says, 'we played ten men against eleven for over an hour, and that is what damaged us most. Now, we know that the odds of us winning are low, but we cannot play thinking that we must score three goals. We must play the perfect match. Our first aim is not giving Liverpool any space to exploit. There is no ready-made solution here, like for instance attacking first and foremost: we must do all that we can, taking time to play well. Being at San Siro can make a difference: the crowd can be a decisive element if the match is looking up, and if we believe that we can recover the score. But it is chiefly up to us. Benitez's Liverpool is not a defensive team, but their defence holds wonderfully. They are all on top shape, they have just reached that level, and then they have Torres, who has really grown after six months in England.' Mancini has also got one last warning to send out: 'If by any chance we go out, we must not turn it into a drama – because when two great clubs face each other, and one is two goals behind, not getting through is a real option. Anyway, I am generally quite an optimistic person, even more so at times like this.'

'We believe in this, nothing is impossible for Inter Milan,' reads the poster before the match. But there is to be no miracle on 11 May 2008. Halfway through the second half, Fabio Aurelio passes to Fernando Torres, who controls it well, turns, and beats Julio Cesar with a low, right-footed shot. Inter Milan, again down to ten men having had Burdisso sent off, freeze. They have tried, but could not get their 'perfect match' quite right. Liverpool are through. The Black-and-Blue supporters are left with a burning disappointment. 'One evening manages to cancel out the excitement from two years of victories,' the papers will say the following day. 'And Inter Milan discover themselves to be quite provincial – that is, only capable of winning in their own back yard.'

The surprises and disappointments don't end there, though. At 11.15pm, in the Meazza press room, after analysing the match, Roberto Mancini takes the floor: 'May I say something to the Italian press here – I don't think the Brits will care that much. Anyway, although I still have a four-year contract with Inter Milan, these will be my last two-and-a-half months with the club. I have already told the team, and now I am saying it officially. I hope they will be two-and-a-half great months, in which we can win the championship and the Coppa Italia again.' Nothing more is added. It is a twist in the story that leaves everyone gasping: directors, players, journalists, fans. Even Roberto's agent is not quite sure of what to make of his announcement.

Possible explanations abound, as do rumours regarding the future. Having flunked the Champions League for the fourth time in a row is undoubtedly a burden for Mancio. The manager also had an argument with Moratti because of his 'If by any chance we go out, we must not turn it into a drama' statement – not one that went down well with the president. Perhaps, too, Mancini wanted to give the team a shock, because they are first in the league but must not rest on their laurels, and must watch out for their opponents. And all in all, the Inter manager has had enough of Italian football, with all of its controversies and tensions. The Black-and-Blues dressing-room is once more a difficult place, with opposing cliques and a sizable contingent of unhappy players. Mancini knows that Moratti has already met up with Mourinho, and he is jumping before being pushed. These are only some of the explanations bandied about: some are real; some are made-up.

Anyway, Mancio dreams about the future; he dreams about England. In the newspapers, on TV and radio, and on supporters' websites, everyone is trying to find the reason for Mancini's statement. They are also trying to figure out what will happen to the manager. Some suggest that Mancini will be asked to stand down immediately, with his assistant Sinisa Mjialovic taking temporary charge until José Mourinho arrives.

The following day, at 1pm, Massimo Moratti does not hide his disappointment. 'His announcement took me by surprise,' the president says. 'No one was expecting this, not even those who are close to him. I believe he was harbouring it since [the first leg in] Liverpool, because it does seem odd that he would suddenly come up with something like this.' At 8pm, though, everything changes: things seem to have been pulled together again. 'I had a little chat with Mancini,' Moratti says. 'He told me he would like to be with Inter Milan next year, and for the rest of his contract. And next season, he wants to win the Champions League. The situation is very different from what the club, the team and I had imagined in the last few hours. I didn't get much of an explanation, but Mancini's love for and interest in the club were both reconfirmed to me. Most of all, he wants to stay at Inter Milan, not because he is being forced to, but because he feels like doing so. So this seems to me like the best solution, but it is now important that the matter is cleared up with the team. Things might have been thrown a little bit off balance, but I think that can be fixed. I suppose this will depend on whether Mancini can persuade everyone that he is honest with them: he looked totally sincere to me, but he did kick up a storm. Now there is some water left on the ground, and it is up to him to dry it up. Maybe words are a bit heavier than the will of he who uttered them.'

Now it is Mancini's turn to explain. 'No one knows better than president Moratti, the Inter Milan fans and the team how it feels to miss out on such an important goal as the one we had set for ourselves,' he says. 'I hope that all those who live football will understand my outburst and the bitterness that one feels at such delicate times. A manager is always the point of reference for the group, but that group feeds on emotions that run deep. After the match, it was my heart and feelings talking. I thank the president for the strength he gave me, for being able to read the circumstances and for being understanding towards me. I am sorry for any misunderstanding that might have arisen: the team knows that already, and we are ready to fight until the last minute, with great intensity, to win our third championship and to conquer the Champions League right from the beginning of next season.'

Mancini does indeed win his third championship with Inter Milan – not hands down like the previous year, but in a nail-biting finale in Parma in the last game of the season. The Mancini gang gets to the final day having dropped points in their previous two games, so that they are now only one point ahead of Roma. The Red-and-Yellows are playing an away match in Catania. The Black-and-Blues, in a swampy

Tardini Stadium, must face a club determined to avoid conceding anything to the Italian champions. Roberto Mancini plays Julio Cesar between the posts; a four-men defence of Maicon, Rivas, Materazzi and Maxwell; Zanetti, Vieira, Stankovic and Cesar in the midfield; and, up front, Cruz and Balotelli. Both team have many chances to score, but the score is still 0–0 at half-time. Six minutes into the second half, Ibrahimovic comes on for Cesar, and it is the Swede, with two goals, who ensures the Black-and-Blues retain their title.

Mancini, soaked with rain, shouts out his joy. He turns to the stands, with his arm held aloft in triumph. He really deserved this title, won at the very end of a gripping championship. What with injuries, suspensions and players who were not at their best, he was forced to shuffle his pack many times. He often had to change formation and tactics, and to face up to adverse circumstances. He was flexible and not at all dogmatic, showing those unpredictable skills, that capacity to improvise, that he had as a playmaker. He managed an international group of players who, one time or another, all put their own interests ahead of the team's. And he motivated them, despite their defeat in Europe. He managed to keep Roma at bay, on and off the pitch, arguing here and there with Luciano Spalletti and Francesco Totti. With this third championship victory, Mancini has finally got rid of the label classing him as 'the one with high connections' – the label he got when he arrived at Fiorentina, without having had to rise through the ranks of youth team or Serie C coaching.

All in all, the comments at the end of the season are mostly positive. And Lele Oriali, one of the Inter Milan directors, declares at the end of the championship-clinching match, 'I don't think there are any doubts – Mancini will stay, 101 per cent.'

He is wrong, though, big time. On 27 May, after having lunch with two old friends of his (Diego Armando Maradona and Salvatore Bagni), Massimo Moratti meets Roberto Mancini in his house in Via Serbelloni, Milan. In twenty minutes, he tells Mancio that this is where his marriage with Inter Milan ends. Seven trophies in four years, including three Serie A titles in a row, have not been not enough to secure his place. Roberto leaves as a champion of Italy, and as the manager who – Helenio Herrera aside – won more trophies than any other Inter manager. It looked like their union was going to last (at least until June 2012, the date on the contract), but instead it ends here. The date on which Moratti bids farewell to his manager is not dictated solely by chance, either: it all happens on 27 May, the date on which Inter Milan won both of their European Cups to date – this underlines the only respect in which the manager from Marche can be said to have underperformed.

So the defeat against Liverpool, it seems, was fatal; the Black-and-Blues president's decision was made then, and only postponed until the end of the championship because of the lack of alternatives. However, by 11 March 2008, Operation Mourinho had begun. By the end of March, Moratti and the former Chelsea manager already had a verbal agreement in place, although both denied it publicly. The Portuguese then signed a three-year contract with the club on 26 May. He will be introduced to the team on 3 June, at Pinetina. Five days before this, in an official statement (eight lines in total), FC Internazionale makes it known that 'Mr Mancini is relieved of his duties as first-team manager, because of the comments he made regarding the Inter–Liverpool match on 11 March 2008 [about leaving Inter], the facts that followed and the latest developments which have recently been made public by the press.' The final part of the statement refers to the leaked transcripts of a series of phone calls between a number of Inter Milan employees – Mancini, Mihajlovic, Salsano, Zanetti, Materazzi, two club officials and Altobelli – and Domenico Brescia, a 55-year-old tailor discovered to be a convicted murderer with Mafia connections. The Anti-Mafia section of the Milan Police Service had been investigating Brescia on suspicion of involvement in a cocaine-dealing circle, connected with 'Ndrangheta (the name of the Mafia organisation in Calabria).

Mancini's response to the club dispatch is firm. Not only does he require the clauses in his contract to be honoured, but he goes well beyond that. 'Realising that the club's decision originates from events which are causing serious damage to my honour and reputation, and their illicit broadcasting being censured by means of multiple legal actions on my behalf by the appropriate authorities,' he says 'I have given my trusted lawyer a mandate to protect my image in all required situations, blaming the conduct of the club – my employer – for taking advantage of false and illicit events.' While some of the legal terminology doesn't necessarily translate well, the sense is clear: Mancini is determined to fight any accusation of wrongdoing, and likewise any suggestion by Inter that recent events have given them grounds to cancel his contract. As his lawyer, Stefano Gagliardi, says, 'My client's reputation is damaged by bringing together the ending of his contract with news reported by the media, which he is completely unaware of.'

Still, in Mancini's counter-offensive against his dismissal, he does not forget to thank the club – a courtesy that Inter Milan failed to extend to him. He thanks 'the president, Massimo Moratti, Gabriele Oriali and the staff that always supported me, the team and especially all those Black-and-Blues supporters who stood by me in the last four years' worth of victories and great emotions, and for the gratitude and esteem they still give to me.'

It is a sign of class, but also an attempt to break through the stand-off that has now developed. The situation, however, does not seem to evolve. There is €24 million up for grabs (€6 million per year, the wage that Mancini is supposed to earn until 2012). The club is ready for legal action, and it is pursuing a rightful dismissal formula so that it will not have to pay, and so that there won't be any trouble for Mourinho. Mancini rejects a proposed €8 million compensation deal; it will be another year before the matter is resolved.

At the end of October 2009, Roberto Mancini – still receiving his pay packet from the Black-and-Blues, despite not working – calls off the contract tying him to the club for another two seasons (and, albeit theoretically now, an optional third one). He reaches an agreement with Moratti and is widely believed to have accepted an €8 million compensation package, although both parties publicly deny it.

At last, Mancini is free from his previous commitments and is back on the market, ready to seize the next opportunity.

He was born a manager

A conversation with Sergio Giosuè Viganò

'Tomorrow is a dear friend's birthday, a person who is very close to me: Sergio Giosuè Viganò. I am wishing him all the best.' During the press conference, before the Coppa Italia final against Roma on 8 May 2007, Roberto Mancini – in order to avoid a question on Claudio Lotito, the Lazio president, who is also celebrating his birthday on that day – comes up with this solution. Viganò never forgot that. 'It was quite exceptional stuff,' says the physiotherapist, the masseur, the guy who knows better than most not only the muscles, but also the brains of Mancio and many of his players.

'I met Roberto when he was 17, maybe 18. He had just arrived at Sampdoria, and he was first on my list. He had a few issues; his muscle structure was quite demanding. He was stocky, with his muscles growing outwards and not extending, so he was often prone to injuries such as strains and sprains. He always believed in me, and I always treated him as if he was my son. I am now 72, he is 47 – just like my boys. We had some big trouble initially, with his muscle issues, but then, little by little, it all turned out alright – which was great news. So we started walking down that road together, and we carried on until the day before yesterday.'

So, let's talk about those 30 years together.
'I took care of him when he played for Sampdoria, then

followed him to Lazio, and again when he managed the White-and-Blue team and then Inter Milan.'

And at City.
'That's right, I left Italy for Manchester 40 days before the end of the season, in a rush, sticking a couple of things into my suitcase, and I returned home only after the party when they won the Premier League. He really needed that; it was important to Mancio that I was there. And I didn't feel like saying no, after knowing him since he was a young boy. So I packed my things and left for Manchester.'

Listen, it sounds like you are some kind of good luck charm for Mancini.
'Well, in a way I am, I bring him good luck … you know, players are always trying to ward off ill luck. You go to one of them, and things don't turn out well; then they see someone else and everything is all right. It is just like with doctors: the one who operates on you and fixes you, well, it's not that he's better than some other doctor, but it is only natural that you end up trusting him more. Perhaps I just suited him well … we won at Sampdoria, at Lazio and at Inter Milan as well. And I managed to contribute to his victory in Manchester, too.'

Which players did you treat at City?
'Kompany, Zabaleta, Nasri and others had a few problems that could have affected their performance in the ensuing weeks. Instead, everything turned out fine. Luckily.'

Had you already met the players who make up the City dressing-room?
'I had already been there a few times, over the past two years – two, three days at most. I would have a look at the player

and see what could be done. Then at one point I said to Mancini, "Look, I cannot come anymore, I can't leave my family; my wife has some problems." So he started sending the guys over to my place, in Lu, in Monferrato – a place that no one knows of.'

No one knows of that place, you say, but Mancini and Vialli, back then, used to take the whole of Sampdoria there.
'We went there to eat donkey stew, with agnolotti pasta and soppressa sausage. No one knew that donkey could be quite tasty, and some just wouldn't have any of that, like Ruud Gullit, for example. "I'm not having any," he used to say, but after cleaning up a couple of dishes, he would take a pot back for his family to try.'

Let's go back to City. What was the atmosphere like, in those last 40 days?
'It was quite tense, because, even though the team was strong, not many had tasted victory before, and very few of them could take that sort of stress. When they started realising just what stress was, that was when injuries began. It is quite normal, because each action becomes more violent, you move in spurts, with no logic of motion. The muscle system is altered, depending on the amount of stress you are subject to. We went into the derby against United with such tensions. That's the reason for that so-and-so match, which we won 1–0: we deserved better. Then we went over to Newcastle – still the same stress, but less apparent. And it [the stress level] went down in the last half-hour, after Yaya Touré scored. On the Friday and Saturday, before the last match, I watched the training sessions and I remember thinking "Dear me, this is electric." And on the Sunday, that tension fried the guys' brains … City shot 44 times at goal; we took 19 corners. Also, QPR played a defensive game – but it wasn't a good match.

And Mancio really suffered. He was tense, and he had to put up with an incredible amount of stress.'

Apart from being subject to that kind of tension, what are the characteristics that you appreciate most in Mancini?
'He can lay out a team, and he knows how it should play.'

Where did he learn that from?
'He learned by himself, he was born a manager. Mancio still does not have one of those clear-cut personalities, by which you are either a goodie or a baddie. He does not want to be bad, and he does not want – he cannot – be too good. Still, he is phenomenal on the football pitch. He managed a really complicated group, he changed tactics an infinite amount of times, in order to adapt to the situation. He managed to win with a team which lacks the history, tradition and attitude for victory that a team like Manchester United has. He won with good players, really good ones, alright – but not the players that Real Madrid had. With Mourinho's players, I could be a coach, too.'

How has Roberto Mancini changed, throughout all these years?
'He is becoming more technical, and more aware. He knows that he has the magic formula that will enable him to run any team. He used to be quite impulsive, but in my opinion he is a lot better now and has become much more calm and collected. He had to adapt his personality to his new job as a manager, and he has become a number one. And in England, he has also toughened up.'

Why do you reckon that is?
'Because, in the Premier League, he faced many different opponents, and that allowed him to improve his mental strength and to have more control over his decisions.'

*Like those he made in the last minutes of that City–QPR match …
speaking of which, how did you manage to get through that
heart-stopping game?*
'I managed just wonderfully …'

*Did you still think you could win, when everything seemed to be
lost?*
'It would be easy to say that I did. But when I saw there were
three minutes left till the end of the game, I thought, "If we
score now, we win." It was not new for City to win a match in
the last 4–5 minutes. The crowd usually goes crazy, everyone
is standing up, chanting, screaming – the team's reaction
to all of that is not normal, either. If you go and watch City
play at the Etihad Stadium, you are in for a show. But it is
like at the theatre: people clap only if you deserve it. Alright,
Mancini usually gets his tribute, but it is during those final
minutes that people really let loose. I must admit, I was
quite tense, but in the end I felt really happy. As I did for all
the championships, the cups and Super Cups that Mancio
and I have won together so far – and in spite of everything
and everyone, we often won. My only regret is that evil
European Cup; we really threw that one out of the window,
because someone did not measure up to the situation and
the stress.'

How do you see Mancini in the future?
'He deserves to stay with City, and not be torn to pieces by
the press, threatening his dismissal in favour of some other
Mourinho or somesuch. He deserves some new players, too.
I really hope he can get some peace and quiet, because I
can tell that he has aged, and he is under a lot of pressure.
Last year, the championship was quite hard; it took quite
a lot out of him. He paid a high price for victory, after
44 years. Fortunately, people appreciate that, and he gets

good feedback for it. The parade through the streets of Manchester was beautiful, really moving – especially for him.'

Will you go back to Manchester, to bring him good luck?
'Well, we'll see about that ...'

And then the sheikh called

It is a week before Christmas. Manchester City are playing at home against Sunderland. Two goals by Roque Santa Cruz earn the Blues a 4–3 win. It is a thrilling victory over a Black Cats side reduced to ten men. At the end of the match, Mark Hughes, the Blues' Welsh manager, raises his hands up to the sky and waves to the crowd. In the press room, Sunderland boss Steve Bruce is surprised when a journalist asks him to comment on a possible early dismissal of Hughes, his former teammate at Manchester United. 'You can't build a football club in 18 months, and one transfer window,' says Bruce. 'You need a bit of time.' However, he adds, 'No one is surprised by these kind of decisions anymore, as ludicrous as they might be.'

Two hours later, the rumours, which have been going around for days, are confirmed. An official notice on the Manchester City website announces that Mark Hughes' contract has been terminated. The reasons are set out: the €200 million investment – used to buy, among others, important and expensive players like Emmanuel Adebayor, Joleon Lescott, and Carlos Tevez – has not yielded the expected results. The team's play has not been brilliant; nor have its achievements. 'Two wins in eleven Premier League games are clearly not in line with the targets that we had agreed and set,' reads the official statement. It goes on to say that 'Sheikh Mansour and the club board felt that there was no evidence that the situation would fundamentally change.' Therefore, Hughes is out and Mancini is in.

'Roberto is a hugely experienced manager with a proven track record of winning trophies and championships,' comments chairman Khaldoon Al Mubarak. 'His experience and track record speak for themselves. What is absolutely clear is that Roberto believes in Manchester City's potential to achieve the highest level and, more importantly, in his own ability to make this happen. My hope is that our incredible fans will join us in welcoming Roberto to the football club.'

Nineteen months after getting the sack from Inter Milan, Mancini is back in the dugout. His decision not to coach for a whole season has been entirely personal. 'I have been working for 30 years non-stop,' he asserts. 'I really needed a break for twelve months.' For an entire season, he has been a high-profile unemployed person, handsomely paid by Massimo Moratti. He travelled, he learned English, he watched a lot of football matches, unofficially scouting for the future; he followed, from not too far away, José Mourinho's adventure with the Black-and-Blues, and he spent some time indulging an old hobby of his: yachts. Mancini has a passion for boats and, having owned several, he took the next step and became a partner in a boat-building business.

Although the concrete offers made to him have numbered four (as he will admit later), his name has been linked with a number of clubs. He has been named as a possible replacement for first Bernd Schuster and then Manuel Pellegrini at Florentino Perez's Real Madrid. He has also been cited as Dick Advocaat's successor at Zenit St Petersburg, and as Jürgen Klinsmann's designated heir at Bayern Munich. Other rumours have had him joining Juventus, CSKA Moscow and AS Monaco, or else going into international management with Russian, Ukraine or Turkey. And Nigeria have enquired whether he would be available to take care of team selection for the Africa Cup and the 2010 World Cup.

Mancini has often had to deny such gossip, while making it clear that, in principle, he does not rule out any option. 'The only team I really wouldn't feel like coaching is Genoa,' he has said, 'as I was Sampdoria's standard-bearer and I hold all these records with the Blucerchiati; I am sure that Genoans would be the first to dislike my being around.' He has had to answer many questions, regarding just as many hypothetical coaching jobs. He has had to point out that 'I love coaching, and I feel like I am at one with football', and to repeat that, having had a break, he is once more ready to take on the responsibilities of club management. And he says that, after 30 years in Italy, he would rather manage abroad next, ideally in the Premier League.

In England, he has been mentioned as a successor to Guus Hiddink at Chelsea, as a replacement for Rafa Benítez at Liverpool, and as a candidate to manage Portsmouth and Sunderland. Sven-Göran Eriksson also enquired whether he would be available to coach Notts County. But most insistent of all has been the rumour about him succeeding Hughes at Manchester City, if and when the Welshman failed to meet the sheikh's expectations.

As early as April 2009, the *Sunday People* suggested that the Manchester City club management were about to meet up with the Italian coach in order to offer him a job, starting in the summer. But such suspicions become reality only in December, although there are claims that the contract was signed back in November – according to this theory, the City directors foresaw bad times coming for the team and chose to postpone the succession for a few weeks.

The question of when Mancini signed for City is scrutinised (and is the subject of the odd diatribe) during the press conference called to introduce the new manager. This takes place on 21 December 2009, and it looks more like an interrogation rather than an introduction. The press are annoyed by the Welsh manager's sudden replacement; and they are not the only ones. He was sacked after suffering only two defeats, with the team in sixth and having progressed to the semi-finals of the League Cup – the furthest the club had progressed in the competition since 1981 – where they were to play their city neighbours Manchester United.

Mark Hughes has said that the events have taken him by surprise, confirming that he was notified of the termination of his contract just after the match against Sunderland. The supporters haven't taken it too well, and nor have several members of the dressing-room who are faithful to Hughes. It is said that six of them – including Craig Bellamy, Gareth Barry, Roque Santa Cruz and Shay Given – actually tried to persuade Garry Cook, the director general, to change his mind and try to get the club owner to reconsider. In short, it is not a pleasant atmosphere in which to meet the press, with their microphones, video cameras and insidious questions.

It is 5.30pm when Mancini turns up to face the media at the City of Manchester Stadium. He is smartly dressed: dark pinstripe suit, crisp white shirt and blue tie. Mancio bravely answers the journalists' questions in his basic English. The questions are as abundant as the snow on the ground outside, and many of them concern his first meeting with Sheikh Mansour. Indeed, the opening question is about the precise moment when Roberto was contacted. He answers, 'Two weeks ago I met Khaldoon and the owner of the club, the sheikh, in London – but they called me after Tottenham, not before.'

So the decision regarding a managerial replacement seems to have been taken only on 16 December, after the match at White Hart Lane, when City lost 3–0 to Spurs. However, this is not enough for the distrustful audience, who already have the bit between their teeth. They want to know more about that London meeting. 'We met to discuss this situation, to speak of football,' explains Mancio. 'He [Khaldoon] is a man of sport, a great person, he wanted to know how I felt about Manchester City.'

The new City manager is doing well, but it is not enough. The questions become insistent. The journalists ask how Italians would view a meeting between an out-of-work manager and, say, Silvio Berlusconi, the AC Milan owner. 'In Italy, this kind of thing is normal,' is Roberto's answer. Garry Cook, sitting by Mancini's side, is forced to intervene, detailing the circumstances of the appointment, in order to expunge the notion of a conspiracy – that is, the suspicion that the City directors went behind poor Hughes's back, reaching an agreement with Mancini much earlier than they are now prepared to admit. Cook has to repeat himself: 'It is important for people to know that Roberto was only offered the job after the Spurs game; we negotiated on Thursday and finalised his agreement on Friday. He was not in the stadium on Saturday, as has been reported.' Cook also adds that 'there is no player rebellion and the playing and train-ing staff have been going about their business this morning very professionally, with Roberto and Brian Kidd.'

Of those present, there are few who believe him. The following day's *Daily Telegraph* comments, 'Not since Bill Clinton glared into a television camera to deny allegations of his relationship with Monica Lewinsky has a man appeared so uncomfortable having had his version of events openly contradicted.' The press gives Cook a good dressing-down, and tries to do the same with Mancini; however, the man from Jesi, little by little, manages to break the ice and win over sections of the crowd, if – as one person remarks – in a somewhat Machiavellian way. He has an answer for every-one, and on every subject. About Hughes's replacement, he says, 'I'm sorry for Mark, but when you start this job, the situation is possible. I was at Inter for four seasons and won seven trophies, and they still sacked me. It's football.' About discontent in the dressing-room, he comments that 'It's normal for players to feel bad when their manager goes, and I hope they will feel like that about me in many years' time, when I go.' Regarding his contract: 'It is six months plus three years' (his salary will be €3.5 million per year). About the risk of being sacked if results are poor: 'My job is to work hard every day, to try to improve the team and to win more games than Mark. I think I can do a good job because we have good players.' About the way he wants his team to play: 'When I played, I always wanted to attack. This is my philosophy. These kind of [attacking] players – Robinho, Tévez – are fantastic. It is important for a big player like Robinho to make history with his club.' On pressure: 'If you are a manager in Italy, living with pressure is the norm, so that won't be a problem for me here. I stayed at Inter for four years, which was a record.' About his friend Sven-Göran Eriksson, a former City manager: 'Sven called me yesterday. He is very happy for me. He told me that Man City is a fantastic club.' On Milan and Manchester: 'Manchester is the same as Milan. The weather is the same, and you have two big clubs fighting against each other. Sir Alex Ferguson is a big manager who has won lots of trophies, but we want to do better than Manchester United.' And, finally, regarding his ambitions: 'My squad usually plays to win, always. My target is top four this season, and I think that is possible, but next season, I want to win the Premier League title.'

Mancio is ambitious, and people like that. He calls City 'a big club' and says, 'I want to stay here for many, many years and I want to contribute to winning many trophies because City has great supporters and I hope we do a good job for them. My job is to work hard every day to improve the play, to improve the victories. This is all.' The talk turns from general issues to more specific ones, such the team's Boxing Day fixture against Stoke City. Mancini is asked whether he knows anything about Rory Delap's long throws. He prepared for this one. 'I know about him. Shay Given will come for the throws,' he says. And with this, the endless press conference finally breaks up, and Mancini walks out on the football pitch for the official photos. Just before this, he promises everyone that he will improve his English by watching *Coronation Street* and *EastEnders* on TV. It seems an absurd idea, and the joke goes a long way towards winning over Hughes's supporters. They take it the right way, and smiles finally break through the ice.

Still, the bookmakers do not seem to have a lot of trust in the new man, and they are already offering odds on his departure. They have the former Inter Milan manager at 11/2 to lose his job before the end of the season. But perhaps he will last at least until the summer (5/4). They are all wrong though, big time. This is clear from 26 December. Mancini has spent his Christmas holidays at work: taking training sessions, meeting with the staff (Fausto Salsano, Ivan Carminati, Brian Kidd), studying his players, watching DVDs of Stoke City matches, over and over again. He needs a good start to win over the crowd, the players and the critics alike.

He gets the start he wants, winning the match and receiving not only applause but also a song just for him – to the tune of the famous Italian song 'Volare'. He leaves the stadium with a smile and a thumbs-up, after shaking hands with his players, while the crowd sing 'In the blue, painted blue – so happy to be up here, too'. City won the match with goals from Martin Petrov and Carlos Tévez and a clean sheet – a real record for the Blues' sieve-like defence. Also of note was a strikingly effective tactical change by the manager: half an hour into the match, Mancini brought Ireland from the right wing in to the centre, moving Petrov across from the left flank to the right and pushing Robinho wider left. One minute later, the opening goal came, from a move started by Ireland and finished off by Petrov.

During the match he stood, composed, a metre from the white line, backed by his assistant Brian Kidd, who translated his instructions to the players on the pitch. Midway through the second half, Mancini took off a flat Robinho and brought on Bellamy, one of Hughes's most strenuous supporters. It was a clever and cunning move, and one that the crowd appreciated, roaring their approval. Mancio has shown that he knows his stuff, and that he is not at all rusty after 19 months off. He is cool, as they say around here, but he has charisma to spare, too. And in a club like City, there is a desperate need for that. Already, those who were looking at him suspiciously only a few days earlier in the press room are now paying him compliments.

The manager says that one half was 'good', while the other was 'so-so', but he adds that 'the first time was for winning only'. So that's what he made sure of doing. He turned up as a real star, with the loudspeakers announcing him to the crowd; around his neck, his blue-and-white scarf. 'Blue is my colour,' he will later comment. 'First at Samp, then at Lazio, at Inter Milan – and now, here.'

His adventure has started well, and it carries on just as well. Four matches, four victories. After Stoke, they win 3–0 in a home match against Wolverhampton Wanderers, then 1–0 against Middlesbrough in the third round of the FA Cup and 4–1 against Blackburn. The first defeat of the Mancini era comes on 16 January 2010, in Liverpool, where Everton win the game 2–0. But three days later, City have the satisfaction of beating Manchester United in the first leg of their League Cup semi-final, with United old boy Carlos Tevez scoring two goals. Unfortunately, Sir Alex Ferguson's team turn it around in the second leg, winning 3–1, so the

Blues are out. Their FA Cup run also comes to an end against Stoke City.

On 9 May, the final day of the Premier League season, it is time to take stock: in five months' work at Eastlands, Roberto Mancini has totalled 11 victories, five defeats and six draws. His primary aim – ranking among the top four – slipped away when they were beaten 1–0 by Spurs in their final home match of the season. This defeat means that City will not compete in the 2010/11 Champions League – something that would have brought the club prestige, as well as money. The ambition to reach the prestigious heights of the Premier League, though, will only be on hold for one more season. In any case, Mancini has recorded some important victories, against Chelsea, for instance.

When the Blues miss out on Champions League qualification, the critics accuse Mancini of being too conservative and defensive. The fact is that Mancio has indeed been working hard on his defence, and on the team's mindset, in order to build a compact group. But there is still a lot to do before City are not just a work in progress, but rather a team capable of looking like the former playmaker who now sits on their bench.

The owners seem persuaded that their project is heading in the right direction, and they come out in support of their manager. In a video broadcast via the club's website, Khaldoon Al Mubarak speaks for ten minutes, sending out the clear message that Mancini is staying. 'Roberto did an excellent job,' he says, 'and I, together with the owner, Sheikh Mansour, are satisfied. He will undoubtedly need some time to prepare and organise the team, but we already know what needs to be made better.' Khaldoon goes on to explain what happened on the day of the Spurs game, when he appeared in the Eastlands changing rooms: 'The owner Sheikh Mansour called me and asked me to go and speak to the players on his behalf. We wanted to thank every person in that dressing-room for the support and effort they have put in this year. There have been some magnificent performances over the year. Some of the players have been phenomenal.' About the Champions League, the one that got away by a hair's breadth, he adds, 'It's difficult when you come close, but come up short. It was disappointing, but we have still had a wonderful season. We have come a long way, and I feel good about next year.'

A masterpiece

A conversation with Pietro and Massimo Battara

'Roberto rang me up a few days before Christmas. We were in the countryside, in Bomporto, a small village in the Modena province where footballers like the Sentimenti brothers and Giorgio Braglia were born. He asked, "What has Massimo been doing lately?" "Not much, at the moment," I answered. "Right," he said, "give me his number, because I might need him."' So Pietro Battara remembers Mancini's call, the one that opened up the doors of Manchester City to his son.

The Battara family has a history of goalkeepers. Pietro, the father, was born in Turin in 1939. He started playing for Lanerossi Vicenza before going to Sampdoria in the mid-1960s and then, eventually, Bologna. He totalled 259 appearances in Serie A and 38 in Serie B. Once his playing career was over, he began an activity that, at the time, the football world did not contemplate.

'When I used to play, we didn't have a goalkeeping coach. No one paid attention to us; no one wanted, or was able, to figure out what we needed to do. At the end of training sessions, we would go between the goalposts, the others would take a few shots, and that was it. We were definitely penalised. So I thought about it, made up a few preparatory skills, codified them in an orderly way, and when I stopped playing for Bologna, I opened an academy for goalkeepers. Many good guys came out of it, who made quite a career afterwards and went on to play in the national team. The idea of a goalkeeping coach made its way to Coverciano, and now finally they have a training course for keepers, too. It is a great satisfaction for me. Today, most of my former students are goalkeeping coaches, and Massimo is one of them.'

Battara senior's academy opened in Casteldebole. It is there that he met Roberto Mancini, a 13-year-old boy whom he then followed to Sampdoria, as a goalkeeping coach for the Blucerchiati team that won the Serie A championship in 1990/91. And when Mancini ended up managing Fiorentina, it was the older Battara again who helped him out with the men between the posts. Years later, it would be up to his son to follow the tradition. 'Massimo and Roberto played as kids in the Bologna youth team, and they came to Sampdoria within a year of each other,' says Pietro. 'From then onwards, they took different paths. Roberto made the career that we all know about. Massimo went to Sanbenedettese as a second-choice goalkeeper, then to Casertana, Salernitana and later to Spal. Then he followed Beppe Dossena to Al-Ittihad FC. He left, because it was impossible for him to work in Saudi Arabia, and came to La Spezia to earn a promotion to Serie B. I am so glad that Mancini thought of Massimo for this role with City when Giulio Nuciari, the goalkeeping coach he had at Inter Milan, could not follow him to the UK – as he was still tied to the Black and Blues, and he also had some family issues he needed to take care of. I must admit, Roberto always paid extra care to the keepers' training.'

From father to son now, as Battara junior reflects on his association with the Blues' manager.

How do you recall that famous phone call and the way you became part of the City staff?
'Roberto asked me if I wanted to help him out. Well, of course I did! So when he asked me if I was ready to move to England, I told him that my suitcase was already packed.

He didn't even mention which club I was going to work for: he only said that, on a given day, Fausto Salsano would come to pick me up. We left at 5pm from Bologna. I remember that it was snowing, we got stuck in Amsterdam and we had to leave on the following day to make it in time for our meeting with Roberto.'

How have these three seasons in Manchester been?
'Quite exceptional really, because City are quite an organised club, with great players. They work with footballers who have great skills, and who are also great professionals. With regard to keepers, I knew I was entering a completely different mind-set from Italy; the gap was much bigger for me than for Roberto, Salsano and the other members of staff ... I tried not to erase what had already been done. I wanted them to get to know me, and I didn't want to disrupt everything with respect to technique and work patterns. I worked with many gifted individuals, such as Shay Gilbert and Stuart Taylor, who did a marvellous job.'

And Joe Hart ...
'Joe Hart came later. When we got to City, he was on loan at Birmingham. Then Eriksson, while talking to Roberto, mentioned that Hart was a guy with good potential. I went to watch him play, and I realised he had great skills, quite rare really, in the world of British goalkeepers. I am sure that, when the great keepers currently at Barcelona and Real Madrid [Victor Valdés and Iker Casillas respectively], together with Italy's Gianluigi Buffon, finish playing, Hart and [Bayern Munich's Manuel] Neuer will contend with each other for the title of best keeper in the world. I also ought to point out that not many managers understand about keepers the way that Mancini does. Suffice to look at Julio Cesar, and his evolution at Inter Milan: from a perfect

stranger, to one of the best keepers in the world. And the same will happen with Joe Hart.'

Let's change subject, let's go back to your first months with City. Was it hard?
'Yes, it was … if you take a look at the papers, in those days everyone wanted Mark Hughes back; everyone was asking the club to change their mind. The club management gave Hughes free rein, so he put people he trusted in every department, from the medical staff to the fitness coaches. We went in every day expecting to be running for cover. Roberto showed great character, and great patience, managing to earn everyone's trust and esteem little by little – the club's, his new team's, the supporters' and all the technical staff's.'

What is Mancini like, seen through the eyes of a person who works with him every day?
'He's great stuff … and I believe he was a surprise for many, at City, too. In England, the managerial approach rules: in other words, the coach is not actually coaching, he is supervising the training, and his assistants carry out the work for him. However, Roberto was on the training pitch from day one, to direct the tactical training. Both his English advisors and the players were impressed – positively, that is. And I must admit that it was worthwhile, seeing a manager getting his hands dirty with the team. He would always know what to do at the right time, while an assistant might not always be quite on the mark. Roberto is great at this kind of stuff, he showed it in the last match of the season, with those two substitutions at the last minute: Dzeko, who equalised, and Balotelli, who made the final pass. As they say in England: a masterpiece.'

Let's talk about that City–QPR game.

'After watching that match, I know for sure that I won't ever have a heart attack. I might die from some other misfortune, but my heart will hold. I couldn't believe that … with ten minutes left to go, sitting one row above Roberto, with Ivan Carminati, the fitness coach, we commented, "We really threw that one away!" It was unthinkable that we still could win, and regrets were deep. You are ahead for a whole season – and you deserve to be ahead, too – then other clubs catch up with you, or rather, you allow them to catch up and overtake you. Then, the last match comes: United score first, and they are ahead; then we score, and we are top of the Premier League until QPR takes that advantage away from us … I was really distressed. Then we had a stroke of genius, that is, the manager's decision regarding substitutions – and a little bit of luck, because that is needed, too. And we won the title. That last match was, for better or worse, the most dramatic moment of the last three years. The most pleasurable was undoubtedly our 6–1 win against United. They have beaten the living daylights out of City for a lifetime; they are one of the strongest clubs around and it is really tough to win against them. We have been getting worked up about this forever, and this time it was the other way round. Listening to Alex Ferguson calling us "noisy neighbours", then seeing all those blue jerseys around Manchester – well, that really was something.'

How do you see the future? Rosy?

'Well, the future is never rosy, because you must work hard, in order to win. This last Premier League shows that. We'll need to get back to work, get our heads down, with the same intensity as before. And never give up. This is my mantra in life. Nevertheless, I am persuaded that City is a club that holds the future in its own hands.'

Just the beginning

'GOAL!!! GOAL!!! GOAL!!! GOAL!!! GOAL BY YAYA TOURÉ!!! MANCHESTER CITY 1 STOKE CITY 0'

In the 74th minute of the game, the Ivory Coast giant does it again. He scores, just like he did before with the goal that beat Manchester United in the semi-final. Same stadium, same net. This time, it is El Apache, Tévez, who makes it all happen, passing the ball to the left of the opponents' penalty area, to David Silva. Silva turns, he has no room to manoeuvre at all, and crosses to 'Super' Mario Balotelli, who unleashes one of his rockets, but the keeper clears it. The ball ends up on Touré's foot and the big man strikes a half-volley from the penalty spot. It is a really powerful shot, which Tévez moves to the side to let through. Thomas Sørensen, who has been saving the unimaginable so far, can't do anything about this one. The goal ensures that the 130th FA Cup is won by Manchester City. It is their first trophy after a 35-year drought.

When the final whistle blows, Mancini lifts his arms to the sky in triumph. Shortly afterwards, he comments, 'I am happy for the fans, they deserved to win this cup. For a long time they didn't win.' Half of Wembley Stadium (the half that's wearing blue, that is) is celebrating. Since their last League Cup success in 1976, City supporters haven't seen any of their players lift a trophy. Now the captain, Tévez, has the honour. It is 14 May 2011 and it is the first tangible success for Mancini's City. Actually, no, it is the second, because they have also secured qualification for the Champions

League, via their league position. Their neighbours United won the Premier League just a few hours before, while City, who were denied the crucial fourth spot by Spurs the year before, this time secured entry to Europe's elite competition at the north Londoners' expense. In fact, Mancini's team achieved a ranking of third, even ahead of Arsenal. 'We have achieved one piece of history by going into the Champions League,' said Mancini. 'If someone had said two or three years ago that City would become one of the top teams in the world, no one would have believed it.'

Going back to the summer of 2010, thanks to the £126 million invested by Sheikh Mansour and Abu Dhabi Group in a sizzling transfer market, City – from a 'wishful thinking' team – were rapidly becoming serious trophy contenders. Worthy reinforcements arrived: David Silva from Valencia, Mario Balotelli from Inter Milan, Yaya Touré from Barcelona, Jérôme Boateng from Hamburg, Alexander Kolarov from Lazio and James Milner from Aston Villa. Joe Hart became first-choice keeper, so Given was on his way out. Bellamy, too, left, going to Cardiff City on loan.

'We are getting there,' Mancini said to the Italian newspaper *La Repubblica* in August. 'Our team is a lot better, although some finishing touches are still needed.' After eight months in a hotel, Mancio had finally settled down in a big house in a residential area outside Manchester. He reflected that 'We had to rebuild the environment, mentality and all. But we have definitely begun walking down a new road, and we are very hopeful. We must start winning now. That's the only thing that's missing.' And in September, in a long interview with the *Daily Mail*, he spoke about his past successes. 'Manchester City is like Sampdoria,' he said. 'If we are successful, we change the history of this club and we change it for life. This is our moment. When people ask why do I come here, I tell them it is because Manchester City never win. For me, that is the best challenge. Inter Milan were a top team but they had not won the league for a long time; Lazio the same; Fiorentina the same; Sampdoria never win. These are good challenges because when you work for Real Madrid or Barcelona it is easy; all managers win at those clubs. But if you build a squad, work very hard for months and years at Manchester City and then you win, for me that would be more important. That would be fantastic.'

Winning would indeed be fantastic for a club that hadn't been in a final since 1981. Then, City lost the FA Cup final in a replay on 14 May, against the Tottenham of Glenn Hoddle, Ossie Ardiles and Ricky Villa. The Blues' last league title came in 1968, and their last major trophy was in 1976. The road to Wembley, and silverware, this year would prove just as fantastic.

For example, the semi-final against United. The Red Devils were dreaming of the treble, but left with shattered nerves. Scholes was sent off for a bad foul on Zabaleta; a dazed Carrick hit a poor pass that went straight to Yaya Toure, who immediately powered past him and scored the only goal of the game. Rooney and Giggs were absent, Park was disappointing, Balotelli's teasing got a rise out of Ferdinand, and Sir Alex Ferguson simply could not find an explanation for City's victory. The answer, however, was simple: Mancini's team prepared well for the match, and played equally well. They let the red jerseys play, waited for Berbatov to make mistakes, and then hit them with surgical precision, making them pay for their mistakes and their Champions League fatigue.

The performance in the Wembley final has been similarly impressive, played in front of a crowd of 88,643. Just to be here was a triumph for Stoke – no one would have expected it at the beginning of the season. It has been the Potters' first final in their 148-year history. And indeed, the 2011 incarnation of Sir Stanley Matthews and Gordon Banks's team falls short of greatness: they lack refinement, playing a stripped-down, rudimentary game and lacking great individual skills. They were not really up to the challenge. And they were not even able to field the line-up that beat Bolton Wanderers comprehensively (5–0) in the semi-final. Thus, it has been no great surprise that they failed to do much against opponents who are strong in every suit, boasting good players, skills, speed and attacking thrust.

Manchester City dominated the match from start to finish, while the men in red and white basically try to blunt their opponents' attacking threat. Carlos Tévez, not quite on top form (he only recovered from injury at the last minute), failed to shine on this occasion, but nonetheless had a good chance to score in the first half – as did Silva and Balotelli (who Mancini preferred to Milner).

In the second half, Stoke are a bit more assertive; they tried to threaten the City goal from Delap's usual long throws, and also with quick, direct counter-attacks. This last option almost brought success when Kenwyne Jones found himself one-on-one with Joe Hart. The blond keeper, though, was good enough – and lucky enough – to stop him. City were happy to wait, to keep possession and pass the ball from one side of the pitch to the other, waiting for spaces to open up. They remained patient and were eventually rewarded with Touré's goal, which gave the Blues the win without having to play extra time. In injury time, Mancini did the rest, bringing on Patrick Vieira and allowing him to claim his fifth cup, after the four he won at Arsenal. And it was the Frenchman who blocked Stoke's final attempt of the game, as they pushed forwards in desperation, Sørensen included. Touré, Wembley's hero, comments afterwards, 'We deserved to win this game because we created a lot of chances and played so well. This win is fantastic for us.'

It is fantastic for the whole team, because, as David Platt says on the BBC, 'that trophy gives to the dressing-room the winning mentality. What nobody can take away from the players is that they have won something.' It is fantastic for the crowd, too: 'Because now,' adds Platt, 'there are a lot of people driving back on the motorway, very happy because they won a major trophy, for the first time in 35 years.' It is, perhaps, especially fantastic for Mario Balotelli, because after the controversy surrounding his conduct in the semi-final, when he enraged the United supporters and players with his provocative behaviour (not for the first time, his manager came to his defence; 'It looks like it is always his fault,' Mancini said. 'What are we gonna do, send him to prison?'), he is officially named Man of the Match.

It is, of course, fantastic for Mancio, too, who can finally say 'mission accomplished'. In his second year in the City dugout, he has brought home a trophy, and he is in Europe, too. He has done what he promised; what the owners and the fans wanted him to do. It is an achievement that acts as a rebuke to all those who wanted his head on a silver plate, and silences the continuous speculation about his future. He has been careful and quick-witted, more so than his predecessors. And just as his team were in the match, he has been patient. His 'blue revolution', as some are already calling it, has already broken the monopoly of the 'Big Four', and is now bearing fruit, subverting the existing order. However, this is just the beginning. Everyone hopes that the revolution continues, and that more titles are coming to Eastlands. Starting with the Premier League.

'Bobby Goal'

A conversation with Attilio Lombardo

'I have been in Manchester since 5 July 2010. Since then, I have worked with Roberto and his other assistants, taking care of the techniques and tactics of the team on the football pitch. On Saturdays and Sundays, I go and watch matches, in England and abroad, in order to take a good look at our opponents' teams and players.'

This is how Attilio Lombardo explains his job at City, with extreme simplicity. He was born near Caserta, but he grew up in Zelo Buon Persico, a little village in the Lodi province. Attilio Lombardo is 46 today. He spent almost 20 years of his life as a right-winger for Pergocrema, Cremonese, Sampdoria, Lazio, and Juventus, winning the Italian championship with three different clubs – a rare achievement – plus various cups and a Champions League medal with the Turin side. After running up and down the wing, he went on to coach Chiasso, the Sampdoria youth team, Legnano and Spezia. For a brief spell in 1998 he was also player-manager at Crystal Palace.

Is it hard to be a coach in England?
'It is hard everywhere. Football is the same in most places, more or less, but what sets British football apart from other championships is its intensity. It is a totally different culture; it is sufficient to watch fans entering the football stadium, 15 minutes before the game. Sometimes, here, it seems to

me that people are going to a football match as if they were going to the theatre. I believe this is the most beautiful thing you can see happening in a stadium.'

Mancini has always been fascinated by British football too, is that right?
'I suppose almost everyone is. Roberto was always attracted to this kind of world. He gained experience as a player in Leicester, and perhaps that was the time when he realised that maybe, one day, he would like to work in the UK.'

What is Mancini like, as a manager?
'For those who played with him – and I did play with him, at Sampdoria and Lazio – Roberto was always managing the team, on the football pitch. I was curious to see him on the job, as a manager, day to day, though. At City, my guesses were confirmed: his ideas are the same ones that he held as a player. Roberto is a very competent manager, who pays no attention to others, and who can make the best out of the work carried out during the week. As he used to play as a striker, he loves having a very competitive team. Today, Roberto is at the height of his success. He won with Fiorentina, with Lazio, with Inter Milan and now here, in Manchester – definitely a bonus on his résumé. He is now among the greatest, he can only be compared to those who – just like him – have won a lot, all over the place. He is very much loved, I realised that in the last two years. There is no football stadium, no match, in which I haven't heard the fans chanting for Roberto.'

And as a person, what is Mr Mancini like?
'He is a great guy, with deep feelings and strong friendships. Sometimes he can be a bit annoying, but he has a good

heart, and he is a truly good person. He has great charisma, and, as people often say, he's a winner.'

In what ways is he different from how he used to be, when you played together?

'When you move over to the other side and become a manager, you become less impulsive and more reasonable. Roberto has undergone this transformation without losing the qualities he had as a playmaker on the football field, though. When you are with him, you always know when it is time to take resolute action and when, instead, you can just behave normally. It is that extra something that distinguishes a real manager.'

What is Mancini's creed, with regard to football?

'We saw it in the past seasons: ball possession, making sure the ball goes around, and finding the right times for striking. Roberto continuously pursues balance in defence, and when his opponents have the ball, he trains his guys to make sure they don't keep it for long. He demands great determination and purpose. You must be swift and sharp in counter-attack, and move quickly in tight spaces. We have been working on this at City, as Roberto really believes in these principles.'

How have these two years been?

'Fantastic. We won the FA Cup after 35 years, and the championship after 44. The only times that were emotionally draining for Roberto were the first four months, when he replaced Mark Hughes, and he still had to win people's respect. And, again, at the end of the 2009/10 season, when he couldn't qualify for the Champions League tournament. Other than that, everything was great, we only missed Europe. We didn't get through in the Champions League, nor in the Uefa Cup. In order to achieve that, you need mental and physical training, and a little bit of luck, too, as was the case with Chelsea in the 2011/12 season.'

Still, despite the last two 'fantastic' years, Mancini's job was often called into question.

'This normally happens in jobs like ours; you are always called into question, especially if you are part of a club which must be competitive until the end in order to win something. A lot of money was spent to reach certain aims, and we did reach them, albeit in the final minutes of the last match of the championship. Of course, what really bothered Roberto was that the names of other managers kept popping up during the season, even before the championship was over. However, this is the world of football, and I believe Roberto has been very good at living with these sorts of situations.'

And you, how did you live through those last five minutes?

'It was a complete and utter disaster. When the score was 1–2, I went into the changing room to watch the last bit of the game with Yaya Touré, so that I would have someone to share emotions and disappointments with.'

So, be completely honest, you didn't believe you could recover the score, did you?

'Well, no one did! You could read disappointment all over the faces of all those people who had flocked in to watch the match ... to lose a championship in a home game, after never ever losing in our own stadium! We were losing the Premier League on the last day, after dominating throughout the whole season, for many months ... we were losing a title we thoroughly deserved, too. It was not easy to take. Let's say it was a real drama. Then, we went from sadness to infinite joy and happiness. After Agüero scored, we leapt out of the changing rooms and went to the pitch, in order to celebrate with the staff and all those players who had made our dream come true.'

During the celebrations, you were caught waving a Sampdoria scarf. And, at the restaurant, you started the chanting.
'We were chanting away with long-time friends; we used to do that when we were at Samp. I did get Bobby Goal started ... but it is true, singing those tunes brought us back to old times, to those seasons when we wore a Blucerchiati jersey. Those were times when Roberto was worshipped, as a player.'

Noisy neighbours

6+1=7 is a simple sum; even a child in elementary school could do it. These are the goals that the 'noisy neighbours' scored in the Premier League against the other team from Manchester – the team who wear red, who play under Sir Alex Ferguson and who have won countless trophies over the years. The team representing what was, until recently, the richest football club in the world, with 330 million supporters all over the globe. In short, the team who are not used to losing against sad old City.

But lose they do. Indeed, they only manage to score one goal against the defence set up by Mancini. So it is 6–1 at Old Trafford, on 23 October 2011, and 1–0 at Eastlands on 30 April 2012. Dates, and scorelines, that frame and summarise a whole season and an incredible head-to-head race between City and United, between Mancini and Ferguson. It is a season just like these two Manchester derbies: full of goals and excitement. A season worth reviewing in slow motion.

7 August 2011. Not even four months have passed since the two halves of Manchester faced each other in the FA Cup semi-finals. Now they are due to meet again. This time, the Red Devils and Citizens are playing for the Community Shield. In their last two visits to Wembley, United have lost: in the City semi and in the 2011 Champions League final against Barcelona. It looks like history will repeat itself when, at the end of the first half, Ferguson's team are 2–0 down (Joleon Lescott and Edin Dzeko with the goals), but

they recover in the second half. After 94 minutes, Nani of Portugal scores the winner. The first trophy of the season is Manchester United's.

15 August 2011. The first day of the Premier League season. At home, City dominate and beat Swansea 4–0.

24 August 2011. Samir Nasri arrives at Eastlands from Arsenal, for £25 million. After Sergio Agüero (€45 million, from Atletico Madrid), he is the most important (and expensive) purchase for City during the transfer window.

28 August 2011. Tottenham 1 Manchester City 5; Manchester United 8 Arsenal 2. Two shocking results for the London clubs. Two results that state, emphatically where the power lies within the Premier League.

27 September 2011. Carlos Tévez apparently refuses to play in a Champions League match against Bayern Munich (although the Argentinian will later claim that he only refused to warm up). Roberto Mancini states that he won't play for City ever again. El Apache leaves for Buenos Aires, where he will stay for three-and-a-half months. He will come back and wear his blue jersey again on 21 March, in order to help his teammates defeat Chelsea.

23 October 2011. Act 1: Manchester United 1 Manchester City 6. Balotelli (2), Agüero, Dzeko (2) Silva. Super Mario, who has been on all the newspapers' front pages for setting his house on fire while trying to light fireworks, lifts his shirt after his first goal to reveal a t-shirt saying 'Why always me?' – and promptly gets a yellow card. It is the first home defeat for United since April 2010, when they lost against Chelsea, and their worst result ever since 1955, when they lost 5–0 to

(funnily enough) City. The Red Devils hadn't conceded six goals at Old Trafford since 1930, when Huddersfield won there 6–0 and Newcastle 7–4. Sir Alex Ferguson comments, 'It is the worst result in my entire history. I can't believe the scoreline. Even as a player I don't think I ever lost 6–1.' He adds that 'it was a horrible defeat but it was suicidal.' Despite the shellacking, he is persuaded that 'we will react, no question about that. It's a perfect result for us to react to because there is a lot of embarrassment in the dressing-room and that will make an impact. That's a challenge for me too.' City are now top of the league, five points ahead of their neighbours in red. But Ferguson swears, 'We'll come back. We usually get the show on the road in the second half of the season and that will have to be the case.'

Roberto Mancini, the winner, treads carefully. He is not easily excited and claims that Ferguson's team are still the favourites for the title because of their history of winning. 'United are still one yard above us and we can only change this if we win the title,' says the Italian. 'After that it might be different but until then United are better than us. I still have big respect for United and for their squad. There are still four or five teams who can win the title and the season is long.' In other words, it is mandatory to avoid getting carried away, although reality cannot be denied: 'I am satisfied because we beat United away. I don't think there are a lot of teams that can win here. This is important for our squad and I am happy for the three points – but in the end it is three points: we don't take six points.' He throws a wet blanket over, as ought to be done in these cases, but he does let go over Mario Balotelli, the player that he wanted at City at all costs: 'I think Mario played very well. If we want to talk about Mario as a football player, I think we can put him among the first five players in the world. The problem is that he is young and can make mistakes.'

7 December 2011. City win in a home match against Bayern Munich, the final fixture in their Champions League group. However, this is the end of their European experience, as City don't get through to the last 16. Their 2–1 defeat against Napoli at the San Paolo Stadium in the penultimate match proved decisive.

12 December 2011. City's first defeat in the league. Despite a goal by Super Mario, Chelsea win 2–1. After a 14-match unbeaten run (12 wins and 2 draws), the blue charge is halted; they will recover quickly though, beating Arsenal 1–0 in their next match.

26 December 2011. City draw in an away match against West Bromwich Albion. United go level with them at the top of the league, on 45 points. 'It was crazy to expect that we could keep such an impossible pace,' Mancini argues in an end-of-year interview with *Gazzetta dello Sport*. 'We are only sorry that we lost points where we least deserved it. We were unlucky against Chelsea, while against West Bromwich Albion we dominated the match for 90 minutes, and for once, we didn't score. Only once did I see our team in difficulty: in the match against Liverpool, in the last 20 minutes, when we were down to ten men. In any case, it is better to be caught up with on Boxing Day than at Easter.'

With this fixture, the adopted Brit from the Marche region marks his two-year anniversary at City. He takes stock. 'We have been growing together,' he says. 'Myself as a man; while City have grown as a team. After 30 years of football in my own country, it has been really important to deal with such an experience abroad. One becomes a better professional, and a better man. I might sound naïve, but I believe I am more civic-minded these days, and I also stepped up in class as a manager.'

8 January 2012. City against United. Another derby, this time in the third round of the FA Cup. The Red Devils have lost their last two league games, against Blackburn and Newcastle, but this time they have their way against the Citizens. Ferguson puts his trust in Giggs's class and Rooney's charisma. Paul Scholes, 37, is also sitting on the bench: although he had bidden farewell to football the previous summer, the ginger magician has been recalled by the Scotsman, who was missing a reliable midfielder. After 59 minutes, when the score is already 3–0 to United and City are down to ten men following Vincent Kompany's sending-off for a dangerous tackle on Nani, Scholes enters the field of play to an ovation from the fans – including famous ones like David Beckham, Roy Keane and Phil Neville. In the pouring rain, City score two goals, perhaps putting the final result in some doubt. But in the end there is too much for them to do. The Blues are out. United go through to the last 16, and the returning Scholes will be a key component of the team for the rest of the season.

25 January 2012. Manchester City go out of the League Cup, too. In the semi-final second leg at Anfield, Liverpool and City draw, with former Blue Craig Bellamy scoring for the Merseysiders. In the end, the crucial stroke was the penalty kick scored by Steven Gerrard in the first leg at the Etihad Stadium.

11 March 2012. City lose 1–0 against Swansea and for the first time since October they slip from first place in the table. For Mancini's team, the hardest month begins, the one in which everything will seem lost; in which the team – what with injuries, suspensions, bad luck, bad shape and an inability to score – seems to have no options left. Like a badly cooked soufflé, they fall, both at home and in Europe.

15 March 2012. Manchester City 3 Sporting Lisbon 2. In the Europa League, thanks to a 1–0 scoreline in the first leg, the Portuguese team go through on away goals. There is nothing doing for City.

24 March 2012. From 35 yards, Peter Crouch scores with an impossible volley – one of the most beautiful goals the Premier League has seen. It is worth Stoke's draw against City.

31 March 2012. The Blues' home game against Sunderland ends 3–3. For Mancini, this is the turning point of the whole season. 'We were down 3–1 but thanks to Mario and Aleksandar we are able to equalise,' he says. 'That result was important because it was a lesson of character. I thank Balotelli and Kolarov for those two goals.'

8 April 2012. Mario Balotelli loses his head and is sent off again, making Arsenal's job much easier: Wenger's team win 1–0. Super Mario risks being suspended for six games and Mancini says that he won't have him on the City team anymore. Even if his suspension is reduced, he won't wear a blue jersey again. Still, Balotelli is the least of his worries. United beat QPR and now, with only six league games remaining, they are eight points ahead of City. The title race appears to be over. Mancini is asked whether he concedes the Premier League title. He answers that 'It's not mathematically over. It's clear now that it's very difficult. We have a game in three days and we will try to win. Never say never in football.'

It sounds like a reference to the Bond film starring Sean Connery, the actor that Mancio loves. Yet it will prove particularly appropriate come the end of the season. Even though everyone is saying that the championship is over, that there is unrest in the City dressing-room and Mancini will be out of a job come the summer, in three days things will look very different indeed.

11 April 2012. Wigan Athletic defeat Manchester United 1–0 at the DW Stadium. This has never happened before, ever. City dismiss West Brom 4–0. So the points gap between the two Manchester clubs is now down to five. And Mancini, knowing and feeling that the pressure will rise, sings a different tune. 'I fight always, every day and so do my team but now I think it's too late,' he says in a press conference after the Blues' success at the Etihad Stadium. It is the right attitude, while City are flying high.

14 April 2012. City win 6–1 away at Norwich, with a rehabilitated Carlos Tévez scoring a hat-trick.

22 April 2012. Another City victory, this time 2–0 against Wolves, who are the first team to be relegated. Unbelievably, while City are winning, United waste a two-goal lead over Everton at Old Trafford. The final score is 4–4. The game is not yet up.

30 April 2012. 'Big Monday'. The greatest derby, the one that will go down in history: a lot more than a local competition, a lot more than the previous 163 derbies. This time, the match is worth a big chunk of the title. When the final whistle blows, Vincent Kompany, the captain, who scored the winner with a header 47 minutes into the game, from a Silva corner, goes down on his knees. Roberto Mancini says, 'We wanted to win and they wanted a draw. They had all their players behind the ball. That is the difference. We wanted to win, we played better and we took our chances.'

The man who has been accused of playing defensively a number of times is now criticising the manager who says that his team always attacks. It is the law of retaliation, a clash of generations and ideas, which ignited at pitchside, too. After Nigel De Jong brought down Danny Welbeck, Sir Alex complained animatedly. Mancio was not happy and waved him off with his hand. Ferguson responded in kind, and the stewards – together with the fourth official – had to come between them. The episode cannot spoil Mancini and City's party. With two games left to the end of the season, they join their eternal rivals at the top of the league. They have won the second act, too. Previously, United had not lost both their league derbies since 1970.

6 May 2012. At St James Park, Mancini dances at the end of the game and his supporters go mad. City have overcome their penultimate obstacle, winning 2–0 against Newcastle. By the same scoreline, United beat Swansea. Now the table reads 86 points for Manchester City, 86 points for Manchester United. But the Citizens' goal difference, which is better by eight goals, gives them the edge. Everything will be decided on Sunday 13 May, when United play Sunderland away, while City face QPR at the Etihad Stadium. Mancini sets everyone on the defensive. 'It's not finished yet,' he says. 'If we think we have won the championship, it will be a big mistake. All the players have to keep their feet on the floor.' However, he admits that they are favourites for the title, saying, 'If we beat QPR, we are champions. It doesn't depend on what Manchester United do any more, it depends on us.'

Sir Alex Ferguson asserts, 'We'll go to Sunderland to win; it's our duty and responsibility. It could be like Devon Loch [the racehorse that famously collapsed when leading the Grand National] – stranger things have happened in football. We just have to keep going with the right spirit. We've won the title on three occasions on the last day and we don't mind doing it again. They're red-hot favourites and will make sure they win the match.' Fergie is really pinning his hopes on the one who was dismissed to make room for Mancini. He is hoping his former player Mark Hughes will lend him a helping hand, and he says it without mincing his words: 'Mark was sacked by City in a very unethical way and he'll remember that. Mark Hughes's teams always fight, but QPR need a point and his players are fighting for survival.'

For now, Ferguson can still hold out a slim hope that his team will triumph against the odds, but in the end he will have to accept what the City supporters are keen to say to him, spelt out on a banner: 'The noisy neighbours are getting louder, Alex.'

Stepping up in class

A conversation with Roberto Martínez

'Big Monday, what about it? It was awesome. Possibly, one of the most important games in the history of both clubs. The apex of a centennial rivalry. Because on 30 April 2012, both United and City could still win the Premiership; the two best teams in the league were facing each other, those teams that will go on and compete for the title in the coming years, too. Players like Carlos Tévez, who have worn both clubs' jersey, ended up generating even more tension.'

This is the opinion of the Wigan manager, who undoubtedly had his hand in the final push for the title on behalf of United and City. It is hard to forget that his guys won 1–0 against the Red Devils in the DW Stadium, thereby reopening a title race that looked to be all over.

The Catalan Roberto Martínez came to England in 1995 to play for Wigan, and ended up starring for the club, together with Jesús Seba and Isidro Diaz. The 'Three Amigos' did it to save their team, and they succeeded: the Latics not only survived; they built on that success and have now been in the highest division of British football for the past three seasons, with Martínez as manager. However, it is impossible to forget their satisfaction in defeating their glorious neighbours, the great Manchester United. All in all, Roberto Martínez is well placed to comment on the duel between City and United, starting from 23 October 2011, the day of that 6–1 win.

'At Old Trafford, for about 20–25 minutes, United were definitely playing better football. City defended well, and they were insidious on counter-attack. The fact that Jonny Evans was sent off, the fact that they were playing with ten men for almost all of the second half, did affect the final score, turning it into something no one would have ever imagined. At Eastlands though, in the FA Cup match, it was just the opposite. City tried to wrap up the match in the first half of the game, but couldn't settle the score and United had a couple of masterstrokes on the counter-attack. When Kompany was sent off, everyone thought that United would be in for an easy stroll, but Mancini changed the outline and the tactics of the team, making life difficult for Ferguson. In fact, the match finished 3–2, a decent result for them. For 'Big Monday', I was expecting a balanced match, because surely both clubs would have learnt from the previous encounters. It was going to be a game in which United would not be ready to take many risks, and City were going to wait for the right chance to strike. In other words, I was expecting the match to be decided by a masterstroke, by an individual moment, by a strategic action. And that's what happened, a corner kick settled the score.'

How do you judge this Premier League, won on the final day? Was it a poor one, as there were only two clubs really competing for the title, and the other claimants disappeared quite quickly?
'Actually, it was quite the contrary. I believe it was a highly competitive championship. This is proved by the amount of points earned by both City and United. In other seasons, fewer points were needed to secure the title. Liverpool, Arsenal, Chelsea, Tottenham did not disappear; only, they had to fight for the other two places to qualify for the Champions League, because they simply couldn't keep up with City and United, who were going great. Even though

they had their ups and downs, they still kept up a hellish pace.'

Sir Alex Ferguson and Roberto Mancini – a few comments.
'They are two different managers, sharing one feature in common: in order to manage teams like United or City, you must be a born leader. And they both are. Possibly, Ferguson has the greatest decision-making skills; it is his natural virtue. He knows when to make the right choice, at the right time. Roberto Mancini, on the other hand, can read a match like only few people can. Therefore, he will help his players to achieve positive results. And he is also very good at putting his tactical ideas across to others in a clear, simple way.'

You lost both games against City in the Premier League, both home and away. What did you think of Mancini's team, then?
'The first time we played against them it was very early in the season, on 10 September. They were absolutely in top shape, both physically and mentally, and some players like Silva and Agüero were just phenomenal. We had no chances to win. Just like everyone else, really. In the first half of the season, City were overwhelming. In the second match, though, City were less confident, they played less smoothly – in short, they weren't 100 per cent. They still managed to defeat us, though, and this goes to Mancini's credit for being able to handle the team through hard times as well, nevertheless obtaining a good score.'

But how did Mr Mancini change City?
'Well, first of all, he definitely did, that's for sure. He made them step up in class; he brought in players with international experience, who had already won titles before, who knew what it meant to be competitive. He built a high-

quality group. But the most important thing, in my opinion, is that Mancini introduced some new techniques and tactics to work on, over time, and with a lot of patience. And, little by little, he created a solid team, capable of defending well. Then he added some creative players, who gave some extra strength and balance to his plan.'

What kind of techniques and tactics are you referring to?
'He created a wonderful mix between Italian mentality, his technical heritage and British football. And those ideas, joined together, worked well. I believe Mancini was very thorough in applying some concepts to his team's play: the way you take control of a match, ball possession, and putting defence first. He suggested having a six-man defence: a back four and two defensive midfielders. And based on this solid defence (it is extremely hard to score against Manchester City), he developed his attack strategies, with high-quality, really fast-paced players, who can penetrate the opponents' lines and create scoring chances.'

Who were the players who were fundamental for Mancini's plan?
'Carlos Tévez, in the 2010/11 season, had both a role and an influence which were most important for the team. At his best, he was unstoppable. Last year, at least for two-thirds of the season, David Silva was sensational, and he really added that extra something to the group. Then his performance dropped, because of some physical issues and the fact that he had to adapt his body to the necessities of the Premier League. There are four tournaments going on simultaneously here: our calendar is packed. We play on Tuesdays and Saturdays and our matches are of a different intensity from the ones in La Liga. It is obvious that, if you play for over 3,000 minutes, and your body is not used to that, your performance decreases.'

Right, Tévez: he was fundamental, but then he was also in the eye of the storm last year, with all that controversy. Just like Mario Balotelli. What's your opinion on them?

'In this case, my observations are those of a simple bystander, because I have no other elements to comment on what happened. I can say that I liked the position of the club, i.e. defending the manager and putting the footballer second. Players have a lot of power nowadays, and only a few clubs dare to question that. Only a few would behave like City have done. In the Tévez case, they sent out a loud and very important warning to the football world: a player who refuses to play is a bad example for any young athlete. And I also think Roberto handled the Balotelli case really well, a guy with great potential, who is growing up, but who needs to face up to his responsibilities, on and off the football pitch.'

What did winning the Premier League mean for City?

'It was an incredible achievement for a club that has suffered so much in the last 15 years. It is enough to remember their two relegations, or the intense play-off at Wembley to climb back up into the higher division. Until a couple of seasons ago, it would have been impossible for City to win the Premier League. Impossible, just as it was to measure up to United. Winning the title meant seeing the end of a long ordeal. It was a reward for those fans who had always supported the team, while putting up with United's triumphs. Sure, the club put a lot of money into this project, and not only into the first team. However, purchasing high-level players is relatively easy today; what's more difficult is changing the group's and the club's mentality, in order to lead them to victory. This is the great job that Mancini did: turning City into a competitive team, with great mental strength, now able to go on and win other titles.'

94 minutes, an entire lifetime

There were men and women losing their faith and leaving, swearing against the entire world as they walked away. Others looked to the heavens, their hands joined together in prayer. Unbounded joy rolled out of a pub. A child covered his eyes, not wanting to see what happened next. Another sat on his daddy's shoulders, screaming, with his fists in the air. Thousands of people danced to a tune which had no music, but plenty of words. A captain spoke about miracles happening, and a manager spoke about God. A fan said that if God exists, He must support Man City. A woman appeared to be in shock, as numb as if she had just escaped from a terrible accident. Another, heavily pregnant, was saying that she couldn't take it anymore. For a moment, there was true happiness. And desperation, too. Black men and white men, stripped to the waist, hugged each other. Big and muscly men, covered in tattoos, cried like babies. A young Argentinian, half naked, flew a blue kite inside the stadium. A parked car was kicked, again and again, in a deserted alley. There was rage, in the same old tales of bitterness and regret. A dream fell apart, and was born again. A movie that had been anticipated for 44 years reached its climax. A goalkeeper ran wildly all over the football field. People in blue-and-black jerseys emblazoned with the Aon logo and the Red Devil crest looked on the verge of tearing their hair out. A roar came from one side of town, while silence fell on the other. There were family celebrations on a green lawn. The past ended, and the future began. Pints were downed, cigarettes were smoked, nails were bitten. Scarves and hats were worried and torn at by nervous hands. Emotions rose, dipped and rose again as on a rollercoaster. Out came the same old sentiments that have been going around forever, about an illness called City-itis, and how easy it is to hurt oneself. Somewhere, a sheikh watched his £1 billion investment on TV. Scarves, jerseys, hats and flags were waved as if they had suddenly become a symbol for future hope. Shirts with 'champions' printed on them were thrown in the bin. Others, with 'pride goes to war' written on them, were retained. A manager wore his national flag around his neck, trying to escape when one of his players went to soak him with Champagne. In a moving tableau, he then stood next to the silver trophy, accompanied by his mother and father, while photos were taken. Fathers told their sons, 'One day, you will be able to tell your grandchildren "I was there".' Piccadilly Gardens appeared painted in sky blue, on a night of celebration. Older men, sitting in the pubs, drank and sang 'Blue Moon' until they had no voice left. One old man said, 'I never imagined I could have a day like this, in my entire life.' A younger man said, 'I'm not going into work tomorrow; they'll be partying for a week at least' while another said, 'Tomorrow I'll be turning up happy for work – how great will it be to see all those fucking Devils?' Smartphones were white-hot, trying to convey all that was going on to a faraway place, burning with anxiety, and willingness to bet on the next winner or loser. Many felt that not even Alfred Hitchcock could have come up with such a perfect thriller. A couple had an argument: him saying, 'It's all over. There is nothing left to do'; her replying that, in life, one should keep one's hope until the very end – things can always change. And, as he obviously wanted the last say, he added, 'This is football, and you don't know anything about football.'

This is what football can do. And the Manchester City–Queens Park Rangers match at the Etihad Stadium on 13 May 2012, the final day of the Premier League season, provided all this and more.

The facts

The events of the afternoon were played out as follows.

3pm. Kick-off in the final round of fixtures in the 2011/12 Premier League. Manchester City are home to QPR, Manchester United are playing away against Sunderland.

3.20pm. Sunderland 0 Man Utd 1
Wayne Rooney, with a header, beats Sunderland keeper Mignolet to put the Red Devils ahead in the race for the title.

3.39pm. Man City 1 QPR 0
Paddy Kenny, the Rangers keeper, tries to clear Pablo Zabaleta's shot but can only help it into his own net. City have their noses in front again.

4.06pm. Man City 1 QPR 1
Djibril Cissé equalises. As things stand, United will top the table. QPR, meanwhile, will be safe from relegation.

4.13pm. QPR's Joey Barton is sent off after elbowing Carlos Tevez and sticking a knee in the back of Sergio Agüero. Rangers are down to ten men.

4.24pm. Man City 1 QPR 2
Connecting with a cross by Armand Traoré, Jamie Mackie finds the back of Joe Hart's net with a headed goal. It appears all over for City. QPR look to have ensured their safety.

4.50pm Man City 2 QPR 2
Edin Dzeko has just come on, but it doesn't take long for him to get on the end of a corner kick and head it into the net. We are one minute and 15 seconds into injury time. But with Manchester United still leading at Sunderland, a draw will not be enough: City need to score again.

4.51pm Stoke 2 Bolton 2
The match at the Britannia Stadium ends. Bolton needed to take all three points if they were to avoid relegation. Their failure to do so means that QPR are now safe, regardless of their own result.

4.51pm. Sunderland 0 Man United 1
The final whistle blows at the Stadium of Light, and the Red Devils are on the brink of being confirmed champions. Sir Alex Ferguson and his players wait for news from the Etihad Stadium.

4.52pm. Man City 3 QPR 2
Sergio Agüero, through a forest of legs, finds enough space to beat Kenny. His goal brings City the title. It is four minutes into injury time.

4.53 Mike Dean blows the final whistle, and City win the Premier League after 44 years. QPR, although defeated, are safe.

The men
The names never to be forgotten, the protagonists of this incredible story were:

Manchester City: J. Hart, P. Zabaleta, V. Kompany, J. Lescott, G. Clichy, D. Silva, Y. Touré (N. de Jong 44), G. Barry (E. Dzecko 69), S. Nasri, C. Tévez (M. Balotelli 76), S. Agüero.

Queens Park Rangers: P. Kenny, N. Onuoha, A. Ferdinand, C. Hill, T. Taiwo, J. Mackie, J. Barton, S. Derry, S. Wright-Phillips, R. Zamora (J. Bothoroyd 76), D. Cissé (A. Traoré 59).

The words
In the aftermath, Roberto Mancini summed up his emotions as follows: 'Five minutes from the end, I didn't think we could win this game, but it was a crazy finish to a crazy season. I have never seen a final like this. I think we changed the history of this club. I'm very proud of my players, because I know that they wanted to win the title. They worked hard for this ... The best team won, in the end. We played the best football. We beat United two times. We scored more goals than them, and conceded fewer goals than them. We deserved to win. We deserved this, for our supporters. But next time, it may be better to win five minutes before. It was the best, but never again, not this way. This was very hard. I feel 90 years old now!'

A winning frame of mind

A conversation with Pablo Zabaleta

He hasn't scored a single goal throughout the whole season. After all, that's not his job: he is a defender. Then comes the last match in the championship, the really important one, the 90 minutes in which the Premier League result will be decided. He moves forward on the right wing, just like he has done so many times during the year, and he strikes the ball. It is half-cross, half-shot, somewhat crooked, but nevertheless beats the Queens Park Rangers keeper. This goal seems to finally put paid to Manchester United's title challenge and give City the breathing space they need. Now they can relax and play their game; they need only hold on to this lead and the title will be theirs.

What were your thoughts, after scoring that opening goal?
'I was over the moon, of course, for scoring in such a decisive match. And I thought, just as everyone else did, that the match was taking a turn for the best. In other words, I hoped that we would live happily ever after.'

And then …
'Then they equalise, and they score a second goal as well. Although we keep attacking, creating one chance after another, we cannot finish any of them. Then, after 90 minutes, the referee adds five minutes' injury time, and you know very well that scoring two goals in five minutes is unlikely –

314

let's say impossible – even though the team is giving everything to recover the result. You can see the opportunity to
become champions fading away; your hopes are vanishing as
the seconds go by. And then, the incredible happens.'

El Kun scores.
'I remember I fell flat on the field from the excitement. I
really could not describe those moments ... during the last
minutes of such a match, the first thing that comes to your
mind are your dear ones, your family, all those who helped
you and made incredible efforts to stand beside you always.'

Pablo Zabaleta, 27, comes from Buenos Aires. He already
has many football matches under his belt, on both sides of
the Atlantic and indeed on both sides of the English
Channel. But he never experienced anything like this, and
he believes that he will never again see a match like that
13 May 2012 clash between Manchester City and Queen's
Park Rangers.

Zabaleta has collected many honours: with the Argentina
team he won the Under-20 World Cup in the Netherlands,
where his teammate, one Lionel Messi, was starting to get
himself noticed. Also with the Albiceleste – and again with
his friends Leo and El Kun – there was the gold medal in
the 2008 Beijing Olympics. Still, the Premier League is the
most prestigious club title he has ever won. Neither with the
Argentinians of San Lorenzo nor with the Catalans of RCD
Espanyol had he reached such heights.

Zabaleta arrived in Manchester from Spain in August
2008, because – as he puts it – it was impossible to turn down
City's offer. And in November 2011 he renewed his contract,
without having to think twice, until the summer of 2015.

'I am happy in Manchester, it's good here,' he says. 'We
used to meet up often with Carlos and Sergio. We founded a

little Argentinian colony around here, although I love English culture and football. In the Premier League, contrary to the Spanish Liga, football is more physical. You are always challenging for the ball, it is a more dynamic sport. I have been playing for four years here now, and I think I've got used to it.'

Zabaleta started his City career under Mark Hughes, but it was with Mancini that he won trophies.

What are the differences between Mancini and Hughes?
'Well, they have different personalities and two different ways of looking at football. A player can't do anything but adapt to his manager's ideas.'

Were Mancini's first days quite complicated?
'When a manager starts in a new club, it is always complicated. He needs time to do his job, to get his ideas through to the club and the team, to build a new plan and a competitive group – in other words, to create a team that can match up to expectations.'

What did the Italian bring to the team?
'A winning frame of mind. He is quite temperamental, a person with a strong character, and that was evident straight away. In order to achieve prestigious titles, you must raise the bar, and Mancini helped us in that respect. What's more, as seems to be the case with most Italian managers, he made some changes to our tactics, to the way we behaved on the football pitch, and that really emerged in the last season. Our way of playing has definitely improved.'

Mancini is said to start building his teams by putting defence first …
'Sure, he starts from defence and works his way towards attack. For me, his way of thinking was fundamental.'

What kind of advice did he give you?
'He especially insists – and not only with me – on intensity, on facing up to each game with great passion. During the week, we work on specific patterns of play, tailored towards the opponent we are going to face. This is something that Mancini is really good at doing.'

What was the most difficult moment in the 2011/12 season
'I believe it was the whole Tevez affair; the only tiny flaw we experienced in the last season.'

You know El Apache very well. How did it all come to that?
'It was a recurrent issue, that grew and grew in magnitude, until it became too big to handle. It hurt Carlos, the club, everyone: a real pity. Luckily, in the end, El Apache came back, started scoring and helped the team with the Premier League.'

The best moment?
'I would say that the most positive thing was the determination showed by the team. Even when Manchester United were eight points ahead, we never stopped believing that we could do it, that we could win the league.'

At times like those, Mancini – according to the British press – was a mastermind, playing his cards just right, denying any chance of a recovery. Did that help to take pressure off the team?
'Mancini did a great psychologist's job for us. To the media, he said that it was impossible to catch up with Manchester United, but for us on the team, the hidden message was quite different.'

Who impressed you most among your teammates, this year?
'David Silva. I knew him already; we played against each

other when I played at Espanyol and he was with Valencia. Now, as a teammate, I can say he is a crack player. He is a football genius.'

And Balotelli?

'He is an amazing player; physically he is very fit, but you never know what's going on in his head. With Mario, you never know what is going to happen. He can be sent off after five minutes of the first half, or win a match all by himself. With him, there is never a middle ground.'

How do you see the future for City?

'We are coming from a wonderful season, having earned a title that the club has not held for 44 years. We saw our supporters' happiness, their joy on the streets of Manchester on the day of the parade. People had been waiting for that moment for so many years. Let's hope we can match that next year. Let's hope we can win again. That's right: there is an ambitious future waiting for us now.'

Absolutely amazing

Clouds are running fast through the sky above Manchester. White and fluffy, or dark and stormy, they come and go, making room for blue skies. Traffic cones are scattered through the city centre, yellow-jacketed figures stand on every crossroad. Access is denied to Princess Street, Portland Street, Deansgate, St Mary's Gate and Corporation Street. It is Monday 14 May 2012, 1.30pm. At Albert Square, everyone has been working since dawn. Over the frontage of the Town Hall – otherwise a monument to the city's Victorian past – hangs a huge poster: Manchester City's official team photo, with the word 'together'. Just across the square, a swarm of cameras, aerials and mobile units. Cameramen and technicians are already down to business. Crowd barriers are already in place, to keep people out of the square.

A man wearing black is making sure no one gets through. He explains that 'The victory parade begins here at 6.30pm, just about the same time Manchester United's players will be sitting down for their end-of-season awards dinner.' He adds that it will be the greatest Blue party the city has ever seen: 'Forget the 50,000 who were here after the FA Cup last year. Today, up to 100,000 people might turn up here!' He is kind and well informed, and he's not finished yet. 'Everything will begin at around 4pm,' he explains, 'with music and various entertainment, waiting for 6pm, when City's players and manager Mancini will emerge' – he points at the Town Hall – 'to present the trophy and to give a question-and-answer session before boarding an open-top bus for the parade.'

There are still two-and-a-half hours to go: time to take a quick look at the papers. 'Blue Heaven but Reds hell as City snatch title in last seconds,' reads the headline in the *Manchester Evening News*. 'Miracle Man: 7.30 City boss prays, 4.53pm injury time title winner' is the *Sun*'s first page, accompanied by a photo of Mancio between Balotelli and Kompany. It tells the exclusive story of the Sunday morning mass attended by devout Catholic Roberto Mancini, together with two other players, at Manchester's Holy Name Church. It does not forget to mention his pilgrimage to Medjugorje back in March (he will return in June with his wife Federica and daughter Camilla). The *Daily Telegraph* goes with 'before' and 'after' shots of Mancini, with the caption 'He thought it was all over ... but it wasn't' and, in the sports pages, 'Miracle Manc: City end 44-year title hoodoo with most dramatic finale in history.' 'Blue Sunday: late goals bring City's first league title for 44 years' is the choice for the *Guardian*, while its supplement features the headline 'Paradise City'. 'Epic finale to City's quest for Premier League glory,' is *The Times*'s take on it, with, afterwards, 'For Mancini's crazy gang every last second counts.'

For any City supporter, it is immensely rewarding to go through the papers on such a morning: history, statistics, epic drama, comment, opinion, match reports, rumours. Some of the opinions expressed by journalists and pundits regarding Mancini are particularly interesting. 'I've not been his biggest fan,' writes Alan Hansen in the *Telegraph*, 'but he did what was asked of him yesterday – on the biggest day of all – and gave City their lifeline when it mattered by bringing on Edin Dzeko. It set up that incredible final five minutes of added time and I already fancy City to retain their title next season.' Alan Shearer, in the *Sun*, exclaims, 'What a great job Mancini has done. People go on about City buying the title, rather forgetting the tens of millions Manchester United have lavished on players down the years.' Richard Williams, for the *Guardian*, writes, 'All charm and *bella figura* in front of the cameras, Mancini is a hard nut who does exactly what it takes to achieve his ambitions. Not many managers, having declared that Tévez and Balotelli would never play for the club again, could have swallowed their pride so readily and restored the miscreants to the team sheet when the going got tough and City needed goalscorers.' *The Times*'s Matt Dickinson, meanwhile, wrote, 'Mancini's capabilities? City know they have a manager of serious purpose, single-mindedness, ambition and, they confidently assert, integrity. A man who can envision the path that will turn City into Champions League winners whether or not he can guide them there. What is undeniable is what is most important of all, a steady progress.'

Persuaded or not, everyone gives it up for Mancini the winner – who also receives Khaldoon's compliments on this Blue Monday. The chairman says, 'I've grown very close to Roberto over the years. I know how he works. He wants to win more than anyone I have ever seen. He is so driven towards winning it gives you confidence and an incredible amount of energy. He is a strong character, who will do a lot of great things for this club.'

But what about all these Blues who are now swarming through and taking over Manchester city centre? What do they think of their manager now? They come fully armed: scarves, jerseys, balloons, horns, blue wigs, 'Balotelli' wigs, banners and signs, which do not spare United, nor Ferguson. 'Thank God for Fergie Time, reads one; 'Forget Fergie time, it's Mancini's time' is another. There is also an 'R.I.P. Fergie', which Carlos Tévez receives from a fan and hangs on their open-top bus. It will obviously ignite more controversy with their neighbours, but still. The fans are happy, the painful knot that has gathered and tightened over 44 years has now come undone, leaving only a great joy. They all queue up outside the City shop, where the sky-blue and red-and-black jerseys hang proudly in the shop window, printed with the number 12 and 'Champions' above. For those trying to save money, there are peddlers on every street corner, with their little stalls set up on supermarket trolleys, selling all merchandise imaginable: horns, jerseys, scarves with 'Noisy Neighbour' on them, or 'Manchester City: Champions of Manchester, Kings of England.'

By the 'Top Dog' stand, supporters are eating hot dogs under a giant poster of Mancini eating a sausage. They swarm noisily, like children out of school, along Prince Street. They take all the seats in the pubs, preparing for what will come next, right into the night. And no one holds back when it comes to talking about their manager. 'He is God,' says a woman in a Kun Agüero jersey. Her friend, sitting next to her, adds, 'I love him.' 'Forget Mourinho, forget everyone else, Roberto is the best,' shouts Steve, a guy who has come from Aberdeen for the party. 'Good, very good manager,' screams someone who overheard the conversation. And another one insists, 'Mancini is the man. Mancini is City's salvation.' A noisy gathering, when invited to comment on the manager, starts singing 'In the Blue, Painted Blue', the Mancini version. And it doesn't sound like they'll be stopping anytime soon, either. 'Amazing, absolutely amazing' is the sentiment expressed most often, together with 'Brilliant', 'Fantastic', 'Lovely', while one person, on realising there is an Italian in their midst, tries to resort to Dante's noble language: 'Bellissimo, Bravissimo.'

'He looks good, he is competitive, calm, and has a great CV both as a player and as a manager. Wherever he went, he won, and he did the same with City. In two-and-a-half seasons, he gave us two titles that we hadn't seen for an entire lifetime,' says Irishman Kevin, a tall and gangly guy. John, standing next to him, adds, 'He turned some good and great players into a real team, not just a sum of individuals. He brought trust into the club, and I imagine that, behind closed doors, his Italian passion played its share in that, too.' Paul, born in 1968, the year of City's last First Division title, joins the conversation: 'Mancini was great in dealing with all the mind games. When we were eight points under, or even five, he kept repeating over and over again: we cannot win the league. A perfect bluff, called by a great poker player. He's very clever and very cunning, Mancini is. What's more, he has a sense of humour, something that most Premier League managers surely lack.' 'Look at how he handled the war of words with Fergie; it was just incredible,' opines Kenny. 'And he hammered him on the field, too. That 6–1 really drove me out of my mind.' Mark, a man with a big beer belly and tattooed arms, says, 'I liked him from the very start, because right from the beginning he understood where he was, he understood City's history and tradition. It makes you feel proud of being part of our club.' 'He is a great motivator, and a brilliant strategist,' holds Jenny. 'He never made a bad move. Look at last night when he played Dzeko and Balotelli.' And Paul, a Korean guy who is studying in Manchester, says with optimism 'He can help us win the Champions League.'

'I love our supporters,' concludes a shattered Roberto Mancini at the end of a long party. 'They're incredible and that's who we won it for.'

I like winning

A conversation with Roberto Mancini

Thirty-five years have gone by since you started playing in the Bologna youth team. Back then, you were just a boy. Football has been your life. What has it given to you?

'Everything. I loved playing football; it was what I wanted to do, and then it became my life. It doesn't get any better than this ... I have had the chance to travel the world, to meet people, and, above all, to play football.'

And you: without false modesty, what have you given back to football?

'I gave – or, should I say, I returned the gift that God gave me: the ability to play football and entertain people.'

Let us take a look once more at your life in football. Starting with the Saint Sebastian parish recreation centre and Aurora sports club.

'That parish recreation centre was where I first started kicking a ball around. Don Roberto and Aurora both mean a lot to me, and not only in a football sense. They gave me a direction, they set me on a good path – morally, ethically, that is.'

Then Bologna.

'Bologna will be in my heart forever, because I was 13 when I got there, and I found a club and many extraordinary people who stood by me and helped me out in a delicate stage of my life. In those four years, the people there were just amazing. It was the first step I took on my way to becoming a footballer.'

But how does it feel to make your debut in Serie A at 16 and score nine goals in your first season?
'Back then, it was really hard to make it at such a young age. I really must thank Burgnich for that, as he put his trust in me. I don't know what it feels like, to be honest, because when you are 16 you don't really realise what is going on. Only with time do you come to understand what happened. Yes, it is easy to lose your head, when you're up there at the top and you are still a boy; but luckily I had great people around me, who kept my feet on the ground.'

Sampdoria.
'Samp is my life. I spent 15 years there and they made me what I am now. With them, I won important trophies; I experienced great disappointments and great joys alike; and I learned a great deal about the world. I watched a big family being born, with Paolo Mantovani as father. In that city, Genoa, I made friends who never left me.'

Lazio – your first spell, as a player.
'It was the last stage of my career as a player, in a big city where football was lived on a very intense level. That was Cragnotti's Lazio: the Lazio of great players, the club that made a comeback and won after many years spent waiting.'

Leicester.
'I didn't stay long enough – only for a month – but it surely gave me a taste for English football.'

Fiorentina – a bittersweet experience?
'No, not really. It was an interesting learning experience, my first one as a manager. It started well, with the Coppa Italia; then came the financial difficulties for the club. Even though it did not end in the best way possible, I still had a good time there … I took Vittorio Cecchi Gori's side, and he didn't have many friends. That's how life goes.'

Then Lazio again, as a manager.
'For me, it was like coming home. We won, we managed to get into the Champions League, but unfortunately financial difficulties hit that club, too. Nevertheless, thanks to those working with us at the time, we still managed to carry out a very interesting project.'

Inter Milan, finally, after the longest engagement in the history of Italian football.
'I should have gone there as a player first, then as a manager, but I made it there in the end. Four years, really busy and full-on. It is not easy to work in Milan, but out of all the managers the club has had in the last 30 years, I believe I am the one who stayed longest, and the one who won the most, after Helenio Herrera.'

What has been the happiest moment, and what was the saddest one, in this tale of yours?
'The happiest moment: my debut in Serie A, playing with Bologna; the saddest moment: Paolo Mantovani's death.'

What has football taught you?
'I reckon that football, just like many other sports, has the same rules as life. It taught me to respect myself and others, to respect hard work, to try to be polite, and to become a good person: a man who football-loving children can look up to.'

What's the worst thing you've witnessed, in all your years in the football world?
'There are so many things that I don't like, and that I would love to erase from this world. Especially as, in my opinion, football should first and foremost be fun. What would I rather not see? Uncivil behaviour, violence, scandals, matches sold and fixed, doping. Those things don't belong in sport.'

And the best thing?
'For me, my life as a footballer. A life made up by daily training sessions, being on the football pitch every day, playing matches, being with my teammates, seeing a group come together little by little, watching happy supporters, spending 15 years with Sampdoria. Wins and losses aren't the most important things. Obviously, one would rather win all the time … but losing is part of the game. I have been very lucky, because I played for many years, and now I'm coaching.'

What kind of manager are you? What's your philosophy?
'I like winning. That's the idea I want my teams to bear in mind, when they take the field. I like winning and I like running the show, entertaining the crowd, making the fans enjoy the game. I like to attack, to amaze, to surprise; and to be in control of the ball and of the game itself. Then, you might still lose, because you make the wrong choices, because luck is not on your side, because you are having a bad day, because – just as in life itself – one day you win, one day you lose. But what's important is to have the right frame of mind, always.'

Who were your mentors? Or else, as Sergio Viganò says, were you born a manager?
'I am not sure whether what Sergio says might be true, but I think you must have that something in yourself. You don't

become a great player or a manager if you haven't got the taste for it, the right skills. I believe you must have that extra something. And then come the mentors. I had some good ones, though not many – three or four, who taught me a lot. Starting from my first coaches at Bologna, when I was 15, to Boskov and Eriksson. I learned a lot from the latter two, because I spent a long time with them. But they all gave me something really special.'

What about Bersellini and Ulivieri, with whom you had some issues in your first years at Samp: does the same apply to them?
'Sure, I learned from them, just as I did from all the managers of the national team.'

Do you know that your friends, your teammates at Samp, really couldn't imagine you as a manager? They couldn't see how you could get by with a temper like yours. Enrico Chiesa said that you were a nightmare on the football pitch, the way you used to behave.
'That's quite a compliment! No, honestly, he's right. Back then, I was really like that. What's important is that they understood my personality. And, in any case, I wasn't the only one behaving like that at Samp that year. There were quite a few like me, but we all stood by one another for 15 years. And they were incredible years, too. Then, as time goes by, you change, you mature, you calm down and you start a different job – football manager, in my case – even though I still feel like a footballer, deep down inside.'

What's it like, being a manager?
'It is a wonderful job, although very difficult. It is immensely draining, and quite stressful. You have to do your best every day, and you are under examination two or three times a week. If you win, you're a genius, if you lose, you're an idiot.'

Since December 2009 you have been an Italian in Manchester.
How would you rate your experience?
'I really miss my country. For an Italian, it is not easy to go abroad, and I really do get quite homesick. Still, I must admit that what I am living is an extraordinary life experience. It has given me a lot, both on a personal and on a professional level. It has made me grow. Football in England is absolutely great, and the people here, too. The club really lets you get on with your work, and everyone respects what you are doing. So altogether it has been an absolutely positive experience. I am happy to be working here. And I like it in Manchester, apart from the weather ...'

But when did your fascination with England begin?
'The Premier League has always been a point of reference for me, a tournament to hold as an example. In Italy, we have always followed English teams. I remember I used to watch Premier League matches 20, 25 years ago: at the time, they were broadcast on Telemontecarlo, and Massimo Caputi used to be the commentator. I have always loved English football, and over time it has only got better. Today – and last season's grand finale showed this – I think it is the best championship in the world.'

What do the English like about you, about your style, about the way in which you manage a team?
'I don't know – I really don't. I hope they appreciate the job I am doing, and my will to do things properly. What I know for sure is that it feels great having not only the appreciation of the City supporters, but also the recognition – or even respect – I have felt when we went to play in other football stadiums.'

How do you see your future? Will you still be coaching at 70 like Sir Alex Ferguson?

'Ferguson is still young at heart. What about myself? I honestly don't know, maybe I won't be the same. It will all depend on how I feel, in body and spirit, and on how things will turn out. It is too early to say whether I shall follow Sir Alex's example.'

How do you remember 13 May 2012, now that the game is over?

'I especially remember our supporters, who were – and are still – brilliant. They feel the colours, they live for the team, they have great respect for the players and they have always stood by us. I remember their happiness at the end of the match, at winning the Premier League after 44 years. It was the best thing about that day. They really deserved that title, because they are great, and they really deserved some happiness after all that suffering.'

So, what did you have in your pocket that day? An amulet? Some sort of lucky charm? Gianluca Vialli wouldn't tell us …

'No, I didn't, I have no such things as lucky charms. I had prayer beads in my pocket that day, but that's nothing out of the ordinary: I always have them on me.'

Do faith and football have something in common?

'Of course they do … or at least, in my opinion, they can have a lot in common.'

During your pilgrimage to Medjugorje, did you thank the Holy Mary for the Premier League title?

'I thanked her for my father's health, because he underwent heart surgery and it all went well, fortunately – that's the most important thing. And I thanked her for all the joys she has brought to me, including the football ones. Medjugorje is an incredible place, you must go there and then return on a pilgrimage. It is a place where I am at peace with myself. It is an important life experience for a believer.'

In Medjugorje, you are also part of several projects …
'That's right, we are helping the orphans from the Balkans war who live in the orphanage run by Sister Cornelia, and we also support two other projects aimed at young people, together with the Franciscan friars in Mostar.'

Let's go back to City. With your new five-year contract, what have you got to say to supporters? What are your hopes, your ambitions, your dreams?
'I can just say that we will give our best, that we mean business here and we want to carry on working just as we have been doing these last years. Saying that we might win this or that title is hard, because football is unpredictable.'

And the Champions League? Is that still a kind of obsession for you, having missed out on it as a player, against Barcelona?
'Nowadays, it is no longer an obsession … if it comes, it comes – sooner or later. I don't know when, but it will come.'

Still, it would be great to win it with City. It is what all supporters are hoping for …
'Sure, that would be great. Winning the Champions League would be grand. It is one of our aims, but we need time for that, together with patience and practice. We want to advance in Europe, that's true, but we also want to defend our Premier League title. That's a priority. And it won't be easy.'

What do you say to your sons, Andrea and Filippo, about football?
'I really hope they can continue being footballers, although it is not easy. I don't know if they'll succeed. Football has

made me a very happy man, and I hope that can be the case for them, too. I teach them to behave properly, to do their best always, and, most of all, to be decent human beings.'

And what do you say to your daughter, Camilla?
'My daughter is 15; she is studying, and, being a girl – and hence much more intelligent than us – she won't be chasing a football.'

Bibliography

Buckely, Andy, *The Pocket Book of Man City* (Kingston upon Thames: Vision Sports Publishing, 2010)

Clayton, David, *The Man City Miscellany* (Stroud: The History Press, 2011)

Colace, Mauro, *Mantovani, Il sogno e la realtà* (Chiavari: Internos, 2010)

Filacchione, Marco, *Nel cuore della lazio* (Roma: Librería Sportiva Heraclea, 2010)

Parodi, Renzo, *Roberto Mancini, Vita opere e miracoli di un artista del pallone* (Genova: Liguria editore, 1995)

Sessarego, Pietro, *Io, Mancini: le piccanti confessioni dell'ultima bandiera del calcio* (Genova nervi, Alkaest, 1996)

Vincent, Bruno, *The Secret Diary of Mario Balotelli* (London: Sphere, 2012)

Magazines
FourFourTwo, London
France Football, Paris
Guerin Sportivo, Bologna

Newspapers – Italy
Corriere della Sera
La Repubblica
La Stampa
La Gazzetta dello Sport
Corriere dello Sport
Tuttosport

Il Manifesto
L'Unità
Il Resto del Carlino
Il Secolo XIX
Il Lavoro

Newspapers – UK
The Times
The Guardian
The Independent
Daily Mirror
Daily Mail
Daily Star
Daily Telegraph
The Sun
Manchester Evening News

Television – Italy
Italy
Rai 1
Rai 2
La Sette
Italia 1
Canale 5
Rete 4

Television – UK
BBC
Sky Sports

Websites
www.robertomancini.com
www.sampdoria.it
www.bolognafc.it

www.sslazio.it
www.lcfc.com
www.acffiorentina.it
www.violachannel.it
www.inter.it
www.mcfc.co.uk
www.manutd.com
www.fifa.com
www.uefa.com

Acknowledgements

I would like to thank Roberto Mancini, Aldo Mancini, Andrea Mancini, Attilio Lombardo, Valentina Vezzali, Giosué Viganó, Gianluca Vialli, Sven-Göran Eriksson, Moreno Mannini, Fausto Pari, Pietro and Massimo Battara, Marco Lanna, Enrico Chiesa, Paolo Bórea, Antonio Soncini, Amedeo Baldari, Franco Bonini, Silvio Cardinali, Roberto Pazienza, Elvio Cittadini, Don Roberto Vico, Aldo Moretti, Doriano Giuliani, Mario Sconcerti, Azeglio Vicini, Pablo Zabaleta, Pietro Vierchowod, Marco Macina, Marino Perani, Tarcisio Burgnich, Franco Colomba, Graeme Souness, Javier Zanetti, Roberto Martínez, Simon Flynn, Duncan Heath, Laure Merle d'Aubigné, Roberto Domínguez, Carlo Corinaldesi, Cora Tiedra, Alia Nardini.

Dedicated to Elvira, Lorenzo, Olmo, Alda and Tullio.